Education for Judgment

EDUCATION
for JUDGMENT

The Artistry of Discussion Leadership

EDITED BY

C. Roland Christensen
David A. Garvin
Ann Sweet

Harvard Business School

Harvard Business School Press

Boston, Massachusetts

© 1991 by C. Roland Christensen, David A. Garvin, Ann Sweet

Printed in the United States of America

95 94 93 92 91   5 4 3 2 1

The paper used in this publication meets the requirements of the American National Standard for Permanence of Paper for Printed Library Materials Z39.49-1984.

Library of Congress Cataloging-in-Publication Data

Education for judgment : the artistry of discussion leadership/
  edited by C. Roland Christensen, David A. Garvin, Ann Sweet.
     p.   cm.
  Includes bibliographical references and index.
  ISBN 0-87584-255-0 (alk. paper) :
  1. College teaching. 2. Discussion—Study and teaching. 3. Critical thinking—Study and teaching. I. Christensen, C. Roland (Carl Roland), 1919–   II. Garvin, David A. III. Sweet, Ann, 1935–
LB2331.E376 1991
378.1'25—dc20   90-26961
                                                        CIP

To
David Riesman

A teacher of scholars,
and a scholar of teaching

Contents

Foreword

RICHARD F. ELMORE

THIS BOOK TOOK SHAPE in unusual circumstances: a group of faculty from diverse disciplinary backgrounds, with a common bond to a distinguished university, came together to reflect on their teaching, to discuss their ideas with each other, and to write about these ideas for a broader audience. Their conversation is a tribute not just to the authors but also to the intellectual stature of Harvard University, the institutional leadership of the Harvard Business School and its dean, John H. McArthur, and, not least, to the persistent efforts of Professor C. Roland Christensen to develop new ways to help instructors learn to practice their craft more effectively.

But why should it be unusual for university faculty to reflect on and write about their teaching? Teaching, after all, is a major part of what university faculty do. Even on campuses where research is highly valued, it is difficult to be a university professor without spending a substantial chunk of one's career in the classroom. Furthermore, teaching involves the sorts of intellectual puzzles that attract people to academic life in the first place—deep, complex, layered problems, which yield answers only in the form of new questions. Also, teaching can provide some of the most profound rewards of academic life—direct experience with the intellectual growth of people coming to grips with problems in the presence of knowledge. Nonetheless, teaching is seldom taken as a subject for serious intellectual discourse in universities; still more rarely are books about teaching written by university faculty. The reasons for this neglect have to do both with the nature of teaching and with the conditions under which teaching occurs.

Confronting the Uncertainty of Teaching

Teaching is a messy, indeterminate, inscrutable, often intimidating, and highly uncertain task. Against this uncertainty, teachers construct defenses. One common tactic is to argue that professors are hired to profess, not really to teach. Becoming a distinguished scholar in one's specialty requires deep immersion in a subject over a long period of time. What students really want is to hear what the professor knows. They do not want to waste their time with contrived exercises in pedagogy.

Another closely related defense is the belief that the higher the level of education, the more students should be motivated by mastery of subject matter, and therefore the less their learning should depend on teaching. We may need "teaching tricks" to engage and motivate children who do not fully appreciate the intrinsic importance of knowledge, but university students should be motivated by a desire to learn the subject matter, not by the mode of its presentation.

A third common defense is to put teaching to one side by glorifying it. Teaching is a gift that descends from heaven onto the shoulders of a few among us. Every university should have its share of brilliant teachers, but only a few can be expected to enjoy this rare gift. We should acknowledge these gifted teachers while they are active, with awards given at solemn occasions, and we should commemorate them after they have gone, with plaques and endowments, but to analyze and understand them would be to trivialize their gift.

A fourth defense is to regard differences in teaching as matters of taste or style. In universities, this view reflects long-standing norms against "meddling" in the classroom affairs of another professor. In schools, this view has its roots in the social isolation of teachers' work. As long as differences in teaching are kept at the level of taste, and as long as teaching is considered an individual creative act, it is subject to the conventions of connoisseurship, in which differences are considered matters of style, with no serious consequences.

Without denying the importance of deep understanding, the intrinsic value of subject matter, the gifts of brilliant teachers, or the variation in individual classroom styles, I think these arguments, and others, are too often used to avoid confronting teaching. Let's be blunt. Exposing one's knowledge, personality, and ego to the regular scrutiny of others in public is not easy work under the best of circumstances. This kind of exposure also accompanies research, but whereas professors spend most of their graduate education preparing to conduct research, their only preparation for teaching is their own, largely unexamined, experience as students. In the peculiar world of universities, one is expected to know how to teach as a condition of employment, but the practical problems of teaching are almost never discussed. It should not be surprising, then, that we develop strong beliefs as a defense against uncertainties. These defenses, however, too often result in an eviscerated, flat, and disappointing experience for both professors and students: an interminable montage of talking heads and illegible overhead transparencies, interspersed with short periods of stark panic at exam time.

On one level, this book is a gentle invitation to confront and demystify the uncertainty of teaching, not just in universities but in any educational setting. It is a book about how individual faculty have solved recurring problems of classroom practice—how to think concretely about the task of teaching, how to organize subject matter, how to get a discussion started, how to guide the course of a discussion without stalling it, and how to create a sense of closure and accomplishment. Read in this way, the book should have a bracing effect. It certainly did for me. Here, on public display, are practical solutions to many of the classroom headaches, quandaries, and embarrassments that we have confronted in our teaching careers, laid end-to-end, discussed thoughtfully and honestly by experienced practitioners. In this context, Melissa Mead's chapter, "Great Beginnings," and Colleen Burke's chapter, "Tulips, Tinfoil, and Teaching," are truly inspiring accounts of what it is like for a novice to confront the uncertainties of teaching and emerge not only with a reasonably intact ego, but also with the beginnings of a deliberate working model of teaching practice. These essays work both as guidance for beginning teachers and as useful perspectives for experienced teachers on how a thoughtful model of teaching practice can be developed from experience, observation, and consultation.

If this book merely diffused the dread that accompanies the uncertainty of teaching, and opened up teaching for serious discussion among colleagues, it would repay the considerable effort made by its contributors. But the book is about something more important. It challenges us to take a deeper view of teaching. Teaching, in this view, is essentially a transformational activity, which aims to get students to take charge of their learning and to make deeply informed judgments about the world. The book also challenges us to examine the institutional conditions that support or undermine this more ambitious view of teaching. In this sense, it urges a transformation of the conditions of teaching.

Teaching as Transformation

The authors of this volume have modest aims. They would like to tell us about their experiences with discussion teaching. They would also like us to understand that discussion teaching can be applied broadly in the curriculum of schools and universities, whether in the liberal arts, the sciences, or the professions. Although they focus on their own experiences with discussion teaching, their insights are deeply connected to a long historical conversation about the nature of teaching and learning.

David Cohen sums up conventional pedagogy as follows: "Teaching is telling, knowledge is facts, and learning is recall."[1] That is, teachers are responsible for delivering content, in the form of factual information. Students are responsible for receiving it. The relationship between teacher and student is satisfactorily completed when the student has successfully transferred factual material back to the teacher at the required moment.

In conventional pedagogy, with its emphasis on factual information, distinctions among students can be based on objective criteria—those who "get it" at some minimally acceptable level succeed; those who don't, fail. Albert Shanker, the iconoclastic president of the American Federation of Teachers, is fond of telling people about a sign in his office. The first line reads, "I taught the material, but the students didn't learn it." The second line says, "Define the meaning of 'teach' in that sentence." These lines capture the essence and limits of conventional pedagogy.

The authors of these essays challenge us to think about teaching quite differently. At the core of discussion teaching, as Roland Christensen argues in Chapter 2 and Abby Hansen develops in her essay on teaching and learning contracts, is the idea of reciprocity between students and teachers. People learn to the degree to which they can actively manipulate facts within some general framework and can relate general ideas to specific events in their experience. We have knowledge, in other words, only as we actively participate in its construction. Students do so by engaging, with other students and with the teacher, in a process of inquiry, critical discourse, and problem-solving. The teacher's role is to foster conditions in which students are encouraged to construct knowledge. In this conception of teaching, the roles of teacher and student are easily reversible. Students teach each other, and they teach the teacher by revealing their understandings of the subject. Teachers learn by this process, not only by being exposed to students' understandings of the subject, but also by steadily accumulating a body of knowledge about the practice of teaching. In this view, teaching is enabling, knowledge is understanding, and learning is the active construction of subject matter.

If teaching can be learned, through collegial inquiry and discussion, then it becomes a subject for professional discourse. Such discourse, however, requires a language and a set of core ideas that spark an argument. These factors have been largely absent from university teaching. Although there is an extensive body of research on teaching in elementary and secondary schools, dialogue has been largely confined to researchers and only rarely penetrates the world of practitioners. The authors here take professional discussion about teaching seriously. They have developed a language for talking about teaching and a set of ideas that can be used to shape arguments about what constitutes effective ways to teach.

The distinction between conventional pedagogy and discussion teaching also raises the question of what teachers should know about how students learn. Conventional pedagogy is essentially ideas about teaching disconnected from ideas about learning. To teach is to convey information; thus teaching consists of organizing and communicating content. We discover whether students have learned by seeing how well they are able to report back what we have told them; *how* they learn is not our concern. To the authors of these essays, on the other hand, knowledge of teaching depends on understanding how students learn. To teach is to engage students in learning; thus teaching consists of getting students involved in the active construction of knowledge. A teacher requires not only knowledge of subject matter, but knowledge of how students learn and how to transform them into active learners. Good teaching, then, requires a commitment to systematic understanding of learning.

In taking this view of teaching and learning, the authors join a conversation that has been under way in Western civilization at least since Socrates questioned the young slave in the *Meno* about his knowledge of geometry. This conversation, as Howard Gardner suggests, "is an extended rumination on the nature of knowledge: where does it come from, what does it consist of, how is it represented in the human mind."[2] Lately, the conversation has grown to include many of the best minds in such areas as psychology, philosophy, linguistics, anthropology, computer science, and neurophysiology.

Current research on human learning has converged on a few key ideas about the nature of learning and their consequences for teaching. These ideas are remarkably parallel with what the authors of these essays have discovered by studying their own teaching. In describing their experience with discussion teaching, they have tapped into a broader set of ideas that could have far-reaching consequences for the way teaching and learning are conducted in our society.

One insight from the current research is that all learning is contextual in at least three senses: new knowledge is acquired by extending and revising prior knowledge; new ideas acquire meaning when they are presented in a coherent relationship to one another; and knowledge becomes usable when it is acquired in situations that entail applications to concrete problem-solving. These three meanings of context set a frame of reference for thinking about effective teaching.

Discussion teaching, as defined and practiced by the authors, is essentially a systematic way of constructing a context for learning from the knowledge and experience of students, rather than exclusively from the canons of disciplinary knowledge. Hence, when Roland Christensen argues, in his essay on questioning, listening, and response, that students should take collective responsibility for determining the direction of the discussion, and that teachers should enable that responsibility, he is acting on a belief that learning occurs when students actively form the relationship of new knowledge to its intellectual and social context. Daniel Goodenough explains that his experience dealing with the physicians treating his wife caused him to rethink his role as a teacher of medical practitioners. "I was helping to train doctors so narrowly specialized that they had difficulty seeing beyond their own areas of expertise," he recalls. For Goodenough, teaching became not just a matter of imparting knowledge of his specialty, histology, but a process of helping physicians understand the human context in which their knowledge would be used.

Another important insight from current research on human learning is that the acquisition and application of knowledge are fundamentally social acts. Children acquire language, for example, through complex social interactions with adults and other children. Carpenters, bookmakers, chefs, surgeons, experimental scientists, and practitioners of other occupations requiring complex strategies of estimation and decision making acquire a large portion of their practical knowledge from observing and interacting with other skilled practitioners. Lauren Resnick has suggested that, although the social dimension of learning is critical to practical application of knowledge, we construct formal learning in schools and universities in ways that discourage social interaction. We emphasize individual cognition over social interaction, abstract manipulation of symbols over concrete application in practical settings, and generalized learning over applications in specific social contexts.[3] As a consequence, learning in school becomes progressively isolated from the kind of learning that affects people's competencies in real life. The problem for teachers is not whether students will learn when they are not in school. People are inveterate learners. Rather, the problem is how to construct learning in school so as to maximize its influence over learning in the world.

The authors of these essays clearly see social interaction as a key component of learning. The basic premise of what David Garvin refers to as "active learning" is to create a community of interest within the classroom in which students think of themselves as enabling each other's learning. The techniques of questioning, listening, and responding described by Herman Leonard and Roland Christensen are the basic constituents of a community of discourse, which values collective support of learning. The close analysis of interaction patterns in the classroom, suggested by Julie Hertenstein, goes to the core of how teachers construct and understand a community of discourse.

The essays also address the ethical dimensions of teaching, a subject that has not received the attention it deserves. Good teachers, Joyce Garvin argues, are powerful and influential people who are often so preoccupied with their own understanding of the subject matter that they are unaware of how much they influence their students. Even if dedicated to enabling students to exercise independent judgment, Garvin suggests, teachers are always at risk of exercising "undue influence" by virtue of their expertise, or alternatively of not exercising enough "due influence" in their role as enablers. Teachers with encyclopedic knowledge of their subjects, John Hildebidle observes, are not necessarily good teachers, even when their students value and respect them. Good teaching, in the ethical sense, enables students to engage in intellectual discourse, to learn how ideas are shaped and used, and to articulate those ideas clearly. Knowledgeable teachers often slip into defining teaching as knowing and telling it all.

The ethical dimensions of teaching, David Garvin argues, usually take the form of dilemmas that require decisions but have no obvious right answers: valuing divergent questions versus keeping the discussion on track, acknowledging right answers versus encouraging deliberate discussion, publicly revealing students' flawed reasoning versus correcting students' understanding, capitalizing on an individual's feelings for the purpose of making a good teaching point versus respecting the individual's personal stake.[4] Teaching, it seems, is a struggle for mastery not only of content and craft, but also of self. Learning to teach is, in important respects, learning to view one's own knowledge and expertise as instrumental to others' learning, rather than as something to be displayed.

This book aims to persuade us that teaching is an essentially transformational vocation. The aim of teaching is not only to transmit information, but also to transform students from passive recipients of other people's knowledge into active constructors of their own and others' knowledge. The teacher cannot transform without the student's active participation, of course. Teaching is fundamentally about creating the pedagogical, social, and ethical conditions under which students agree to take charge of their own learning, individually and collectively. These essays help us to understand what those conditions are.

To introduce more ambitious conceptions of teaching, however, we must not only change the way teachers and students think about teaching and learning; we must also transform the institutional conditions in which teaching and learning occur.

The Transformation of Teaching

Suppose a group of teachers decide to develop their teaching more consistently in the directions suggested by this book. How would they go about it? These essays suggest a number of useful ideas. They also expose a deeper set of problems in the organization of teaching and the culture that surrounds that organization.

For most practitioners, teaching is an intensely private and personal matter. The way we think about our subject, design our courses, deal with students in classrooms, and the way we evaluate them—these dimensions of teaching are all deeply affected by personal beliefs. But these personal matters have rather large public effects. For the vast majority of students who do not aspire to become academic experts in the subjects we teach, what we teach *is* the subject. So we are responsible not just for teaching our view of the subject, but also for giving a sense of how that view fits with those of a broader professional community. Moreover, the main value that students take away from our classes is not their knowledge of the subject, but a predisposition to learn. If this predisposition is not consistently communicated across the curriculum, then we have failed students, both intellectually and ethically. No matter how personal teaching is, the teacher's responsibility to a broader community cannot be avoided.

The way universities and schools are organized does little to encourage collective responsibility toward teaching. In schools, the sheer volume of work and custodial responsibilities for students restrict teachers' attention largely to their own classrooms. Even in universities, which pride themselves on free and open commerce of ideas, teaching is a socially isolated experience. Professorial roles are increasingly organized around ever more tightly defined specialties; to offer an opinion about a colleague's work is to risk exposing oneself as a dilettante. Courses are increasingly specialized, to the extent that only one or two faculty members in a department or school are typically judged to be competent to teach a given course. (The norms of specialization imply that if many professors could teach a course, its content would necessarily have to be superficial and not worth teaching at all.) Furthermore, professors assert something close to property rights over certain courses. To volunteer to teach a course currently taught by someone else can easily be interpreted as an act of aggression against a colleague. Under these conditions, it should be no surprise that conversation among colleagues turns to baseball, parking spaces, divorce, psychotherapy, common enemies in school or university administration, and even the weather before it focuses on what we teach and how. These conditions are not immutable. Changing them, however, requires thoughtful action.

The authors of these essays gently suggest that the improvement of teaching requires a significant relaxation of the norms of privacy and social isolation that surround teaching. This book is itself a monument to the idea that teaching can be a subject of serious and useful discourse among colleagues. The essays offer an abundance of more specific ideas.

Co-teaching and observation of one's teaching by colleagues are direct means of opening up discourse about teaching and learning. Although inviting a colleague into one's classroom may require a large measure of courage, James Austin, Ann Sweet, and Catherine Overholt suggest that the gamble will be amply rewarded by insight and understanding on the part of both the observer and the observed. They explain how to make the process of working with a colleague less intimidating and more helpful.

Collegial support for beginning teachers can also be important, both in helping them solve initial problems of how to teach and in creating a sense of opportunity, rather than dread, in the early stages of teaching. Both Melissa Mead and Colleen Burke testify to the influence of collegial support in forming their early views on the practice of teaching.

Students can also be important allies in the improvement of teaching. An important message of Julie Hertenstein's and Herman Leonard's essays is the need to get students to reflect on patterns of participation, the nature of questioning, and the progress of the class. Roland Christensen suggests an active role for students in evaluating the progress of teaching and learning in their classes. Reflective students promote reflective teaching in at least three ways. First, students become more active and responsible participants in learning when they are explicitly engaged in the improvement of class discussion. In addition, their expectations for ambitious forms of teaching can be an important source of motivation for teachers. And, after a class is completed, students can provide useful information to influence future students' opportunities to learn.

Whether teachers receive appropriate incentives and support depends very much on the organizational context of teaching. But the problems of nurturing good teaching run deeper than organization; they are rooted in the culture of universities. Few institutions have been able to create and sustain norms that foster continuous attention to teaching and learning, as opposed to the transmission of subject matter. Daniel Goodenough's chapter captures what it was like to confront the improvement of teaching and learning in the New Pathways program at the Harvard Medical School. The program involves a basic change in culture, away from the individual, competitive model of medical education to one in which "students could succeed only through teamwork," and away from a conception of curriculum as discrete bits of factual information to one in which students are introduced to powerful synthetic, analytic structures for ideas.

The most telling example of institutional support for teaching comes from the Harvard Business School, which contributed considerable talent to this project. The business school has been distinguished virtually from its founding, in the first decade of this century, by its concern for *what* is taught to future business executives, *how* it is taught, and the connection between the two. The school developed a distinctive pedagogical approach, a form of discussion teaching that has come to be called the case method; more important, it developed an organizational structure and culture to support and reinforce the development of that approach. The early stages of that development were very much influenced by the intellectual heritage of Alfred North Whitehead and William James, which attached high value to the practical application of ideas. What students were taught and how they were taught were central to the institution's agenda, and these subjects were considered to be legitimate subjects for inquiry, development of new knowledge, and professional discourse. To build bridges between traditional disciplinary knowledge and the active world of management, the business school knew it would require new conceptions of content and pedagogy.[5] The school and Harvard University have made a long-term commitment to putting issues of teaching and learning front and center on the institutional agenda, and to investing resources to develop a new conception of teaching and learning. Teaching and learning can, it seems, be made an enduring issue in the intellectual life of serious academic institutions.

The improvement of teaching and learning in universities is an important matter. Its purpose is not only to provide students with a more pleasant and rewarding educational experience, but also to prepare them to take charge of their own learning and to participate in a society in which learning is a cooperative more than a competitive act. This goal requires teachers to examine teaching with something like the level of inquisitiveness they bring to their own subjects, to appreciate the social complexities of learning as they do the complex structure of knowledge in their disciplines, and to think about how to nurture student engagement in learning with the same playfulness and creativity as they exercise in thinking about creating the next layer of knowledge in their field. These essays are an invitation to join an important and fascinating conversation about the nature and conditions of teaching and learning, a conversation that will ultimately transform both teaching and the institutions in which teaching and learning occur.

NOTES

1. David K. Cohen, "Teaching Practice: Plus ça Change . . . ," in Philip W. Jackson, ed., *Contributing to Educational Change: Perspectives on Research and Practice* (Berkeley, CA: McCutchan, 1989), pp. 27–84.
2. Howard Gardner, *The Mind's New Science: A History of the Cognitive Revolution* (New York: Basic Books, 1985), p. 4.
3. Lauren Resnick, "Learning in School and Out," *Educational Researcher*, vol. 69, no. 9 (1987), pp. 13–20.
4. For a parallel discussion of these issues in the education research literature, see Magdalene Lampert, "How Do Teachers Manage to Teach?" *Harvard Educational Review*, vol. 55, no. 2 (1985), pp. 178–194.
5. Andrew Towl, *To Study Administration by Cases* (Boston: Graduate School of Business Administration, Harvard University, 1969); F. J. Roethlisberger, *The Elusive Phenomena* (Cambridge, MA: Harvard University Press, 1977).

Preface

DAVID A. GARVIN

THIS BOOK HAS A LONG HISTORY and deep institutional roots. It grew from wider efforts at the Harvard Business School to improve the practice of teaching and ensure continued excellence in the classroom. These efforts were reinforced by the commitment of the university as a whole, and especially its Danforth Center for Teaching and Learning. One result has been an environment unusually well suited to the thoughtful consideration of teaching practice.

The business school, for example, has long emphasized the importance of teaching, and its program relies heavily on case studies and discussion methods. Instructors meet regularly with one another to plan classes and develop effective classroom strategies. Still, special efforts were required to develop a more systematic understanding of case method teaching. An extended program of observation was begun in the late 1960s; it led eventually to a series of case studies examining teachers in action and a seminar for instructors based on those case studies. At first the seminar was limited to Harvard Business School faculty, but it soon broadened to include teachers throughout the university. In 1984, a further step was taken with the convening of the Colloquium on Case Method Teaching, a three-day seminar attended by eighty teachers, primarily professional school faculty, from around the world.

These efforts helped individual instructors improve their classroom performance and better understand the challenges and rewards of teaching. They also suggested an essential next step: capturing our oral and experiential tradition in a format less evanescent than cases and seminars. Many of the colloquium participants, for example, requested further explanatory material for use at their home institutions. This book is a response to such concerns.

We began slowly and experimentally, matching authors with broad, open-ended topics drawn from a rough outline. Although almost all our authors were graduates of the teaching seminar, many found it difficult to pull their thoughts together in an essay. Often, the core ideas were still inchoate or required further development. We therefore began a

series of authors' meetings to flesh out concepts, critique work in progress, and learn from one another. These meetings quickly became forums
for exploration; in many ways they mirrored the approach to teaching
that we advocate in this book. All of the essays evolved and improved as
they journeyed through this process.

Our approach to authors, topics, and essay development has several
important implications for readers. First, *Education for Judgment* is a
book by practitioners, for practitioners. It is operational rather than theoretical in tone, and is based primarily on distilled, articulated experience.
We have tried to keep the academic literature in the background, focusing instead on lessons and themes that emerged from our collective
experience.

Second, because we selected authors before either topics or the overall
book outline was finely honed, *Education for Judgment* offers diverse
and often highly personal perspectives. The book is very much a "mixed
bouquet," an eclectic blending of voices, teaching approaches, institutional settings, and topics. Whenever possible, we have followed our
authors' interests, rather than striving to be comprehensive. And because
we represent multiple educational levels (high schools, colleges, universities, and professional schools), speak in varied voices (personal, autobiographical, philosophical, and tactical), and reflect a range of fields and
interests (statistics, literature, business, and ethics), readers will seldom
find us advocating a single best approach.

Despite this diversity, the essays are unified by a common philosophy
and some shared beliefs. All of us view teaching as an activity of central
human concern, deserving careful and systematic study. For us, teaching, whether conducted by discussion or other methods, is not simply
a gift, a talent one is born with, or a black art; it can be analyzed and
assessed objectively. Good classes are distinguished from poor ones not
by instructional magic, but by a set of identifiable practices. Yet we
continue to believe that teaching will never be fully codified or reduced
to cookbook rules, because it is an essentially human activity, fraught
with uncertainties and unresolved dilemmas. In the classroom, there will
always be room for judgment.

Our favored approach is teaching by discussion. Those of us at Harvard Business School go a step further, preferring discussions based on
case studies. Cases are teaching documents that have been designed with
two goals in mind: a substantive lesson and effective pedagogy. They are
thus unusually well suited to classroom debate. But whether or not they
use cases, our authors prefer discussions to lectures. They believe, as the

book's early chapters indicate, that discussion methods do a better job of stimulating student learning and developing critical skills. In this they are not alone, for recent reports on educational reform have repeatedly called for greater use of discussion methods.

We agree with these reports in many respects, especially their argument that institutional support is essential for the success of discussion methods. We have a somewhat different view, however, of the other barriers to change. As we see it, the deficiencies in discussion teaching today, including its limited use, have less to do with theoretical problems, a lack of supporting evidence, inadequate resources, or professional indifference than with a need for clear and unambiguous operational advice. We lack an effective vocabulary for talking about the practice of teaching and a system other than apprenticeship for transferring knowledge from experts to novices. The existing oral tradition has failed to produce the desired results. Hence, there is a need for a book like *Education for Judgment*.

The book is organized as follows. Part I introduces many of the key principles and premises underlying discussion teaching. Its two essays serve as the cornerstone of the book, exploring such fundamentals as instructor and student roles, the centrality of process, skill requirements, and barriers to change. Part II covers similar issues, but from a vastly different perspective. Each essay in Part II is personal and autobiographical, featuring an individual instructor coming to terms with discussion teaching. Some of the instructors are making their first forays into the classroom; others are skilled lecturers shifting to a new mode. Each, however, describes a personal odyssey and the reflections it prompted. The lessons they learned range from gracefully managing one's first year of teaching to enlisting the support of peers, dealing with self-doubt and uncertainty, and mastering new skills and attitudes.

Parts III and IV are more operational in tone. Like the introductory essays, those of Part III examine the building blocks of the discussion approach. But here the point of view is applied rather than conceptual. Two themes dominate: the need to develop group norms, especially those that create an effective learning environment, and the need for distinctive instructional skills, revolving around questioning, listening, and response. In each of these areas, the essays provide detailed practical advice. Part IV has similar objectives, although its essays are more focused. Each considers a critical challenge of discussion teaching— evaluating student participation, teaching technical material, learning from classroom observation, reaping the benefits of a lengthy semester, encouraging independent thinking—and offers operational suggestions. The essay on technical material, for example, speaks eloquently about the need for structure and clear direction, while the essay on classroom observation articulates what the observer might look for, how teacher and observer might prepare for such a class, and how the after-class debriefing might be conducted.

The concluding section of *Education for Judgment* is the most philosophical. Part V explores the limits, dilemmas, and joys of our craft. The questions are timeless: Can an instructor know too much to be effective? At what point does a teacher's impact become so pervasive that it leads to undue influence? How should the delicate ethical dilemmas of discussion classes be resolved, as the instructor tries to satisfy competing norms of fairness? These are complex issues, for they involve paradoxes and trade-offs. Few have simple solutions. Yet they must be thoughtfully addressed if we are to act wisely in our chosen careers.

Given the broad sweep of the topics addressed, how should one read this book? Our advice is to dip in and sample, to read selectively rather than from beginning to end. And then, we suggest, to try out what you have learned. Some of you may wish to experiment independently in the privacy of your classrooms; others will collaborate with like-minded colleagues. Whatever your approach, we hope that the spirit of our book stays with you. For us, *Education for Judgment* is a celebration of teaching.

Acknowledgments

THIS BOOK IS A TRIBUTE to the Harvard Business School's long tradition of support for teaching. It takes many forms. For example, all incoming faculty are encouraged to participate in the teaching seminar from which this book grew. Courses are developed and taught by teams of teachers who meet regularly to plan the teaching of individual cases. Even the school's classroom construction (a tiered horseshoe, now widely copied) has, since the 1950s, been guided by a commitment to encouraging students to talk to one another, as well as to the professor. Committed leadership has been equally important, and we thank the deans whose vision gave top priority to teaching for judgment. In particular, John H. McArthur, the most recent of those deans, has for ten years, with the assistance of Associate Deans Dean Currie and Linda Doyle, provided the physical and intellectual space for the growth of the teaching seminar that so significantly influenced the contents of this book.

We are especially grateful to the authors of the essays, whose devotion to discussion teaching and to sharing their enthusiasm with peers around the world has sustained them—and us—during the lengthy process of preparing the essays for publication. They have educated us in many ways.

To Abby J. Hansen the editors of this book, along with many of the contributors, owe special thanks. Her creative participation in virtually every developmental phase has helped bring the project from dream to reality. We value her contributions and colleagueship.

Dyanne Holdman Cleary, as project manager, coordinated the multiple planning and operational activities so essential for our book's successful completion.

We are grateful to Nancy Jackson, our editor, for her scrupulous attention to making every phrase speak clearly.

The discernment and responsiveness of Carol Franco and Natalie Greenberg at the press accelerated the production of this book, and added further refinement.

Our families' warm interest and thoughtful suggestions sustained and buoyed us throughout the project.

Each of us remembers with thankfulness our own teachers, whose sensitivity to the tentativeness of our skills nourished their growth over time.

Most of all, we are grateful to our students, from whom we continue to learn how to be better discussion leaders.

Boston, Massachusetts   *C. Roland Christensen*
December 1990   *David A. Garvin*
                                      Ann Sweet

Education for Judgment

PART I
Learning and Teaching

1

Barriers and Gateways to Learning

DAVID A. GARVIN

DEBATES ABOUT EDUCATIONAL REFORM tend to be impassioned, intense, and remarkably repetitious. For decades, two models of education
have coexisted in uneasy peace; when debates have arisen, they have
invariably pitted the model in practice against an appealing, but less
used, alternative. These models might be called the *teacher-centered* and
the *active learning* approaches. The former is the more traditional, with
deep roots in our educational system; the latter is the foundation for the
essays in this book.

The traditional model is based on the idea of teaching as telling. The
primary goal is the transfer of information from an expert (the teacher)
to novices (the students), with the expert controlling such critical elements of the process as the syllabus, pace and sequencing, and mode of
presentation. In practice, this usually means that the expert lectures and
the novices record and absorb. Interchanges between teacher and student
are limited to brief question-and-answer sessions, and there is little or no
interaction among students.

This approach dominates modern education. From kindergarten to
graduate school, teacher talk takes up the vast majority of class time.
Some studies estimate that as much as 80 percent of class periods are
spent in this fashion.[1] And why not? If the goals are information transfer
and the accumulation of knowledge, the process is practical, efficient,
and well understood.

Yet, over time, the traditional model has been raked by repeated
criticism. The latest wave of reports calling for educational reform, including A *Nation at Risk, Horace's Compromise, Involvement in Learning,* and many others, revives a host of earlier complaints. It is old wine
in new bottles. In fact, the most eloquent critiques of the teacher-
centered approach date back to such master vintners as John Dewey,
Alfred North Whitehead, Jean Piaget, and Carl Rogers. Their concerns
are as timely today as they were when they first appeared.

Objections to the traditional model can be grouped into three broad categories: cognitive, philosophic, and pragmatic. Cognitive concerns arise because of the shakiness of the traditional model's assumption that students can assimilate and retain information independent of its use. A number of studies have found that, when lecturing is the dominant mode of teaching, students forget as much as 50 percent of course content within a few months.[2] For real learning to occur—what Whitehead calls "the mastery of knowledge," or "wisdom"—students need to be active participants in the learning process, rather than passive recipients of information.[3] Retention, it appears, increases markedly when learning is solidly anchored in the experience and interests of students.

A second objection to the traditional model is philosophic. Here, the debate is over ends rather than means. The traditional model implies that the primary goal of education is information transfer. Facts, theories, and modes of analysis must be communicated so that each generation can build upon the successes of its predecessors. According to this view, knowledge lies at the core of learning, and that knowledge is best transferred from experts to novices via lectures.

Lectures are an extremely efficient method of transferring information. Even with low retention rates, they are a powerful tool, especially when complex concepts must be conveyed and facts and theories are unequivocal. But lectures are of only limited value if the goals of education go beyond information transfer. The development of clinical judgment, the formation of critical skills, the shaping of artistic sensibility—such achievements are difficult to nurture through lectures. Preparing students to think independently is an enormous challenge. And if the goal of education is to help students grow as individuals and forge their own identities, the teacher-centered model has even less appeal. Rather than immersing students in learning opportunities, it floods them with facts. All too often, the result is loss of interest and a deadening of curiosity.

Such effects suggest a third objection to the traditional model: many students don't like it. The recent rash of reports on educational reform is in part a response to poor student performance and the associated boredom and apathy. Students today are distressingly disaffected with formal education. For many of them, class time is more of a chore than a delight. For such students, any alternative to the traditional approach is certain to be an improvement.

Not surprisingly, these criticisms have reinforced the appeal of an alternative model of education. It goes by various names, including active learning, self-directed learning, student-centered education, humanistic education, and progressive education. But in every case, the central tenet is the same: students must be actively involved in the learning process. The implications of this philosophy are both subtle and profound. At heart, they suggest a radically different notion of how education should proceed.

In the traditional model, the core concept is teaching; here, it is learning. The distinction is more than mere semantics or rhetorical sleight of hand. The teacher-centered approach puts the instructor front and center; it implies that teaching can be evaluated without any reference to the depth or extent of student learning. Good teaching is thought to flow almost inevitably from the instructor's mastery of content and clarity of presentation. It is a one-way street, a monologue rather than an interchange.

For years this assumption has ruled education, especially at colleges and universities. Skilled teachers are commonly identified by their ability to deliver pithy summaries or to untangle complex truths. Students are seldom factored into the equation, and for the simplest of reasons: learning is assumed to have little relationship to their contributions or level of involvement.

Dewey, for one, found this notion absurd:

> Teaching can be compared to selling commodities. No one can sell unless someone buys . . . [yet] there are teachers who think they have done a good day's teaching irrespective of what pupils have learned.[4]

Dewey's comment reflects an abiding faith in learning as a shared activity. Only if teachers and students work as partners will the true ends of education—the ability to use knowledge, to think creatively, and to continue learning on one's own—be achieved. Such goals are unlikely to be met in a process dominated by teachers, because true education requires students to be personally invested in the learning process. And that will occur, say the critics, only when students have had a hand in shaping the content, direction, and pacing of classes.

This is indeed a radical idea, requiring a wholly new perspective. Interchange and jointness become the watchwords, and instructors no longer exercise total control over class time. Nor do they speak as frequently or commandingly. Students take more responsibility for articulating and developing ideas, and discussions and jointly sponsored projects substitute for lectures. In such environments, the teacher's role is to facilitate and guide. For many instructors, this means a sharp change in outlook and an entirely new set of skills. No longer is mastery of content enough to ensure a successful class. Now, attention must be focused equally on classroom climate, group process, and the needs, interests, and backgrounds of students.

The active learning model has long been a fixture in debates over educational reform. Yet surprisingly, the model has been honored more in theory than in practice. Despite the popularity of the underlying concepts—virtually all recent reports on education have included an anguished plea for more involved students and more active learning—examples of successful application are scarce. The model has gained a considerable following, but there appear to be tremendous barriers impeding its adoption. If active learning is such a good idea, why is it so seldom seen?

Points of Resistance

Powerful forces sustain the traditional teacher-centered approach to education. Some are as simple as inertia and an unwillingness to change. Others are rooted in the norms, values, and incentives that govern modern education. And still others reflect assorted myths and misconceptions that bedevil active learning and result in a lack of practical guidelines. For simplicity, these forces can be grouped into three general categories: political and institutional barriers, epistemological barriers, and practical barriers.

Political and institutional barriers reflect the difficulty of introducing change in today's schools, colleges, and universities. One problem is financial, or, more precisely, the perception that large sums of money are at stake. Many administrators see active learning as an expensive proposition; the phrase suggests small, intimate classes and low student-teacher ratios. Personal coaching is assumed to be the norm, and the implicit model is a seminar or one-on-one tutorial. Yet active learning is possible with much larger groups, *provided* classrooms have been designed to support discussion and encourage student-to-student interchange. Amphitheaters with slightly elevated tiers of seats, chairs that swivel, multiple blackboards, and comfortable seating for eighty to a hundred students seem to work best; they allow for direct involvement without the expense of expanded teaching staffs. As a noted teacher has observed: "How do you get active learning with a large group of students? Start by hiring a good architect."

There are, however, other institutional barriers to this approach. Incentives, for example, often point in the wrong direction: they elevate research over teaching, or suggest that little is to be gained by excellence in the classroom. The "publish or perish" mentality has long been identified with a devaluation of teaching and a lack of concern for students. At few colleges or universities does the promotion process reward superior teaching; if teaching is considered at all, the aim is usually to weed out the poorest performers, who lack even the most basic classroom skills. But the problem goes beyond values. Experimentation with unfamiliar teaching methods takes time, and, especially at secondary schools, time and energy are at a premium. Most instructors are already spending long hours, both in and out of the classroom, grading papers, preparing exams, reviewing lesson plans, and meeting with students. They have little time left for wholly new efforts, or for the emotional involvement that is required in active learning. This approach demands a willingness to meet students on their own terms and to get to know them as individuals; both responsibilities exact a heavy emotional toll. Moreover, school systems and state universities are often subject to tight centralized control, with governing boards that dictate content and regulate instructional practices by imposing standardized tests or uniform requirements. In such settings, the traditional teacher-centered approach is clearly the path of least resistance for many instructors.

Students are often equally uncomfortable with the new approaches. From the students' perspective, active learning is risky: it requires a change in roles and responsibilities, but with an uncertain payoff. Especially where these methods are rarely or partially practiced, students tend to resist their introduction, fearing that they will learn less in their classes. After all, the argument runs, if the teacher speaks less, isn't less information being conveyed? And won't learning be correspondingly reduced?

Arguments of this sort reflect the *epistemological barriers* that impede active learning. Such barriers arise because followers of the traditional model and believers in active learning hold fundamentally different assumptions about knowledge, the learning process, and the role of education. Frequently, the result is unconnected debate and poor communication. On the surface, the disagreement appears to be about the day-to-day details of classroom management; in reality, it reflects opposing premises and educational philosophies. Thus discussion is confused, the underlying issues are obscured, and resistance to the new model persists because it is far easier to change methods than it is to alter fundamental assumptions and beliefs.

What, then, are the core assumptions of the teacher-centered and active learning models? The teacher-centered model sees information transfer as the primary goal of education; active learning focuses on skill development, the integration and use of knowledge, and the cultivation of lifelong learning. The teacher-centered model assumes that facts and concepts can be learned without experiencing or directly applying them; the active learning model is wary, in Whitehead's words, of "inert ideas . . . that are merely received into the mind without being utilized, or tested, or thrown into fresh combinations."[5] The teacher-centered model insists on the primacy of content and subject matter; active learning gives equal weight to process and classroom climate. The teacher-centered model regards the classroom as the instructor's private preserve; active learning sees teaching as important enough to be subject to the same standards of oversight, assistance, and review as scholarly research. And the teacher-centered model believes that instructors are the hub around which the classroom revolves, while active learning grants students far more authority and autonomy.

Some followers of the dominant model reject active learning because they consciously disagree with its basic tenets. In the past, such resistance was undoubtedly a major barrier to change. But today educators are increasingly vocal in their support of a more student-centered approach, and evidence of its effectiveness is rapidly accumulating. Whether or not there has been a genuine shift in allegiance, the public posture of educators has certainly begun to change.

Yet a less overt and more insidious form of resistance has continued. Some instructors who profess to accept the basic tenets of active learning are in reality doubters or agnostics. They may experiment with new approaches—occasionally under duress—by altering their classroom behavior and normal teaching styles. Unfortunately, their efforts usually fail because of what Robert Rosenthal, the psychologist, has termed the Pygmalion Effect.[6] Rosenthal and his colleagues found that, in teaching, what you get from students is what you expect. Instructors who were told that their students were unusually talented produced better results than instructors who were told that their students were average or mediocre, even when there was no real difference in student mix. Apparently, instructors were communicating their prior expectations through inflection, tone, and nonverbal behavior, and students were responding in kind.

Similar results are likely when instructors merely go through the motions of active learning. Students will quickly sense a teacher's lingering doubts: an absence of real interest in their comments, perhaps, or an uneasiness when some point in the lesson plan does not emerge sponta-neously in a discussion. If the instructor lacks faith, students will wonder why they should trust themselves to an unfamiliar and unproven ap-proach. Not surprisingly, such halfhearted experiments seldom succeed.

The same thing may happen when traditional instructors, who do not fully understand active learning, claim that they are already practicing its precepts. In their classrooms, they feel, students are involved and enthusiastic; the teacher is a partner, not a policeman; and the climate is one of trust and openness. Unfortunately, in many cases this is self-delusion. To take a simple example, teachers routinely overestimate the proportion of class time they devote to students' comments and underesti-mate the proportion of time taken up by their own lecturing and talk. Similarly, surveys of students often reveal a much less positive assessment of the degree of trust that prevails in a classroom judged "open" by the instructor.

Active learning is further impeded by various *practical barriers*. One of the most serious involves evaluation. It is exceedingly difficult to measure and document the success of this approach, especially over the short time span that most schools, colleges, and universities use for evaluative purposes. Many of the desired objectives—creativity, a willingness and ability to continue learning, enthusiasm for education, greater personal initiative and self-direction—emerge slowly and tenta-tively over time; they are hard to detect with the usual standardized tests. For this reason, believers in active learning frequently fall back on anecdotal evidence. Occasionally, they simply proceed on faith, marshal-ing broad theories to support their cause. Neither approach is likely to impress the uncommitted or the disbelieving.

Perhaps the most deeply rooted barrier to active learning is a lack of clear precepts for practice. Teaching of this sort is exceedingly hard to do. It requires a shift in the role, preparation, knowledge, and skills of instructors. Yet relatively few reformers have dealt with such operational matters, or have translated their lofty goals into the gritty details of class-room management. For the most part, they have argued educational philosophy (the "why" question), rather than effective implementation (the "what" and "how" questions).

This inattention to practice has led to two problems. First, improve-ment efforts have often foundered on the shoals of imprecise terminol-ogy. Because we lack a vocabulary for talking cogently about the teaching process, advice to practitioners has normally been couched in the most general of terms. Such ambiguous advice is extremely difficult to implement. A recommendation that instructors "involve students in discussions by drawing on their experience" can mean a number of different things, as can the suggestion that teachers try to be "more supportive and less controlling." For similar reasons, we currently lack effective methods for training discussion leaders. Artistry continues to be emphasized, and little attempt has been made to distill common principles or to translate individual expertise into broader, more practical guidance.

The second problem is the persistence of assorted myths and misconceptions about active learning. Most of these notions involve some aspect of classroom process: for example, the view that active learning is identical to the Socratic method, that student-centered discussions are unstructured bull sessions, that active learning eliminates the instructor's responsibility for mastering content, or that facts cannot be communicated successfully by this approach. None of these claims seems to stand up under careful examination. But because each is so widely held, and because confusion about this method abounds, it is important to lay out precisely the foundations of the active learning model.

Cornerstones and Building Blocks

The successful practice of discussion teaching—or, for that matter, any other form of education aimed at active learning—requires three fundamental shifts. The first is a shift in the balance of power: from an autocratic classroom, where the instructor is all-powerful, to a more democratic environment, where students share in decision making. The second is a shift in the locus of attention: from a concern for the material alone to an equal focus on content, classroom process, and the learning climate. The third is a shift in instructional skills: from declarative explanations, rooted in analytical understanding and knowledge of subject matter, to questioning, listening, and responding, which draw equally on interpersonal skills and a sensitivity to group development.

At the core of active learning is a deceptively simple requirement: students must be personally invested in the learning process. They must care—deeply—about their own education and the contributions that they themselves can make. But when the instructor calls all the shots, students are unlikely to feel that the class is theirs. Instead, they will see themselves as compelled to study topics that the instructor finds particularly interesting or that the state requires. Class time seems to be arbitrarily controlled and unresponsive to their desires. The fact that students tune out in such settings is hardly surprising.

One way of overcoming these problems is to give discussion a more prominent role in the classroom. But for the change to be more than cosmetic, teaching style must also change. The instructor's dominant activity must shift from telling to facilitating learning and encouraging discussion. In practice, this usually means that the instructor speaks less and students speak more. Moreover, the instructor speaks about different things. He or she turns from definitive summaries to questions that open up discussion, from preplanned speeches to transitional and bridging comments that link together students' observations, and from establishing a party line to open-ended responses that stimulate and provoke thinking. Yet the instructor's responsibility for what happens in the classroom is in no way diminished. Indeed, teachers are now responsible for both process—the who, how, and when of discussion—and content. Democracy, whether in politics or the classroom, functions poorly without leaders, and it is the instructor who must check anarchy and shoddy thinking.

To that end, proper preparation is essential. But preparation now means exploring multiple paths of inquiry, rather than mapping out a single linear flow. A lecturer has total control over the order in which material appears and can present it in the most economical and logical fashion. Discussions, in contrast, are inherently uncertain. Conclusions and points of view are difficult to predict, and surprises are inevitable. Genuine discussions are thus quite different from the Socratic method, in which conclusions are preordained and the instructor's goal is to lead students to a particular answer or through an established line of reasoning. When students are actively involved in shaping discussions, the instructor's job is infinitely more complex. Uncertainty is high; with it come countless questions that must be weighed before class begins. In what direction is the discussion likely to evolve? How long will a critical piece of analysis take? Are there alternative approaches to the problem, and does each yield the same answer? What topics are likely to be of special interest to students? When the instructor must anticipate the probable flow of discussion and plan for in-class dynamics, preparation is a far more complex task than it was when content alone was king.

With uncertainty comes risk. Many instructors are uncomfortable with the loss of control implied by active learning, and find the lack of predictability unsettling. Students accustomed to lectures often have a similar reaction. But their concerns have different roots. Active learning requires high levels of personal involvement, and such involvement is lacking in most students' educational backgrounds. Many fear that they will fail in the new environment or, worse yet, will expose their true selves. This creates enormous self-doubt and vulnerability; without a supportive learning climate, cultivated and led by the instructor, resistance is inevitable.

Any form of active learning thus requires high levels of empathy and trust. Discussion classes provide an obvious example. If students are fearful of being "shot down," by either the instructor or fellow classmates, they will never participate fully or with real engagement. Some will retreat into stylized roles; others will withdraw altogether. For most students, participation is fraught with emotional risks. A guarded response is a safe response, especially early in the semester. As one business school student observed: "Before we got to know one another informally, people *were* their classroom comments."

In the active learning approach, then, instructors have the additional responsibility of ensuring a supportive classroom environment. Their goal is to create a setting in which students are comfortable taking risks and throwing themselves into the fray. Instructors must become more sensitive to tone and affect—the emotional undercurrents of students' comments—without losing their grasp of content. They must work consciously to foster the group norms that keep discussions afloat. They must begin to expose more of their own true selves in class, rather than their teaching personas, if they expect students to behave similarly. And they must learn to set standards explicitly and by personal example, creating an environment in which students will not be shot down because of honest mistakes or flawed responses. Yet at the same time, they must show that shoddy thinking will not be tolerated.

These considerations suggest a critical shift in the skills needed for successful teaching. An instructor's knowledge of subject matter and analytical prowess are no longer enough; they must be coupled with social and communication skills if active learning is to be effective. Lecturers spend limited time dealing directly with students and are little concerned with group behavior. Many lecturers, for example, would prepare identically for a class of fifteen and a class of five hundred. But in a discussion class, there is constant interchange, sometimes between the instructor and students, sometimes among students themselves. Group size, group norms, and group behavior are all critical to success. Skillful discussion leaders therefore try to assist students in the process of discovery. Their initial aim is to move the entire class forward, using a combination of probing questions, sensitive listening, and encouraging responses; their long-term goal is to build the group's capacity for self-discovery and self-management.

Such thinking lies at the heart of *Education for Judgment*. The essays that follow extend these ideas in several directions, and in diverse formats. Some essays are personal and autobiographical; they describe an individual instructor's coming to terms with active learning, often after years of teaching in the traditional mode. Other essays are more practical and direct; they include detailed suggestions about preparation, classroom management, postclass review, and other essentials of the active learning approach. Still other essays attempt to describe phenomena that are ill-defined by the existing literature, but vital to the practice of discussion teaching—for example, student-teacher learning contracts and learning groups. And a few essays are contemplative and reflective; they assess active learning from a higher philosophical perch. Yet, despite their diversity, the essays share a core of common concerns: a desire for increased student involvement, an interest in improving the skills of discussion leaders, and a goal of raising the level of discourse about teaching. Each essay, in its own way, is thus a gateway to learning.

NOTES

1. Cited in K. Patricia Cross, "A Proposal to Improve Teaching or What 'Taking Teaching Seriously' Should Mean," *American Association for Higher Education* (September 1986).
2. Ibid.
3. Alfred North Whitehead, *The Aims of Education and Other Essays* (New York: Free Press, 1929), p. 30.
4. John Dewey, *How We Think* (Lexington, MA: D.C. Heath, 1933), p. 35.
5. Whitehead, *The Aims of Education*, p. 1.
6. R. Rosenthal and L. Jacobson, *Pygmalion in the Classroom* (New York: Holt, Rinehart, and Winston, 1968).

2

Premises and Practices of Discussion Teaching

C. ROLAND CHRISTENSEN

THIS BOOK IS LIKE a group discussion among experienced, committed discussion teachers. Although the authors of this book share a common purpose—to lower the barriers to discussion teaching, as David Garvin puts it—our statements will reflect the individuality of personal judgments. We do not speak from a mountain peak of ultimate truth but, like all discussion participants, from vantage points along a path that winds from insight to insight.

That diversity is healthy, and inevitable. As Alexander Pope reminds us, "'Tis with our judgments as our watches, none go just alike, yet each believes his own." This essay, which describes some basic hypotheses about discussion pedagogy, is offered in the hope that other teachers will consider my reflections, and then consult their own "watches."

The most fundamental observation I can make about discussion teaching is this: however mysterious or elusive the process may seem, it can be learned. Through collaboration and cooperation with friends and colleagues, and through self-observation and reflection, teachers can master both principles and techniques of discussion leadership. But the task is complex. Discussion teachers' responsibilities are as varied as their rewards. With greater vitality in the classroom, the satisfaction of true intellectual collaboration and synergy, and improved retention on the part of students, the rewards are considerable. The responsibilties may be difficult to appreciate at first. For example, effective preparation for discussion classes takes more time, because instructors must consider not only *what* they will teach, but also *whom* and *how*. And the classroom encounter consumes a great deal of energy; simultaneous attention to process (the flow of activities that make up a discussion) and content (the material discussed) requires emotional as well as intellectual engagement.

15

Effective discussion leadership requires competency in both areas; it can be achieved only with patience.

The discussion teacher is planner, host, moderator, devil's advocate, fellow-student, and judge—a potentially confusing set of roles. Even the most seasoned group leader must be content with uncertainty, because discussion teaching is the art of managing spontaneity. Nonetheless, a good chart can help a mariner navigate safely even in fog. The premises and associated operational practices described here are my personal chart, tested over years of practice and found dependable in groups that range in size from twenty to eighty or even a hundred participants. Four premises seem fundamental:

1. A discussion class is a *partnership* in which students and instructor share the responsibilities and power of teaching, and the privilege of learning together.
2. A discussion group must evolve from a collection of individuals into a learning *community* with shared values and common goals.
3. By forging a primary (although not exclusive) *alliance with students*, the discussion leader can help them gain command of the course material.
4. Discussion teaching requires *dual competency*: the ability to manage content and process.

A Partnership between Teacher and Students

Lecturing, which emphasizes the instructor's power over the student, is a master-apprentice relationship of great power when the transfer of knowledge is the primary academic objective. But when the objective is critical thinking (in the liberal arts setting, for example) or problem-solving (in the professional school milieu), and the development of qualities such as sensitivity, cooperation, and zest for discovery, discussion pedagogy offers substantial advantages. To achieve these complex, value-laden educational goals, both teachers and students must modify their traditional roles and responsibilities.

In discussion teaching, partnership—a collegial sharing of power, accountability, and tasks—supplants hierarchy and asymmetry in the teacher-student relationship. The discussion process itself requires students to become profoundly and actively involved in their own learning, to discover for themselves rather than accept verbal or written pronouncements. They must explore the intellectual terrain without maps, step by step, blazing trails, struggling past obstacles, dealing with disappointments. How different from simply following others' itineraries!

Such creative activity cannot be ordered or imposed upon the unwilling. Teachers can police attendance and monitor the memorization of theory and fact by tests. But we cannot order our students to be committed to learning and willing to risk experimentation, error, and the uncertainty of exploration. Such attitudes are gifts from one partner to another.

Professor McGregor of MIT used to tell a story to illustrate the true dependency of superior on subordinates. A young executive arrived at a unionized textile mill and told the union officer, "I am the new manager here, and when I manage a mill, I run it. Do you understand?" The union agent nodded and waved his hand. Every worker stopped; every loom stopped. Then the agent turned to the manager and said, "Go ahead, run it." Students, at least in North America, are not unionized, but they possess the power to turn a discussion class into an academic charade by withholding involvement.

Another force mandating partnership in the teacher-student relationship is the fundamental need for students' input to the leadership of a group—a fact of life that lucky instructors discover in the adolescence of their teaching careers. Students not only teach themselves, and one another, they participate in leadership tasks traditionally counted as the teacher's—such as setting the discussion agenda and determining pacing and emphasis.

When students are unaccustomed to discussion pedagogy, the instructor must take practical steps to promote partnership. Students may greet the notion of sharing power and responsibility with skepticism based on years of contrary experience. To the instructor's promise that "we're all partners here," hardened skeptics may silently respond, "Fat chance!" But even they may feel a twinge of hope: "What if he really means it?" This twinge can prompt further questions: "I know the rules of the regular classroom game. But now the professor's changing them. To what?"

When students feel uncertain about the rules of the game, they try to resolve their doubts by testing the instructor. They ask—explicitly or indirectly—does this teacher genuinely want my contributions? Is she interested in knowing me as a special person, and will she keep my individuality in mind when she listens to my comments? Does he receive my suggestions with a positive attitude (there are some fascinating ideas here), or a negative bias (I'll find something wrong)? Does she really listen at all, or just pause while I talk? Does he ask for my help, work with my suggestions, demonstrate respect for my judgment? How does she react when I question her methods or conclusions? When we teachers repeatedly pass these tests, we communicate respect and validate our students' role as co-teachers. Our confidence in them encourages cooperation and friendship—and friendship is a marvelous ingredient in partnership.

Partnership is fragile and difficult to regain once lost. It needs continual nourishment, which can be provided in part by operational rituals and procedures. How a professor starts the day's session, for example, sends a message about the working relationship of the whole class. If the instructor lays out a step-by-step outline for the discussion—orally or on the blackboard—the class picks up a clear signal: follow my lead or be lost! Any partnership between a leader and followers is clearly a limited one.

In contrast, when the instructor invites students to set the agenda for the day's discussion, the openness of the invitation communicates a different message: you, the students bear the responsibility for this discussion. It belongs to you. As the classroom dialogue evolves, the instructor can further underscore the principle of joint ownership by asking students to summarize points or lines of argument, or to suggest the next question the group should discuss.

Direct participation in the leadership of their class enhances students' self-esteem—essential for effective learning—and gives them an opportunity to consolidate what they know by teaching others. Instructors can increase the value of students' input by publicly acknowledging its importance. We all tend to exert our best efforts when we feel appreciated.

Instructors can also benefit from the sharing inherent in partnership. By bringing unexpected points of view and creative, upsetting questions to material that has become extremely familiar to the instructor, fresh and energetic students play a particularly useful role in class: they wake us up. Moreover, when students function as co-teachers, their growing mastery of discussion leadership permits the instructor to step back— mentally, and sometimes even physically—to observe the class from their perspective. This opportunity to focus on how students listen, react, make notes, prepare to pounce, or perhaps "tune out" is invaluable. Such observation provides instant feedback on the progress, or lack thereof, of individual students as well as the group as a whole. By watching our own classes unfold, we can assess our performance from the most meaningful point of view: that of the students. And when students become skilled partners, their after-class comments can help us answer every teacher's inescapable question: How am I doing?

Partnership is both a window through which students can observe the teaching/learning process and a mirror that reveals them to themselves (surely a major element in any education). In deepening their personal involvement, taking responsibility for the quality of the discussion, and making an emotional investment in the outcome of the course, students claim ownership of their own education. This ownership not only stimulates them to excel, it also enhances our effectiveness as instructors.

Finally, partnership makes teaching more joyful. We teachers trade the aloneness and distance of hierarchy for the cooperation and closeness of colleagueship. Partnership with students gives us an incentive to be students again—and what are great teachers if not great students?

A Learning Community

Quality of context—the milieu in which the collective dialogue takes place—is fundamental to effective discussion. Where the context supports rigorous intellectual analyses and group collaboration, where an operational contract defines how teacher and students work together, and where there is mutual respect among all participants, a community dedicated to learning emerges.

Even a casual observer can tell when a group lacks the spirit of community. "If the tone of a class is confrontational, critical, and acerbic," a colleague once noted, "students will retreat—all except those who are 'red in tooth and claw.'" Gresham's Law (bad money drives out good) applies to the class that lacks community: the vocally aggressive and personally superconfident "drive out" the contributions of their measured and reflective, but perhaps less articulate, fellow students. In the absence of understood, trustworthy boundaries for appropriate behavior, attack—not exploration—often becomes the predominant activity. When participants compete to score individual points rather than collaborate to build group themes, they damage the fabric of discussion. In such a milieu students resist modifying early conclusions even when contrary evidence emerges—a particularly dangerous practice for intellectual growth.

In a true learning community, by contrast, diverse backgrounds blend and individuals bond into an association dedicated to collective as well as personal learning. The students seem interested in one another and the academic assignment of the day. And their dialogue has the open-ended quality of exploration. Speakers not only present points of view but test and modify their ideas; instead of doggedly defending personal conclusions, they listen to one another with interest, not fear. Differences of opinion produce inquiries, not disputes. Working as a unit, the class learns to value measured progress without expecting instant gratification.

The basic academic drive to master a body of knowledge, and its application to practice, power all education ventures, including solo study. But what turns a collection of students into a learning community? Not the mere assignment to the same room and time slot. The instructor must take concrete steps to promote collaboration and comradeship. He or she needs to develop strategies that will reflect the values that enable a group of individuals to work together productively. Here are the basic values I endorse for this purpose.

Civility—courtesy in working with one's associates—is a simple but powerful virtue. In class as elsewhere, politeness sets a cooperative tone and encourages the openness that lets people help one another by sharing experience and insight. *Willingness to take risks*, both individual and collective, not only helps students understand the topic of the day, but encourages daring and innovation. Finally, *an appreciation of diversity*—in backgrounds, personalities, questions posed, learning styles, frames of inquiry, and spectrums of interpretation—ensures that the group will avoid the rigidity of single-track paths to single-point destinations. Instead, the group will feel free to venture into intellectual terra incognita, where explorers need one another's help and support. The totality of these values can determine the tone of the group's discussions, and their collective impact creates an ethos that can activate, permeate, and enrich a group's minute-by-minute dialogue.

Instructors who build community reinforce these values by their own behavior. It helps simply to welcome the class to each session before plunging into the business of the day, or to greet individual students by name as they arrive. We can demonstrate our commitment to honest sharing by helping discussion participants who run into difficulties, and by asking for students' help when we find ourselves in an intellectual or procedural quandary.

Reinforcing the values of community can also take the form of being candid about ourselves. Hugh Prather puts the point pragmatically when he notes, "In order to see, one must be willing to be seen."[1] To promote openness in students, we must reveal our own areas of certitude and uncertainty, our dreams and our defeats. And, if we want our students to take the risks that make creativity possible, we must show we are willing and able to assist them when they stumble. To make independence practical and enfranchise all the members of the group, we must support students when their comments depart from the consensus of the moment or their proposals collide with firmly held convictions of the class. One way I do this is by explicitly including the iconoclast in a "majority of two" to make it clear that I will abet honest exploration, even when the group finds it unorthodox.

When the instructor both endorses and models a set of positive common values, the group will usually adopt them. Physical attendance then is transformed to academic belonging, and the group can achieve high quality in its discussions and its relationships.

We instructors can also strengthen the sense of community by paying attention to our teacher-student learning contracts. As Abby Hansen notes elsewhere in this book, a pedagogical contract is a pattern of understood and accepted ground rules that guide the protocols, rituals, mutual obligations, and standards of behavior of a class. We teachers build contracts with our words and our behavior. As we ask questions and respond to students' contributions, we give them material with which to form judgments of our leadership style and values. To communicate our genuine appreciation for the knowledge and judgment of our students, we can invite them to join us in defining the terms of our academic collaboration—and then make sure to honor their terms with our practice.

Implementing the teacher-student learning contract is complicated, for three reasons. First, since teaching contracts are set both explicitly (by statements) and implicitly (by the often inadvertent acceleration of precedents), instructors must attend to both dialogue and behavior. Second, because much of our behavior originates on the intuitive or preconscious level, it can be difficult to know what contract we are promulgating. (A hint: students' readings of our actions provide important clues.) Third, since contracts are organic, they change. Untended, they can either grow wild or decay. As students' interests and command of the course materials evolve throughout the semester, the contract must reflect these sometimes subtle changes.

When we let students share in the governance of their own course, they are less likely to feel like second-class citizens. And since people who contribute to setting standards often feel moved to surpass them, the best teacher-student learning contracts can also transcend themselves. When this happens, they evolve beyond formal procedures, legality, and details of enforcement to become covenants rather than mere contracts:

solemn compacts among members of a group to pursue common goals for mutual benefit. Covenants promote the deep commitment that encourages accountability and mutual responsibility. They nurture true community, for who will reveal his innermost beliefs, dreams, doubts, and most adventuresome ideas in an atmosphere of distrust?

One can be a good lecturer without giving these matters much thought. But in the extemporaneous face-to-face dialogue of discussion teaching, all parties are vulnerable, and students in particular feel their exposure keenly. Learning means leaving the known for the unknown— an exhilarating, but scary venture. In a discussion class, students often feel they are undergoing a private, even intimate, recreation of their personae in public view. A mature student speaks poignantly about this experience:

> It is extremely important for me to be in a classroom where there is acceptance and hospitality, an absolute hospitality of teacher and classmates that will allow ideas to be born for the first time. I feel very vulnerable. The teacher is in the privileged position of knowing me before I change and after. In a way it is similar to being a parent. The teacher holds my continuity because he or she knows me before, yet sees me leave my earlier self behind. School needs to be a safe place to leave my old self behind and change.

While discussion classrooms will never be perfectly safe, instructors can minimize students' vulnerability by promoting trust and respect. It is not enough to espouse these worthy goals in the abstract, for students readily detect empty idea-worship; they believe our actions more than our words. Two skills are especially valuable as teachers attempt to make the discussion classroom hospitable.

First, we can *listen* to students' comments with discipline and sensitivity; second, we can *respond* to them constructively. When discussion participants realize that the instructor treats their comments seriously and takes pains to build them into the discussion, they feel valued. And when this respect is maintained over time, students develop a sense of trust, a sine qua non for a true learning community. Disciplined listening elevates students' comments to the status of contributions. A wise instructor once commented that we should give—not pay—attention to what students say. Paying implies a cold, impersonal commercial transaction; giving communicates colleagueship, sharing, community.

As disciplined listeners, we try to hear the unspoken. Perhaps Bob's terse "Boston isn't moving very fast to integrate public housing" carries a message about his ghetto youth, repeated difficulties in getting good housing for his own family, and aggressive leadership of a tenants' union. If Betty, who has held forth often and forcefully against sending arms to Central America, fails to speak out in today's emotional discussion of the same issue, a disciplined listener will hear her silence and wonder about its cause. Does she expect the teacher to hear yesterday's comments again today? Has she changed her views? The sharpness of questions and responses and the vividness of language employed are useful clues to the intensity of students' feelings.

Treating students' comments with respect does not necessarily mean accepting them at face value. Discussion participants sometimes float verbal trial balloons filled with hot air. When we spot such bloated assertions, the trick is to suppress the tendency (ours or the students') to sarcastic harpoonery and let the discussion bring these balloons gently back to earth.

As teachers, we also build community with our constructive responses to students' comments. If we view all comments as potentially positive contributions to the group's learning process, our task as teachers is to integrate this raw material so as to further the discussion. I have found certain practical mechanisms useful in putting these ideals to work. For example, one can honor participants' contributions by giving speakers time to complete their arguments. Although teachers feel pressed to keep dialogue moving quickly (doodling can spring up at a moment's notice), haste can produce damaging cutoffs that belittle and stymie speakers. A suggestion: after a student finishes talking, watch her eyes. Do they indicate that her thought is now complete? If you feel unsure, wait a few seconds and recheck. A five-second pause often produces a contributor's most insightful thought.

At the most elementary level, an instructor shows respect for a student's statement by making sure that the group has understood its basic analysis. To promote a true community of learning, however, it is also valuable to ensure that a spirit of colleagueship characterizes the way the group will test and explore that analysis. How? By taking care that our comments convey appreciation for the time and effort the student expended to prepare the contribution—and for his or her courage, if the contribution espoused an unpopular view. A learning community needs brave, as well as adroit, students.

Community is strengthened when we put students' comments to work, immediately if possible. We can use their questions to subject conclusions (both students' and the instructor's) to scrutiny. We can link their contributions from earlier classes to the current dialogue; we can follow their leads for next-step inquiry; we can build summaries around their formulations and use their words.

Community-minded instructors will be cautious in introducing their personal judgments into the classroom dialogue, and will state such judgments in a manner that clearly invites students to differ. "Ruth, many experts disagree on the question of increasing the federal gasoline tax. I'm in favor of it, but where do you come out on this question, and why?"

Constructive response appreciates the conditional tense. *Would* this approach seem right? *Might* this be the route to take? *Should* the evidence lead us to this conclusion? Such an approach leaves maneuvering room for students and instructor alike. It eschews false absolutes such as "This is the way to lay out the factory work flow," or "It is wrong to subsidize low-cost housing." It encourages the cultivation of balanced judgment and lets disagreement flourish without confrontation.

Shared values, a mutually understood teacher-student learning contract, and a relationship of mutual trust and respect all nurture community. When discussion groups become communities, instructors can transcend their own uncertainties and vulnerabilities and enter into genuine covenants with their students. Doing so, they can unleash, and then slowly harness, a powerful energy of experience and creativity that students often did not know they possessed.

Alliance with Students

Effective discussion leadership, unlike lecturing, requires instructors to forge a primary alliance with students. We do not bring the material to them, but rather help them find their own ways to it. The subject matter defines the boundaries of the intellectual territory, but the students' intellects, personalities, learning styles, fears, and aspirations shape the paths they will take. Students hunger for wholeness. They want recognition, not just as novice learners, but as persons with the competence to contribute to their own education and that of their fellow students. Alliance with them means learning about them. Students' family, social, and institutional affiliations affect both the style and content of their discussion contributions. Our personal reward for getting to know students is obvious; the experience of teaching becomes a warmer, emotionally enriched pursuit. But there is a pedagogical reward as well: we become more effective in leading the discussion process.

Of course forging an alliance with students has its costs as well as benefits. Learning about them requires an investment of scarce resources—time, emotional energy, and research ingenuity. The more we learn about the complexities of discussion participants, the more daunting the pedagogical tasks may seem. A colleague once asked, "Can one ever learn enough about a student?" Certainly, there are limits. But what are they? In a formal, but friendly relationship, what is appropriate information? And learning about students can be intimidating, too, for the more we understand the many worlds in which they live, the more we appreciate the gulf between those worlds and ours.

Despite these costs, I have found that the rewards prevail. Knowledge of students enables us to meet the first obligation of all instructors—at the very least to avoid injuring those whom we seek to help. I recall, with chagrin, asking a student to comment on a one-page statement I had distributed a few minutes earlier in class. He blushed and declined. After class he explained his frustration: he was dyslexic. And I recall the story of a secondary-school science instructor who began his methods class early in the semester by calling on the boy who sat directly in front of him in the first row. The instructor did not know that the boy, although fascinated by science, was shy and clumsy in public speaking. The student stammered some sort of answer, and the instructor handled the ensuing dialogue equally badly. That boy—a Boston Brahmin now ninety years old—still recounts the incident with fresh pain and anger in his voice. Its ultimate impact was a poor orientation in course substance and subsequent avoidance of science in college and career—despite an early, passionate interest in the subject. How easily we can damage students' confidence, scar their spirits!

Many of the techniques of our craft carry some dangers. Role playing, for example, requires us to be particularly sensitive to students' backgrounds. I would not lightly assign a student a role that might give personal offense—ask a devout Mormon to pretend to be the sales manager of a liquor firm, or a member of a minority group to play the role of a bigoted manufacturing executive. It is easy to mistake labels for people, unless we know our students as individuals. One young woman recalled that most of her college instructors had used her as "our Korean resource" because of her name, appearance, and birthplace. In fact, the daughter of a diplomat, she knew little of Seoul, and much about Paris and Madrid.

Knowing students can also help us humanize the all-too-often cold and formal setting of a classroom in which students, as we know from experience, sometimes feel like necessary nuisances. The Nobel laureate Robert Solow has embroidered on Arthur Guiterman's definition of education—a student sitting on one end of a log and a great teacher on the other—by noting that some professors appear to be sitting on their students and talking to the log. How true! Students appreciate our taking an interest in them, and as a result, the whole class has more fun. And when we sense the students' good feelings, our own efforts seem more positive to us. "This is a first-rate group," we say. "The class is really rolling this year." We telegraph our buoyant mood with our step and posture as we enter the classroom. Our energy level is high as we lead the discussion. And communication improves. We hear the message in students' comments with greater appreciation when we understand something of their background and current interests. And the teacher-student dynamic improves, too. As we learn about students, they are encouraged to learn about us. And learning brings appreciation.

Our knowledge of students helps us meet them "where they are." And that is where learning begins. No matter what the curriculum or course plan may assume, students occupy unique intellectual and emotional spaces, and the discussion teacher is well advised to seek out their locations. What sort of a learner is Tim? Does he know when and how to get help, and how to test its appropriateness? Is he frightened or excited by the unknown? Does he cut corners in defending his points of view? Is he self-aware? Does he know his own blind spots and "hot buttons"? How does he work with classmates? Is he willing to have his ideas tested rigorously, to explore a classmate's argument, even though it contradicts a strongly held conviction of his own? How does he view peer "error," as a chance to demonstrate personal superiority or an opportunity to help a classmate learn? Does he have the leadership skills to contribute to the educational objectives of the day? Does he frame questions that catch the current "drift" and extend its range? Does he truly listen? Can he accumulate and integrate prior comments and construct a unified whole? Wasn't it T. S. Eliot who said that hell is where nothing connects? Does Tim see the connections?

As discussion teachers, we need to see our students on life's wider screen. What academic and work experiences do they bring to the discussion classroom? Have they tutored in secondary school, sold encyclopedias in poor neighborhoods, worked as systems analysts, done research for a state regulatory agency, or managed an overseas branch of a corporation? In what other worlds do they live? What current interests, whether social, political, or recreational, consume them?

Such knowledge can help us in our minute-by-minute leadership of a discussion. If Carol is at her best when given time to reflect on an issue, I would not "cold call" her. If Sam's father is dying, or if Hal is in the final week of producing the second-year class play, perhaps they should not open the discussion. If Ida has managed a day care center and the topic of the day is child care in the workplace, how should I bring her into the dialogue—as an expert, an advocate, a challenger, or a backup resource? What will do her, as well as the class, the most good?

Meeting students where they are encourages us to ask ourselves where *we* are. What are our wider worlds, current interests? How do they affect our leadership of the group? Our own circumstances can have an enormous, inadvertent impact on what we do in class. In planning the course, for example, we may tend to teach first what we ourselves learned last. We often want to give priority to our discovery of the moment, because we find it fresh and exciting. But this may not help our students. They may need to learn first what we also learned first, because it tends to be basic.

Knowing where we and our students are, intellectually and emotionally, can help us with the ever-present problem of how to choose among several students with raised hands and anxious expressions. Almost inevitably, it is a mistake to be guided by the democratic instinct to favor the person whose hand has been raised the longest. Most likely, that student's comment will be "out of phase" because it will address whatever points were in play when the student first raised his or her hand.

Often inexperienced instructors assume it is desirable to *always* recognize the participant whose background experience best matches the point under discussion; it is, however, but one factor to be considered. If the class is discussing federal revenue policy and Arlene is an experienced tax accountant, should one call on her? The simple fact of her experience might lead to a boring or intimidating barrage of information. Given a choice between a participant with a specialized background and one skilled in making cogent comments and relating them to the flow of discussion, I would choose the latter. Or I might call on the student who could best profit from tackling the problem under examination and working with the specific comments just made. At points where the flow of discussion has become sufficiently turbulent (or turbid) to warrant summary, the instructor might do well to recognize a participant with a sophisticated command of intellectual synthesis and a talent for clear expression.

Since knowing our students in depth can confer such palpable benefits, why is it not the norm? I have mentioned some of the costs, but there is also a perceptual barrier to be overcome. All too often we see only what we want to see or what we are accustomed to seeing. Marcel Proust wrote of the simple act of looking at someone we know:

> We pack the physical outline of the creature we see with all the ideas we have already formed about him, and in the complete picture of him which we compose in our minds those ideas have certainly the principal place. In the end they come to fill out so completely the curve of his cheeks, to follow so exactly the line of his nose, they blend so harmoniously in the sound of his voice that these seem to be no more than a transparent envelope, so that each time we see the face or hear the voice, it is our own ideas of him which we recognize and to which we listen.[2]

As Proust suggests, the difference between "our own ideas of him" and a student's ideas about himself can be substantial. We need to ask ourselves how to narrow the gap by obtaining appropriate and useful information.

Let's take a look at my former student "Bob Smith." Like all students, he was a complex of past happenings, present circumstances, and future aspirations, a melange of roles and responsibilities. The richness of this complexity emerged as I began to understand him in the round. According to the registrar's sheet, he was "Robert W. Smith, 27, graduate of Wainsworth College, candidate for the MBA degree with a major in entrepreneurial management." That was just the tip of the iceberg.

There was Bob Smith, spouse, who lived with his wife and two young children in a mixed industrial-residential area of Boston. Bob belonged to several community service clubs and headed a program for physically disadvantaged inner-city children. And there was the former Lt. Robert W. Smith, U.S. Infantry, veteran of two years' duty in Vietnam. Wounded in combat, Lt. Smith had been awarded the Silver Star for bravery. And there was R. Wainsworth Smith, a graduate of the college his great-grandfather had founded, who left school with average grades and a record noting a two-week suspension from classes for having participated in a student protest. And there was Rob Smith, the youngest child in his family, with two older brothers in political and professional careers. There was also Bobbie Smith, son of two academic parents, both active in the Society of Friends.

Bob's background—prominent family, social concerns, military experience—made itself felt in the classroom. It conditioned his choice of issues and levels of involvement in the discussion at large, as well as his relationship with peers, students outside the class, and the instructor. Faulkner's *Requiem for a Nun* puts the point well: "The past is never dead. It's not even past."[3] Students bring their pasts to the classroom, as well as their hopes for the future. We teachers need to understand both dimensions in order to teach them well in the present.

But where, and how, can we obtain the intelligence needed to turn each student from a cipher to an ally in the learning process? Just around the campus—the classroom, our offices, the local coffee shop or hangout—there is a rich lode of information to be mined. The student newspaper and various campus social functions also offer ample opportunity for teachers to get an informal sense of what's going on, as well as specific information—who made the dean's list, who was awarded a prize. Coming to class quite early during the first weeks of a semester can prove rewarding. Students who arrive at about the same time as you do—early birds—usually have a song to sing: a personal concern or request for help or understanding. These pleas may not be verbalized at the first meeting, but they are generally communicated soon after that. I have found them inevitably of major significance to working with the individual, and sometimes to working with the whole group. But the discussion class itself is the richest source of all, for it allows us to take continual readings of our students' academic accomplishments, their skill in helping to guide the discussion, and their involvement in specific topics.

The office is but a more intimate classroom, the most appropriate setting for individualized instruction. When students initiate appointments, we can usually assume that the topic they raise is important to them. Often the items on their agendas are problems of some sort, and chats about their difficulties with course materials can move on to requests for the instructor's thoughts on career planning or more personal matters. In this regard, we teachers need to be wary of moving too far into areas that are not merely personal, but private. There's an enormous difference between knowing that Hans is an avid stamp collector and knowing the details of his current romantic life. We are guides, not professional counselors. Nonetheless, when professionally handled, personal conversations can provide rich opportunties for insight and, in turn, feed the educational process.

A colleague observed that a group of students is like a pack of cards face-down. To read those cards most accurately, to gain maximum useful personal data, we need to formalize our informational search a bit. I have found it useful to ask students, on a voluntary basis, for personal statements that provide information in three areas. Initially, I inquire about the student's view of the course, asking questions such as: What is your preparation for this course? How do you see it relating to past and upcoming studies? Which of the topics in the syllabus hold the most—or least—interest for you? In what areas do you feel most confident, and where might you appreciate special assistance? By what measures and in what ways will you evaluate the worth of this course? How might I make the ritual of academic grading personally useful for you?

Second, I seek to learn about participants' backgrounds. I ask the students to describe, in whatever detail they consider appropriate, two or three particularly meaningful incidents from their academic or professional experience and to explain why they chose these episodes. I ask: What did you learn? What questions do these experiences pose for you now? The "critical incidents" sections of student information statements have proven extremely useful. Almost inevitably they provide a clue to understanding the "real" person, as well as leads to help link his or her experience to classroom dialogue.

Third, I inquire about the future. What are your academic plans for the remainder of the degree program? What are your plans for a job search? What are your career and life goals at this point? Students' answers to such questions often illuminate their motivations.

Experimenting with personal information statements is not complicated. A few administrative suggestions, however, may be in order. I explain the purpose of the statements in class by proposing that students help me so that I may help them. I stress that their cooperation is completely voluntary and that all the information they provide will be held in confidence. I encourage them to modify my questions in any way that seems appropriate to them—and many do this with great creativity. I conclude by asking if there are any physical challenges—sight or hearing problems, for example—with which I might help them cope in this course. I keep the number of questions to a minimum and give no due date for completed statements. Nor do I pressure students who choose not to provide information.

Forging a primary alliance with students means investing intellect, time, energy, and emotion in discovering who they are, where they are, and how they may best find their way to the material. Such efforts help the instructor become a true teacher.

Like the bedrock of partnership and community, alliance with students is both a lofty goal and a matter of everyday practice. All of these converge in the fourth, most practical-minded premise: that discussion teachers must develop skill in managing both the content and the process of the discussion.

Dual Instructional Competency

Most of the rest of the essays in this book focus, from their authors' various perspectives, on the teaching and learning process as it unfolds in the discussion classroom. They assume that discussion teachers must not only (like lecturers) have mastered the content of their courses, but must be equally adept in process. The *what* of teaching (concepts and facts) is no more crucial than the *who* (knowledge of students) and *how*. By mastering the how of teaching the instructor unites the other two aspects and influences the moment-to-moment flow of events. These distinctions, of course, are integral parts of an organic gestalt; they run together and overlap like freshly applied watercolors.

Taken as a whole, mastery of process and content grant what I call dual competency, the central element in effective discussion leadership. But how does one begin to develop this complex mastery? Concentrating on the most fundamental level, I shall offer suggestions about teaching preparation as grounding for the advice presented in much of the rest of this volume. What better foundation for dual competency than dual preparation? The instructor who takes time to think not only about the material, but also about how to "play it" with a particular group of students, will enjoy a double advantage of confidence and competence.

Preparation can never completely eliminate anxiety. After all, one is attempting to foresee the unforeseeable. Discussions are group improvisations; how can one possibly know in advance what students will want to say? Although I have no simple answers, I can offer the following well-tested method based on my own experience with case discussions in Business Policy courses. My preparation begins on familiar turf, with a careful review of content, but it also includes assessment of students' and the group's capacity to work in concert, and speculation about teaching tactics to promote effective collaboration. Taken as a whole, this exercise can give an instructor a running start toward dual instructional competency.

First, I evaluate the academic progress of the class as a whole. How well does this group understand basic course concepts and their application to practice? Where has this class developed mastery; where is it still struggling? What specific topics have been covered? Which remain, and where and how might these materials best be introduced? I make certain that I am in command of the case to be discussed, and I assess it as a learning instrument. What are its strengths, its limitations? Does it include material with the potential to offend? Where is it likely to excite and intrigue? And I try to predict what the students' attitude toward it might be and how well they are likely to prepare it.

Second, I assess the class as a learning group. How does the participants' skill at working together measure up against the challenge of the case? What is their mood—are they having fun or are they glum? What is happening in the wider academic scene that might affect tomorrow's discussions?

Third, I try to estimate each student's current circumstances, his or her academic strengths and weaknesses as well as abilities to contribute to the discussion process. Who might learn most from the upcoming discussion? Will the case be of special interest to students with particular backgrounds or career interests? Will it offer quiet students a useful entry point into the class discussion? Who might find the case intimidating? Which students might be good "coaches" for their peers with difficulties? Which students are likely to take leadership roles in the anticipated dialogues, and who will probably remain on the sidelines?

Fourth, I consider my own mood. How do I feel about this material? Is this a fun section of the course or an academic chore? Are there some sour apples in the group? Where might my personal biases and prejudices affect my leadership of the discussion? All these considerations—as well as family and personal concerns—influence a teacher's behavior in the classroom.

Fifth, I think about the mode, pace, and flow of the upcoming class. Is it to be a drill in applying analytic techniques to the problem defined in the case of the day, or an open-ended search for stimulating and creative solutions to a broader range of problems? What is an appropriate pace—do I want the dialogue to move briskly, cover a large number of topics, and include the maximum possible number of student contributions? Or do I want to probe a limited number of issues in depth—with fewer students speaking at greater length? In terms of flow, do I want the group to build a single construct of the issues involved, by accretion, or would I hope for a more competitive series of arguments and rebuttals presented by individual students in defense of their positions?

Sixth, I work out a rough-cut process plan for the upcoming discussion. What leadership choices might help the group deal most effectively with this material? How should class time be divided between discussions of analysis and action? How should the chalkboard be used—what would I hope to see there at the beginning and end of the class? How active a role do I want to play—should I intervene often or only when changes in direction seem necessary?

Seventh, and last, I think about possible openings and endings for the class. Should I begin with a comment on the previous session and announce my expectations for this one? Should I open with a narrowly focused question, or a broad one? Whom should I invite to speak? What might the student's response be, and how might the whole group, in turn, react? I give similar attention to the end of the discussion. Should I, for example, offer a prepared general wrap-up, let one evolve extemporaneously, or end the discussion without a summary? What mind-benders might I give the students when they leave class? What suggestions, if any, for the next class meeting?

Systematically previewing both content and the major process dimensions—the group dynamic, student needs and ambitions, instructor's interests and biases, and the interplay among material, discussion mode, and larger course concepts—can help an instructor anticipate, at least in a general sense, the paths a class might want to explore. At the minimum, such planning can prevent a few errors (and terrors) and build the confidence and clearheadedness necessary to seeing and seizing teaching opportunities when they arise. Most teachers who work through this, or a similar, protocol several times feel that it sensitizes them to the complexities of discussion teaching. At its best, this preparation can help us harness the learning power generated by the fusion of process and content.

Conclusion

The territory of discussion teaching has never been well mapped. This chapter's four basic premises and accompanying suggestions for practice are but one instructor's sketch. I still find it richly rewarding to explore this world of wonders, and I hope that teachers who practice other modes of instruction might undertake similar explorations. All of us share a splendid vocation with limitless potential. My observations about one type of pedagogy should, therefore, be placed within the context of a premise that I consider even more basic: there is magnificence in *all* teaching. In any form—tutorial, laboratories, and lectures—our efforts bring bountiful rewards. We enjoy the privilege of lifelong learning, a constant link to youth, growth, search, and the world of ideas, and the knowledge that our work has fundamental worth to others. The potential of our daily routines to create impressive results—some of the moment, the most intriguing of the future, makes our work a service of ever-unfolding fulfillment. We are part of something great.

NOTES

1. Hugh Prather, *Notes to Myself* (Moab, UT: Real People Press, 1970), unpaged.
2. Marcel Proust, *Remembrance of Things Past*, tr. C. K. Scott Moncrieff (New York: Random House, 1935), I, 15.
3. William Faulkner, *Requiem for a Nun* (New York: Random House, 1951), p. 92. Gavin Stevens is speaking to Temple Drake.

PART II
Personal Odysseys

3

Tulips, Tinfoil, and Teaching: Journal of a Freshman Teacher

COLLEEN BURKE

RICHARD, MY NEIGHBOR, is an artist. He makes colorful marks on the world. I am a businesswoman trying to become a teacher of business. We teach at the same liberal arts college, and we share a backyard border, where Richard has a very artistic garden, and I simply have a successful one. As a stranger, you might not know whose garden is whose, but once you had been told, you too would probably see Richard's garden as artistic and mine as successful. Our perceptions, our labels, depend on more than just our eyes.

Late in the spring, a huge cluster of tulips bloomed on the border of our gardens. The bulbs were obviously Richard's, but the blossoms belonged to both of us. I sat next to the tulips, absorbed in Fritz Roethlisberger's autobiography, *The Elusive Phenomena*.[1] Suddenly, Richard's bulking presence shadowed the page.

I tried to explain to Richard why I was so excited by Roethlisberger's account of his work in organizational behavior. It reminded me of what I was trying to do in the classroom: place behavior on a mathematical matrix, graph its multidimensionality, try to hold it still as it squirms like a puppy seeing its first squirrel. I described to him the process by which I tried to take students in a discussion class beyond the outline of a situation into its subtleties—a process of accepting and then mitigating ambiguity. His obvious surprise at what I was saying caused me to reconsider what I assumed was a common observational skill. How simple is it to look at a group, an organization, an interaction? It seemed to me I was trying to give my students some tools to see better.

Richard asked me to describe the tulips. I said they were white. He was silent, so I looked harder. And harder. Perhaps they were not white; perhaps there weren't even individual tulips. There was yellow (sort of tarnished cream), and there was pink (well, maybe bleached coral), and there was something like blue-gray, and veins of off-green edged with a noncolor. And the shape? There were overlapping petals creating rich shadows, new nonforms. The whole disappeared in its unmappable complexity only to reappear in multidimensional subtleties of individual petals, stamen, and flowers—an interwoven cluster.

Could it possibly be this hard and confusing for my students to look at a simple business situation case study? Is this why they rush to the outline? Is this why we place organizations in boxes connected by straight lines and point with pride to their clarity? Is this the source of classroom resistance to discussion? Perhaps students feel threatened by ambiguity, the unknown, and the seemingly unchartable as I push them toward the excitement, the analytical richness, and then the discoveries beneath the surface of cases. Whose definition of excitement is it? Maybe it's only mine. Maybe I haven't understood enough of my students' journey.

Is it possible that Richard and I are teaching the same thing in a similar process with different media? With the right tools, with matrixes and measurings, Richard's art students can be trained to re-create a graphically accurate tulip on a two-dimensional canvas. They can learn the precise formulas for color variations. Yet no two of his students will interpret the same image in the same way as they stand before the same still life.

Why is the aesthetic of my classroom so important to me? Why do I push my students toward artistic analyses of secular situations? They may never be the first person to recognize and capture a new market opportunity; they may never create or lead an organization. But they will be the people who make up the organization, who give it life and derive meaning from it. As I look for the artist in each of my students, am I really looking for myself?

As I will never again see a white tulip as a white tulip, I hope my students will never again see a simple group as a simple group. A tulip is not a tulip. The dialectic of abstraction and specificity, of ambiguity and certainty, is part of the case discussion phenomenon. But where on the ladder of abstraction should I, the teacher, focus?

I must not ask my students to see everything with such rich detail or they will never move forward: analysis paralysis. Selection is the key to action. The art of the photographer: framing, focusing. How do I introduce my students to the complexity of a situation yet focus on specifics as well?

I am glad I sat in the garden that day.

How does an art teacher communicate the skills of seeing, analyzing, measuring, interpreting, and presenting? Perhaps I could learn from a studio instructor's techniques something that would help me in my own teaching. I enrolled in an elementary painting class. Secretly I had always wanted to take an art course. Now I could rationalize that I was there to learn not how to paint but, rather, how painting is taught.

Forgetting (or perhaps never consciously recognizing) how hard it is to be a student, I skipped arrogantly over the prerequisite courses of one-, two-, and three-dimensional design. I wanted to get to where the color was. Thus I suddenly found myself face-to-face with my first painting assignment. Each of us was to paint a still life of crumpled tinfoil. All of my competitive juices began to flow. It was the tinfoil and me, and I was determined to win. But I simply could not do it. I could not paint tinfoil, and there was plenty of public evidence on my easel. Side by side with some of the very students whom I would be teaching in the afternoon, I found myself unable to see, to interpret, to present.

First I tried gray, which I had to mix from many colors, because we were allowed no black on our palette. But gray did not look at all like tinfoil. I tried self-mixed black. Still no tinfoil. I tried white, but it looked chalky and dull. Nothing worked. Tinfoil, especially when crumpled, seems to be a conglomeration of darkly reflective geometric surfaces— reflecting the whole visual world. Is this how my students feel when I ask them to deal with ambiguity? There is no black and white. Worse, even gray is in fact a dull reflection.

After three exasperating hours in the studio I dashed over to teach my introductory business class of twenty-five college freshmen who had just read a turgid handout on the structural analysis of industries. They looked at me as if they had just been handed a piece of crumpled tinfoil. Now I could recognize the look, the feeling. To understand teaching, perhaps we ourselves must reexperience being students of the foreign.

How can I teach my students to mix gray from diverse facts and to be comfortable with the gray? Can I build their tolerance for ambiguity? Can I help them shape their own analytical canvases, even with seemingly uncontrollable, ever-changing surfaces? Can I teach them to know their palette, mix their own colors, paint their own pictures?

I tell my students they need a sense of humor and a sense of perspective to make it through my class (and through life). Yet in the art studio, my ill-formed oranges roll off the tilted tables of my canvases. Perspective setting is a skill, not an accident. You experiment with it and experience it. It is not only seeing, but measuring. It is a detailed and sensitive understanding of the relationships of objects and the spaces between objects. How many student-written case analyses resemble formless still lifes with tilting floating oranges or tables?

The art studio seems to have little in common with my business classroom. No student walks into the studio expecting a lecture. There are no desks, no standing teacher, no sitting students. The teacher teaches while wandering around. The students wander, too, exchanging insights, then going back to their canvases to try again. Discipline comes from within the student; the wandering is purposeful. Everyone seems to know that the responsibility for interpreting, presenting, and learning is within him- or herself.

Mistakes made in the studio are not seen as failures. Rather, they are an inevitable step in the constructive affirmative process; they are an attempt to reach a visual resolution of a complex interpretive problem. The visual experiment requires trial and error; the error is proof of trying. So why do students in my business class think that making a mistake is dumb, scary, and risky?

In the studio, grading is a social event. At the end of each assignment, our interpretations (presumably of the same subject, but sometimes unrecognizably so) are hung on the wall. We sit on the floor and tear them apart. My fellow students seem to be enjoying this "peer crit," which is not a criticism, but an opportunity. Led by our teacher, we look first for the successes in each canvas. Is it this exciting, constructive, verbal exchange that motivates those late-night efforts in the studio? Can I encourage this spirit in my class?

The art teacher seldom "teaches." Once he calls us to his canvas to watch him tackle the tinfoil. I can feel the students' uneasiness, impatience. Everyone wants to get back to his or her own effort. We can't learn by watching him. We don't want to know how smart he is. I can see that it is hard for our young teacher to restrain himself. He reaches for my brush as he tries to explain where I am going wrong. He keeps telling me to "lay in the color," and I have absolutely no idea what he means. Experience slowly tells me.

Our interpretive vocabulary is becoming richer as we experiment with more color variations on our palette. We have become both bolder and subtler. One night our homework assignment is to paint a matrix of one hundred grays of incremental value and tone, never using black. What assignments can I give that would help my business students to see the grays between the inevitable either/or of black-and-white analyses?

Everything in the painting course seems to reinforce the student's responsibility for learning. The product of effort is so tangible, so public. Each person's canvas seems to be a personal metaphor. There is pride, specialness, and meaning. Instead of defensiveness, there are dialogue and interaction, spontaneous communication, and constructive criticism, experimentation, and innovation. There is a common value, a common aesthetic.

There is no right or wrong as our coach wanders among our easels. Yet the mammoth room is filled with learning. Critiques are invited, welcomed, valued. Mistakes are accepted, encouraged, and rewarded. My business classroom, several hundred yards across the campus, seems worlds away. Can I carry any piece of this experience across that distance?

The tulips in my garden marked the end of my first year of teaching—and the beginning of my understanding of the journey of that first year.

The tulips were undeniably beautiful. Up too close, they were bewildering. In focus, they were exciting. So, too, was my first year of teaching, whether in its finite, focused moments, or its confused experiential cluster. Beneath the comfortable outline, the chronological academic calendar, are the nonforms, the unseen or unappreciated colors, the shadows, the subtleties, the individuals.

The tulips led me to the tinfoil, my personal experiment in learning visual resolutions. The tinfoil, with its mini-mirrored quality, moved me toward a reflective understanding. It represented the struggle, the trial and error of my teaching journey. The tinfoil became my metaphor for the case discussion classroom, with its interactions of student, teacher, and subject. I had learned a great deal in that first year.

New Appointment for a "Lecturer"

In late August of the previous year my contract for a one-year nontenure-track position was finally confirmed. I now had the opportunity to become a case discussion teacher. Ironically, the job title was "lecturer."

My lateral slide into academia had not been long meditated. A month or so earlier I had telephoned the dean of faculty and asked if there were any openings on the business department faculty for the fall. By chance the chairmanship of the department had just passed to a man whose personal agenda called for a gradual conversion from the lecture method to student-centered discussions and case analyses.

Over lunch I was asked to give the new chairman an oral résumé. Since graduating from business school at twenty-three, I explained, I had been on an intense, high-ambition, nonlinear fast track. Never once in those eleven years had I thought of myself as a prospective teacher. After serving as the executive assistant to the president of a *Fortune* 500 company, I had become a venture capitalist and apprentice entrepreneur. I had had a stint in government as a policy person, and had served with the state arts council, at a time when fiscal reality clobbered cultural ideals. I had given birth to a wonderful son and to a direct-mail catalogue of children's products whose success took me around the country on television talk shows. And I had also become a single parent in a small town, looking for a job—assuming I could be a discussion teacher.

After all, I told the chairman, I had done a lot. I had touched life and it had responded (though not always as I had planned). I had touched power and knew its potential as well as its price. I had known "success" at the superficial levels of net worth and press releases, and I had known failure and loss.

Fortunately, the new chairman was not risk-averse. With two weeks remaining before the start of classes, I was hired.

Two weeks to become a teacher. No textbooks ordered. No course plan. No syllabus. I telephoned one of my former professors and asked how I could become an effective teacher in two weeks. He laughed. And then he said something that kept me afloat during many a near-drowning that first semester: "You will make a fantastic teacher."

I let those words ring in my head during the inevitable moments of self-doubt while I was learning to accept my own ignorance and tolerate my imperfections as a teacher. Knowing that someone I respected as a teacher thought I had the potential to be effective in the classroom was most heartening. What he gave me in that comment was what I had to pass on to my students. They needed to be told that they could be fantastic students.

"Think only about what the students are experiencing," my professor continued. "Know that you are OK and make your students feel that they are. You will be scared, but they will be more scared." Our conversation closed with his suggestion that I obtain a copy of *Teaching as a Subversive Activity*, which challenged the traditional structure of student-teacher relationships and the teaching-learning process.[2]

At last, I thought as I hung up, I have something tangible—a book! Maybe it would have the magic formula that would turn me into a teacher. I was soon disappointed, however. The book was not an operations manual for teaching. What I found in it was more philosophy, more theory, and another critique of teaching methods. My anxiety rose.

I was scheduled to have a preparatory meeting with the department chair. Perhaps he would give me the answers I sought.

The chairman began by explaining that I would be teaching over a hundred students, broken down into three sections. Two of those sections would be a direct transplant of the leadership course that he had developed at his previous institution. The course gave students a quick overview of the key functional disciplines of business through cases—descriptions of business situations—and accompanying notes. But I would be teaching eighteen-year-old college freshmen on a liberal arts campus, whereas the course had been created for graduate engineers. (I considered that a mighty big difference.) The course materials, which seemed overwhelming in relation to the time I had to prepare, were packaged. Multiple copies of the cases had been ordered. Assignment sheets for each day of the course had already been photocopied. All I had to do was "teach" it!

The chair explained that six instructors would be teaching the course to a total of three hundred introductory students. We would meet weekly as a team to discuss content and process. Not one member of the team had ever taught a case discussion course before.

My third section, said the chairman, carried the title "Management Theory" in the college catalogue, but it would be up to me to create the content. He hoped I would use a case discussion format with some experiential learning in human behavior in organizations. (For this little task I had a whole week to prepare!) Now was my chance to ask what I should know in order to become an effective case discussion teacher. Glancing at his freshly painted bookshelves, I asked if he had any books I could read on how to teach. There was no such book, he replied. What in the world had I gotten myself into?

The chair emphasized that he would evaluate my effectiveness on the basis of my ability to "transfer my residual power as teacher over to my students." He must have uttered that phrase fifteen times in a one-hour meeting. What did he mean? I was too embarrassed to ask, lest my ignorance on how one transfers power might preclude the signing of my contract.

While he rambled on about the introductory course and its specific cases, I found myself lost in images of how one transfers power. I conjured up a picture of the first day of class. Solemnly I would enter the room carrying high a sacred vessel filled with power. Each student would rise and partake. Everyone would be *required* to receive (if I were to be evaluated on transferring it, I would make its acceptance a requirement). One at a time the students thus became empowered, first those who craved power but had never been offered it before, next those who feared power and clung to their pseudo-innocence, and finally, those who thought they desired power, but who ran away when it became available. The classroom ritual ended with my powerful students matriculating and my being pronounced an effective teacher.

My new boss cleared his throat and asked what I was thinking about. I responded that I simply did not understand how one transfers power when one is standing in front of a classroom of students. "In front?" I laughed at my semantic imprisonment. I still had programmed word pictures of what a classroom should be: a teacher standing in front, imparting wisdom to students at the rear taking notes. In fact, most of my professors at business school had leaped, lounged, lunged, knelt, and charged anywhere but in the front of the classroom. Earlier, my undergraduate professors had sat comfortably in small seminar circles in living rooms and talked with us, not to us.

I was baffled by this mandate to transfer power. I knew that I had touched power, exercised it, avoided it, and intimately watched others play with it. I knew that one cannot feign its absence or its presence. I knew that I had perceived my teachers—especially the best ones—as powerful figures. They were older, wiser, more talented, more experienced. They had the power to affect me, my life. And they exercised it. They could create new power within me, but they could not give me theirs. I struggled in vain with the concept.

The First Day of Class

Too quickly the first day of school came. I was anxious. I did not want to fail, but I did not know what it might take to succeed. The textbooks for my Management Theory class had not arrived. I had no lesson plan. No teacher's manual. I was winging it, and it was the first day of college.

Remember the first day of school? What is that emotion? Is it excitement or fear? There is that special smell in the air, a crispness, an almost-autumnness. Won't everything and nothing happen on that emotionally explosive day? The first day.

As on any other first day of school, I transferred some of my fears about my potential performance to my clothes. I dressed with considerable premeditation. I tried to dress unpowerfully. In fact, I dressed young. Too young.

As I drove to campus in my Jeep, I tried to psych myself free of my fears and my anxieties. I silently counseled myself to get inside my students' feelings; to care about where they were at, not where I was. They would be freshmen. This would be their first impression of a college classroom, a college professor, a college teaching style. Wouldn't they be worried about the impressions they were making on each other and on me? They would be hearing what I did not say, and not hearing what I did say.

I was scared, too. The corridors were foreign territory for me. I did not know where the classroom was or even where the ladies' room was. In both my personal and professional life, I was as much a freshman as they were. I had not yet assimilated my new role as single or divorced. I didn't know how others perceived me (and I cared). I did not even know how I perceived myself! I had no frame of reference of myself as teacher. There was but one nubbin of confidence deep inside me: I knew that I was a good storyteller and, if all else failed, I could probably just talk to them.

I knew so little about the territory I was walking into. In my previous career I researched markets before entering; I knew who would be at a meeting before presenting. Now I was entering a classroom without data. Who were the players? Where did they come from? What were their values? their assumptions about college? their goals? Who would be competing against whom, for what stakes? What expectations had their new community already set for them? I felt uneasy knowing that they would get their first impression of me before I had any important data about them.

That first day in the classroom I felt as if I were lost in the wilderness without a map or compass. Really lost. Fear takes over for a minute, and then the drive for survival hushes the fear so that one's senses can be fully tuned to any sign or signal. Lost, I saw signs that I would not normally have seen or would have taken for granted. I heard better, as if I were listening for rippling water. I saw better, as if I were searching for a moss-sided tree. I became one large antenna. Maybe the real job that first day is not to teach, but to let your antennae tingle, to process more oblique information faster than you ever have before.

In the previous two weeks—while committing to memory the tips about making students feel OK and pondering the transfer of power—I had thought a lot about what it was I had learned in business school.

The blurring filter of eleven years simplified my inquiry. The specific skills, specific cases, specific courses had smudged in memory, allowing me to conclude quickly that what I had learned was how to think. So, after a deep breath, I walked in to the classroom and said, "Welcome to Thinking 107."

I was startled by the disorientation that resulted from my thoughtful welcome. One student glanced at his registration form and left the class-room before I got a chance to add that this was also "Business 107." In those first few moments I learned very, very quickly how scared, insecure, and confused my thirty-five freshmen really were. Clearly I had not made them feel OK at all.

Words began to flow from I know not where. I asked the students if they had ever boarded a plane, fastened the seatbelt, relaxed, and then suddenly been hit by the anxiety that they had boarded the wrong flight. My analogy must have hit a common experience, because heads were nodding in recognition and grins began to appear. And what if after taxiing, the stewardess had announced an unplanned destination? Perhaps my greeting had produced an equivalent sense of lost control in the classroom. I explained that in this course, everyone would be driving his or her own car. No pilot would control either their destiny or their destination. This would be *their* journey. I would only provide road maps and, when necessary, attempt to prevent deadly collisions. Perhaps I would point out some interesting scenery along the way. At their own chosen speed, behind their own steering wheel, they could control where they would go.

Phew! my quickened heartbeat slowed. Students began to realize that the teacher really did mean that this was a course in thinking, and the analogy about control at least brushed the surface of their consciousness. Still, my actions would speak louder than my analogies, and I still did not know what those actions should be.

Once I had relaxed enough to look around the classroom, I could not believe what I saw. I was sitting on a twelve-foot-long black chemistry table that formed a barrier between two spaces: out there, neat linear rows of student desks and up here, the blackboard. The space had nothing to do with my image of how I would teach. I had pictured some form of spatial interchange between the students and myself, some form of movement and energy between students' comments and blackboard no-tations. Why had no one warned me to check out the space before the opening day of class?

The first class proceeded. It had to. I pushed the chemistry desk into the hall (only to be reprimanded later by both the registrar and the janitorial service department), and we began the Desert Survival Exercise that every member of the introductory course had agreed to use in the first class.

I had been skeptical about the exercise, but it worked! The students broke down into small groups to play the roles of survivors of an airplane crash in the desert; they had to decide how to handle limited resources like water, salt tablets, blankets, knives, mirrors, maps, and even trench coats and gin. It turned out to be a particularly appropriate exercise for the first day, as it came so close to some of our real survival emotions. An important lesson that emerged was the need to determine objectives or strategy before allocating materials. Student-survivors who didn't first figure out whether to signal for help or to walk out of the desert ended up with the wrong mixture of resources.

Students also discovered that decision making in groups, though less efficient, led them to make better choices because of the information exchange, the disagreement, even the conflict in deciding which resources they wanted. Learning to accept and even seek out the intellectual interdependence and to respect conflict as well as cooperation would be a key to making our case discussions work. The very idea of disagreeing with others and arguing a position went against the norms of this campus—especially on the first day of class, when everyone wanted to be liked and no one wanted an argument. But no one person can tackle a case alone. Only the rich exchange of ideas and divergent values would lead to solid analysis, understanding, and creative solutions. The exercise also worked magic with our physical space, as the students divided into groups and broke up those orderly rows of chairs.

While students tried to figure out how to survive their airplane crashes, I asked them to fill out name cards and data cards. On the data cards each student filled in his or her name, its phonetic pronunciation, his or her hometown, work experience, college phone number, expectations from the course, major area of study or intended major, other courses taken this semester, and so on. These cards, suggested by the chair, proved invaluable throughout the semester. They provided a place for recording students' daily participation and, more important, helped me choose opening presenters on the basis of their experiences and interests. If a student was an art history major, I could use an art metaphor to pull out her analysis. If a student was taking introductory psychology, I could avoid calling on him during the week of the major psych midterm. If a student had been on the ski patrol or worked in a sporting goods store,

I could call on her to begin the Head Ski Company case.[3] The data cards helped me find creative ways to give these eighteen-year-olds confidence in the validity of their experiences and thus to expand our discussions. The students, I was to discover, were my subject matter for the semester. The data cards were my textbook.

Each card also had a place for the student's photograph. The next step, therefore, was for me to get out my camera and snap individual mug shots during the first class. I walked around the room, asking each student to hold up his or her name card, and then captured the labeled face. I am amazed at how well the personalities I got to know during the semester—the laughers, the hiders, the aloof, the hesitant, the bold— were captured in those first-day photos. But as I snapped these pictures I felt the tensions in the room begin to rise again. I thought of Susan Sontag's essays on photography, in which she describes the camera as a weapon, something that primitive peoples believe can steal a piece of their soul. So, as I shot, I began talking about Sontag's observations and the phenomenon of control through the camera. We all relaxed as we chatted about this new subject. With only one shot left on my roll of thirty-six, the ninety-minute class ended. Everything had worked. It had almost been easy. Maybe even fun. I felt energized and confident. I was a teacher!

Two hours later I walked into my second section of the same introduc- tory course, assured that everything would be even better now that I knew the formula. This time, the space was right. I had gotten a good room with encircling blackboards, and I had rearranged the chairs into a double semicircle before the class bell rang.

In walked the students, and immediately, it seemed, everything went wrong. The human dimension was awry. Once filled with students, the classroom seemed to be almost exploding with aggression and threat. As I scanned the room, I saw only caught hostile faces. Do you think you're good enough to teach us? How quickly I reflected this perceived challenge back onto students I did not know. Perhaps I was the original source of the feelings and not the reflector.

We broke into groups for the Desert Survival Exercise. In one group a rugged young man assumed almost immediate leadership of the resource decisions. There was no discussion or debate about alternative strategies or resources in his group. He made a unilateral ranked list of survival items for the whole group.

Later, as each group described its decision-making processes, it emerged that this student had told his group that he had survived a real airplane crash and therefore knew the right answers. I picked up the theme and talked a bit about experience as a means to knowledge and knowledge as a means of legitimating leadership. At this point, the student boldly boasted that he had been lying, that he never survived an airplane crash but had learned just enough in his Outward Bound program that summer to bluff his teammates into silence. I was personally offended, even angry, at this revelation. Ethics would be an important topic in the upcoming course. Could I let this student get away with his misrepresentation and his pride in it? Should I condemn him in front of the whole class on the first day? If I did not, would I lose even more of the trust and cohesion that I had hoped for and that already was slipping from my grasp? How could I bring this section back to me? In my management experience I had always had more privacy and more time to think such problems through before taking action. But here thirty-five sets of eyes seemed riveted on me, waiting for my decision. Irreversible impressions would be made no matter what I did. I felt so vulnerable, so exposed. I wanted a script to read from, and there was none.

When the ninety minutes of my afternoon section were finally over, I left the classroom enervated. Why had this class zapped my energy, milked my enthusiasm, left me so used up?

Two Very Different Sections

Though there were many surprises in that first week of teaching, the biggest was the discovery of how different two sections could be. I assumed that both groups were randomly composed of freshmen in a school not known for its heterogeneity. I was the same teacher in both sections. After a room reassignment for the morning class, both sections now occupied similar spaces. Both used identical materials. Why did one section continue to work and one continue to fall apart? The fact that I had already taught the material once in the morning should have made me better prepared, if anything, for the afternoon class. Was I a better teacher in the morning? The incredible contrast between the two sections left me in awe of the dynamics of a case discussion group. Can a section have a personality of its own that just does not fit with the teacher's? How could I ever create a personal teaching formula if my words had such different results in different contexts?

By the end of the second week I was really hurting. My style and its apparent success in the morning made the pain and the frustration of the afternoon even more poignant. I looked forward to entering the friendly territory of my morning class and dreaded the afternoon. When the students from the two sections began talking to each other and comparing notes, the situation became tense. In the halls I started hearing rumors that I favored the morning students and did not like the afternoon ones. The enthusiasm and preparation of the morning section grew even better; the hostility and resistance of the afternoon section grew even worse.

I knew I needed help, but I did not know where to turn. Writing in my journal clarified some of my feelings, but did not offer a lot of advice. I thought about sharing the problem with our teaching team, which was urged to discuss just this kind of process issue at its weekly meetings. But the kind of trust that such a team needs to talk openly about real problems had not yet been built. In fact, I felt there were several members of the team who had mixed feelings about whether they wanted me to succeed. (I was, after all, a nonteacher, and they were experienced teachers who were all being shaken by this new experiment with case discussion.) Our insecurities resulted in isolationism rather than sharing. At the team meetings only the success stories were told, never the defeats. Outwardly, it appeared that everyone else was doing great and only I had a problem.

I could have called my business school professor again, but I was reluctant to tell him that he was wrong—that I was not going to be a fantastic teacher. Finally, help came from an unexpected source: my own students in the afternoon section.

By late September my students began to become individuals to me. As I got to know them, I began to learn from them. In the afternoon section, for example, there was the young woman whom I had asked to begin our first case discussion. The case was about how Howard Head had introduced America to the metal ski. From her data card I knew she had worked in her family's sporting goods store, and I figured she might get us started discussing the importance of a loyal distribution system for a product such as skis. But she seemed scared to talk, even offended that I had memorized her data card.

I myself had never been called upon to start a case in business school, and I did not fully appreciate the impact of hearing one's own name called in this situation. A friend recently told me that he still remembers acutely being the first person ever called upon in our business school section, and still puzzles over why he was chosen. If a very secure forty-year-old businessman still wonders why he was chosen almost fifteen years ago, the impact must be enormous. It certainly was so for my student. After two weeks of classes she told me she was going to drop the course.

As we walked from the class to the parking lot, I asked her to explain her decision. Her words, though guarded, were filled with information that I was not sure how to interpret. First she said there was no room in the classroom for her. "No room?" I asked. "Well, you know," she said, "no space." I still did not understand. She then blurted out, "Well, you're there and you run around too much, you talk too fast, and you make me nervous. There is not room for me!"

I was simply astounded. Had I been too effective at following the advice to get inside the students? Had I gotten too close? Was I taking up their space? Had my data cards trespassed on their privacy? Had the maleness that I felt in the classroom anything to do with her comments?

I liked this student. If she dropped the course, it would be a defeat for me. So I started confiding in her. I told her how very scared I had been in business school. How painful it had been to be one of the three women in a section of one hundred men; to be young and inexperienced and scared. And to be called upon only to give a woman's view of a consumer product like a Singer sewing machine. I wanted her to understand that it was out of respect for her that I called on her to open the first case.

I don't think she believed me. She said she perceived me as someone who could never be scared. Moreover, she had discussed her reactions with several other women in the class, and they were also planning to drop the course. When she finally reached my car, she exclaimed, "I just knew you would drive a Jeep!" and the hostility in her voice filled the parking lot.

Soon afterward, another student from the afternoon section came to tell me that she had asked to transfer to a "safer" section. My section was scary, she explained, and she was uncomfortable. Friends had told her about another teacher's section of the course and it sounded more like her kind of environment. I asked her to explain exactly what she meant about my section being scary. She said that she did not know what was scary; it was just that the other section sounded safe. The other teacher did not make his students sit in a semicircle, and he used a textbook and lectures to supplement his cases.

So, maybe *I* wasn't scary, but *cases* were scary. Discussion was scary. The process, the uncertainty, and the openness were scary. How could I make an environment secure enough that learning could go forward, especially when other teachers were reverting to safer methods for the same course? The discussion environment is risky for teachers as well as students. Is it the responsibility of the teacher to assume all the risks so that the students can feel OK?

Meanwhile, my morning section got better and better. At ease, I found the perfect words to put on the board. I could choose the right person to ask the right question and the right person to follow up on the initial analysis. I found metaphors, examples, and anecdotes that brought forth more ideas and better analysis. I wanted to learn from the success of the morning section, but its signals were just as difficult to decipher. Why was this section working so beautifully? Why did the students seek me out or just stop to chat about a case when we met by chance? Why did they feel comfortable calling me at home? Why were their study groups vital and involved? Why was there so much positive energy in that class?

I sought more help from two students in my afternoon section, meeting with them outside class. One was a dance major who came to class in her leotard and leg warmers and moved easily into my discussion choreography. She had, in fact, transferred into my section after hearing how "great" it was. She was a safe adviser for me, as I knew she was really digging into the materials. Still, it might help to learn whether the afternoon section was meeting her expectations. She said there was no problem at all. Was I creating one by heeding the dissatisfied?

The second student I consulted was a blind woman who had first been assigned to my morning section but had transferred to the afternoon because of schedule conflicts. She had special sensitivities as well as a section-comparative basis for commenting. As cases are not published in Braille, her study group read the cases aloud and, in the process, paid much more attention to details. She surprised me by saying she loved the afternoon section. She felt no claustrophobia. In fact, the discussion method gave her more confidence to fill her own space than other courses, where she felt her handicap precluded involvement. Further, she distinctly preferred the afternoon to the morning section, which she felt was too gentle, too agreeable, too conformist.

With this confusing and contradictory information I telephoned my professor again. He generously listened and expanded upon his insights and advice. It takes at least three years to become a really effective teacher, he said. I should not blame myself if every classroom moment wasn't magic in the first three weeks.

He expanded on the concept of being one with the class: getting into the students' roles and seeing their world through their eyes in order to understand what they wanted to learn, what they were ready to learn. There were limits, he reminded me, and I should always be aware that

I was working when I was with students. You are a teacher even when you are playing. You have a drink with your students, he said, because you are working to know them better and thus influence their growth. On the possibility that I was taking up too much space in the classroom, he gently reminded me about the hormone levels of eighteen-year-olds. The teacher is an object that is stared at from every angle for ninety minutes. Whether male or female, the teacher takes up physical and emotional space.

Effective case discussion teachers do not do it alone, my professor added. He urged me to find someone with whom I could discuss the process, bounce off the fears, unravel the failures, share the victories. Somehow I had to share honestly with the other teachers on my team. I was relieved. This would not be a solo flight.

The next day, however, I had to go back into that section, and it was still a very uncomfortable place for me. If a similar situation had arisen in my own company, I realized, I would never have let it go on this long. I would have gathered everyone around a table and kicked around the issues. I wondered if I could do that in a classroom; the downside risk seemed minimal. But before staging a dramatic confrontation, I decided to check with the chairman.

There was no such thing as a right answer in cases or in classrooms, he said. I should figure my problem out myself. He would trust my analysis, my instincts, and my judgment. But he cautioned me against expecting too much from a let's-get-it-all-out-on-the-table session. Usually a class will not want to talk about its feelings for more than ten minutes, he said. He doubted that an open forum would turn the section around.

As he ended the meeting, the chairman remarked that I was probably just in the process of becoming a REAL teacher. When I asked what he meant, he took from his bookshelf a copy of a children's book, *The Velveteen Rabbit*. In it, a stuffed bunny asks his nursery colleague, the Skin Horse, "What is REAL?"

> "Real isn't how you are made," said the Skin Horse. "It's a thing that happens to you. When a child loves you for a long, long time, not just to play with, but REALLY loves you, then you become Real."
>
> "Does it hurt?" asked the Rabbit.
>
> "Sometimes," said the Skin Horse, for he was always truthful, "when you are Real, you don't mind being hurt."
>
> "Does it happen all at once, like being wound up," he asked, "or bit by bit?"
>
> "It doesn't happen all at once," said the Skin Horse. "You become. It

takes a long time. That's why it doesn't often happen to people who break easily, or have sharp edges, or who have to be carefully kept. Generally by the time you are Real, most of your hair has been loved off, and your eyes drop out and you get loose in the joints and very shabby. But these things don't matter at all, because once you are Real, you can't be ugly, except to people who don't understand."[4]

Well, if my boss thought I was becoming REAL like the Velveteen Rabbit, then I had the courage to go in and make that section work, even if it hurt.

I knew that a dramatic confrontation in the classroom was not my only option. I could wait out the situation, or I might try to work with a few students as change agents and see if they could influence the direction of the afternoon section. But I was impatient for a resolution. So, trusting myself, I went forward with the idea of throwing open the class discussion to what was happening in class.

Lest students perceive that I was treating the two sections differently, I threw open the topic in my morning section as well. Just as the chair had predicted, the morning section's discussion lasted about ten minutes. It was less revealing, as most students said they were enjoying class and felt they were growing.

The afternoon section, however, started off with full engagement. The students had analyzed themselves and me and the class much more thoroughly than they had ever analyzed a case. They were suddenly outspoken. One after another had a point to make, even the normally silent students. I had a sense that the students were angry at me for making them be grown-ups in the class. Only four weeks before they had been enjoying the irresponsibility of a high school summer; now they were struggling with some very grown-up decision making in their coed dorms and in downtown bars. It was not fair that I should force them to make adult decisions in the classroom too. At least in their lecture classes they could be children again, free of decision making.

The students also said that they felt inadequate, intimidated by the analyses and comments of others. Everyone else seemed so smart, had a better idea, raised their hands faster. Each one seemed to feel that when he or she finally had formulated a comment and had built up the courage to speak, I called on someone else. By the end of the class, they felt how stupid they had been when they prepared their individual analyses the night before.

One student aimed his critique directly at me. He *knew* that the business world was an orderly place, offering clear black-and-white choices, though I used case analysis to make it look chaotic; his stepfather had told him so. Ultimately, the student took his complaint all the way to the dean, saying he had not come to college to talk to other students, but to learn from orderly lectures. He was particularly offended that he had not even one full page of notes to show from my class.

It was this student, it turned out, who most intimidated his classmates, for he spoke with an air of authority and precision that made others sure they did not know what they were talking about. He was offended if I did not call upon him, and when I did recognize him, he often asked extraneous questions, using business terminology unknown to the rest of the class. In a macro-level discussion of organizational design and culture, he asked, "What is a transfer price?" No one in the class had even heard of transfer prices, which had nothing to do with our discussion. When I did not let the discussion go in his direction, he accused me of not knowing what a transfer price was. Meanwhile, the other students became silently sick at their own ignorance.

The full ninety minutes of my afternoon section surfaced these insights. For the first time, the students were not talking at me, but with each other. They seemed to have directed all their energies over the previous three weeks to an analysis of me and the course. I now at least knew they had the capacity to analyze and discuss if only I would give them the right topic.

My two sections. So very different. Like two different gardens. One, orderly rows of impatiens, easily tended, easily weeded. One, wild, verging always on being out of control. In my morning garden I knew the spacing, the colors, the individuals, and the whole. I gave late bloomers time and gave egos space. I walked in my morning garden and enjoyed it. It repaid all the effort, tending, and love.

In my afternoon garden I could not relax. There was no formula. I had to look very hard for its uniqueness, its beauty, and its opportunities. I wanted to cling to its outline, its personality. I wanted to see it only from a distance. But the beauty of a wild garden, though much harder to achieve, is also worth the effort. Organized chaos. It looks so casual but takes twice as much effort. Maybe I wasn't secure enough or flexible enough to enjoy my afternoon section. I had selective sensitivities in that room. Once I felt threatened and unappreciated, I sent that same message back to my students. I heard the complaints, but not beyond them.

Having received so little concrete advice on how to become an effective teacher, I tended to hold on desperately to the few tips I had been given. Sure, you have to get to know where your students are coming from, but you can't get too close. When you transfer power, you don't reverse roles. The students need their own specialness, their own space. The teacher has to avoid looking to them for love or appreciation. Maybe at times I was too lonesome. There is so much going on in an open discussion forum that the classroom does become crowded with exposure for all. And, there are contingencies beyond one's control. The classroom design, the assignment of individual students to a given section, even the scheduling of the class can influence what happens, and yet the new teacher cannot manipulate these variables. At the business school I attended, classrooms were perfectly designed for case discussions, for special interaction between professor and students, for student-to-student exchange. Students were assigned to sections in a careful process designed to ensure heterogeneity, value diversity, and vibrating discussions. Even the dormitories were designed with alcoves of circular tables inviting study groups to exchange ideas the night before a discussion. There was an institutional commitment to the case discussion methodology. And no professor was expected to do it all alone.

You cannot do it alone. Every teacher needs trusted and trusting peers—who seem particularly hard to find during the first year, when exposure is so high, vulnerability so obvious, and tenure so distant.

A graduate school professor once told me that you don't solve big problems, you just massage them until they become more manageable, smaller problems. I felt I had massaged my afternoon section. I could live with it. I could manage it. But it would never be easy.

Learning to Grade

After so many years out of school, I found it hard to readjust to the rhythm of academia: the inexorable pace at which weeks roll into weeks, assignments into assignments. There seemed no time for reflection and realignment. My metabolism was used to long hours and hard work, but not to the intensity—punctuated by the too-silent lulls of vacations. So, as class followed upon class, crisis followed upon crisis. No sooner was the afternoon section beginning to settle in than it was time to grade the first papers.

Just as I disliked giving employee evaluations, I hated giving students grades. My boss offered me but one guideline: "Only grade the student's work, never grade his or her self-worth."

Face to face with seventy written analyses of the same case, I could not figure out how to grade them. I even suggested to our teaching team that we give qualitative comments only; my colleagues wisely advised me that the students need the tangible feedback of a hard grade, which they compare with their own expectations and with the work of others. If I independently ducked giving hard grades now, they warned, I would really be lost when the end-of-semester grades were due.

So I began to wade through the seventy papers. It seemed like reading the same Sunday *New York Times* over and over. For each paper I assigned a grade and wrote a one-page memo to the student. Each memo began by complimenting the author on what had worked in the paper. Then I listed questions I wanted the student to ask himself about the case, the paper, and the analysis. I tried never to say outright that the student had missed something or was wrong; I only asked a lot of questions, hoping he or she would see the missing pieces, the internal inconsistencies. Since I had said I would accept limitless rewrites of any paper, several students used those questions to develop second drafts with more comprehensive analyses of the same case.

Though grueling and time-consuming, the process of grading students' written work served me well. The papers proved to be a rich source of data about individual students. I became better able to predict the flow of a discussion because I began to learn how particular students would approach a case. I found it remarkable how the written analyses of cases could reveal an individual writer's personal framework. Those first papers were concerned with the dilemma that faced Volkswagen when the United States passed clean air regulations making the company's bread-and-butter Beetle illegal to sell in this country. The American market then represented 25 percent of VW's total sales. Of all seventy papers I read, only one recommended that Volkswagen withdrew from the U.S. market until it was safe to reenter. That paper came from the student who had petitioned to withdraw from my classroom to seek a safer section. We are all so consistently ourselves.

My approach to commenting on student papers forced me to read them carefully. Asking fifteen or twenty probing questions is a lot more difficult than writing a declaratory statement. This exercise also honed my understanding of the cases and allowed me to be more skillful in formulating questions spontaneously in class. Unfortunately, I was never able to complete the grading quickly, and the impact of my work was diminished by the passage of time between assignment and feedback. Each paper took me more than half an hour to grade (when I was going strong), and there weren't that many thirty-five-hour blocks of free time in my schedule.

It occurred to me that the students might learn a lot from the insights and the mistakes of their peers. For subsequent papers, I asked students not to sign their names, but to use an identifying number I assigned them. Then, after grading and commenting, I put the whole batch of numbered papers on reserve in the library for anyone to read. Students could identify only their own paper, but they could read my memo and the original paper of every other student. The sophistication of classroom discussion improved noticeably.

My last set of papers was probably the most fun because my six-year-old son helped me by writing the letter grade at the top of each student's memo. When Bill got the first "A" paper, he asked why I hadn't put a sticker on it. First-graders were accustomed to finding excellent work rewarded by a scratch-and-sniff sticker redolent of chocolate, banana, or strawberry bubble gum. Convinced that college students deserved no less, my son went to his own sticker collection, and rewarded those "A" papers properly. The students loved the stickers, which took some of the sting out of the grading process.

The course design specified that 20 percent of each student's grade would be based on a team assignment, a group oral presentation of an analysis and recommendation that would be evaluated by real business executives against real-world criteria. Four or five students worked together for months, made a presentation, and then, as a team, received a single grade from the executives, who sat with the students afterward and discussed the performance. This arrangement freed me from the role of judge and allowed me to function as the coach and the mentor for my teams—a role I truly enjoyed. During the weeks of anxious preparation for these presentations, I became closer to my students than ever before. The executives were also far more dispassionate in grading than I, as they considered only performance, not effort. Their evaluations gave my students a solid perspective in which to view my overall grade for the course.

It was during these executive-graded presentations that I first came close to thinking that I might have transferred power. As long as I was giving the grades, I could not feel any real mingling of power. During the preparation for our oral presentations, I was as anxious for my students as they were, and they knew it. But I was not in control. A coach does not decide whether his team wins or loses a game—he takes them as far as he can toward the goal.

Grading classroom participation remained a puzzle. I emphasized the importance of participation—it represented 40 percent of the students' grade—yet I didn't quite know what I was grading. How do you grade a good listener? How do you even know if someone *is* a good listener? How do you grade the overtalkative? If the teacher is the catalyst for discussion, isn't the participation grade really the teacher's self-evaluation as well?

One Section of Upperclassmen

My third section, an upperclass course on Management Theory, presented wholly new challenges. Whereas the introductory course was entirely predesigned and prepackaged, with everything from daily assignment sheets to grading formulas, I had not had time to put anything in writing for my upperclassmen.

I learned the hard way that there is enough ambiguity in a case discussion course without adding more levels of uncertainty and confusion. Even if alternative routes are possible, you still need a road map. Otherwise, energies are diverted from the real challenge of the case discussion. The more I preplanned, the more successful my daily spontaneity.

Another challenge was trying to decide whom I should be teaching. After a few weeks, I realized that about 20 percent of my students were really capable, interested, and enthusiastic; 60 percent had average interests and skills; and 20 percent verged on being listless, indifferent, and unprepared. Should I teach to the really capable and let the rest muddle? Should I teach to the average and risk boring the best students? Should I nurture the lowest common denominator and make sure I didn't lose them?

The upperclassmen also offered a new form of resistance to discussion. They had already established their college learning patterns, which were largely passive. They had seldom been exposed to case discussion before, and for many it was disorienting, even threatening. Some of them, I learned, even felt cheated: once they began to experience the challenge of case discussion learning, of thinking and analyzing and solving problems, they wondered if they had missed something important in their first years at college. In the end, some members of the section took on the challenge and the adventure of the new way of learning, while others lashed out at me and the course as symbolic of threat and loss.

Office Hours

My office, part of a partitioned hallway, was about three feet wide and twelve feet long. When I was talking to more than one student, their chairs had to be lined up Indian file. Yet some real teaching and real learning took place during my office hours.

It is not surprising that freshmen, whose other courses are mostly large lecture classes, should begin to feel close to their discussion teacher. The methodology sets you up to be perceived as an available person, a friendly ear, an adviser. After all, only you seem to know the student by name!

My office hours expanded until I wasn't sure when they began or ended. I learned I had to draw the line between offering a friendly ear and acting as a therapist, and to set limits on my availability. Even if I held round-the-clock office hours, it seemed there would still be students waiting in line to talk.

In that first year I was asked to write about fifty recommendations for students, many of whom claimed that I was the only teacher who really knew them. Teaching in the discussion mode had certainly left me knowing them better than if I had lectured and they had passively taken notes. But the reward system seemed perverse: the more effective you are in class, the more is demanded of you outside class.

Office hours, however, do present an opportunity. This is where the teacher can focus on the individual, not just the outline. Whereas the sections had taken on personalities that sometimes consumed the individuals, the peace and privacy of the office afforded time for personalization and reflection. Had I not had this opportunity to know the individuals, I wonder whether the sections would have worked as wholes.

In Search of a Comfortable Teaching Style

By late November I had survived more than two months of learning with a little bit of teaching on the side. I felt I must be getting closer to becoming REAL. I could almost walk into class and be myself. Myself as a teacher, that is. There is more to developing a personal teaching style than being yourself. The effective self is so much determined by the environment in which you seek to be effective. Though still myself, I am a bit different at a dinner party (or at a business meeting, or as a mother) from when I am teaching.

In the process of becoming myself as teacher, I modeled my performance after the wonderful case teachers I had known. I tried charging up aisles as one former teacher had. I aimed for the precision of thought and the perfect summaries of another teacher. And, especially in my Management Theory class, I tried to replicate my Organizational Behavior professor's ability to role-play any character in a case while maintaining a perfectly orchestrated set of notes on the blackboard.

These multiple personalities must have seemed bizarre to my students. Once, when one of them asked me what it was really like at business school, I framed my answer in terms of teachers. I told him about my Marketing professor who began class by jumping over the front desk as if it were a tennis net. And I told him about my Business Policy teacher, not yet used to having women in the classroom, who was struggling to tone down the locker room references in his classroom remarks. He liked to call on a student, leading his victim deeper and deeper into trouble, and then step back and say, "When rape is inevitable, relax and enjoy it." (That comment always terrified me—no one at Vassar ever said anything like that!) One day the student with whom I had shared these anecdotes came into class in a particularly good humor and asked, "Who are you going to be today, the leaper or the raper?" Though amused, I knew it was time for me to develop a style of my own.

In effect, I think I became a synthesis (not always a smooth one) of all my past teachers, at their best and at their worst. I tried hard to avoid their mistakes—while carefully making new ones of my own.

In November, my boss, remarking on the continual flow of students into my office, asked me if I was trying to be like my former Organizational Behavior teacher. In all seriousness, I replied that I was trying to be my freshman-year English teacher. Quietly discontented, I had decided to drop out of college, convinced that I wasn't as smart as everyone else. After listening to my plans to leave Vassar, the teacher asked if I would first do one final assignment for him. The assignment related directly to my concerns, as it interwove issues of creativity with the Catholic religion and with Irish authors.

He made me feel special just when I thought I didn't fit. It was he whom I emulated when self-doubt flooded my freshman in midsemester, their shallow college confidence used up, their anxiety turned into panic. As my own teacher had done for me, I tried to listen and to give each student something special, some meaning to hold onto.

My personal style as a teacher was a reflection of my own education. The best teachers I had had became the best of me. My openness and involvement with the students came directly from the way I was taught in college, with teachers casually joining students at dormitory dining room tables to discuss life, our common subject. My students came to my home, sometimes uninvited, knowing that I would welcome them just as I had been welcomed in my professors' living rooms. I remembered college as an experience of being touched, changed, and educated through involvement. Now that style would be mine.

My teaching style also reflected my life experiences and my willingness to share them. Some self-knowledge and self-acceptance are probably critical to success as a discussion teacher. There is no place to hide; exposure, though sometimes controlled, is complete.

My personal experiences of success and failure, joy and pain, had left me with a hidden teaching agenda. I wanted to share with my students an awareness of and tolerance for ambiguity. I wanted them to become flexible and adaptable to the inevitable changes their lives would bring. I wanted them to probe their personal definitions of success and fulfillment. Yet as soon as I saw my students' idealism and innocence, I knew that life, not I, would have to be their teacher on many of these subjects. Learning occurs when the idea and the experience meet in real time.

I do think, however, that this hidden agenda, a set of values derived from experience, is what makes a teacher special. It influences what happens in the classroom, no matter what case is being discussed. I am a slightly different teacher with slightly different styles in each section, depending on the section's personality and on the subject matter, but my values eventually surface everywhere.

My personal teaching style became highly anecdotal. Almost every case I taught involved something that came forth from my life. To teach the romance of entrepreneurship in the Head Ski Company case, I drew on my experience starting companies. It was easy for me to empathize with Howard Head as he wrote every word of his ad copy and tinkered with each ski-making machine. When I taught about Charlie Butcher's efforts to take his floor wax out of the hardware stores and into the supermarkets, regardless of his break-even point and his competition, I was often thinking of how my partner and I had taken sparkling mineral water into the supermarkets, learning the painful reality of that distribution route.

I tried to develop a very liberal-artsy style in the classroom, partly because I was teaching on a liberal-arts campus and wanted to build psychological bridges between disciplines and partly because of my own liberal-arts education. I tried to weave references to art, literature, and philosophy into my courses, hoping to give the students a sense that business is not a separate discipline in life but an aspect of their search for fulfillment.

My style became more and more dependent on metaphor, which seemed to give meaning to cases when students had no real-world experience to apply to their analyses. When one of my best students wrote about a case involving an insensitive relocation of employees in a large insurance firm, his paper began with an almost poetic paragraph about transplanting a tree. Not only are the roots affected, he wrote, but now there is shade where there used to be none, and no shade where there once had been. I knew he grasped the behavioral complexity of the case. Similarly, when students made presentations to visiting executives, I found them using metaphors to explain complex situations. One team of students used a flip chart picturing a canoe full of executives headed for a three-way fork in the river. One branch would lead to clear sailing, another to the risks and excitement of rapids, another to a dead end. The personal metaphors of students' own lives made the material real and communicable for them. Metaphors seemed to bring meaning closer than anecdote, for the anecdotes were mine; the metaphors were theirs.

Though a personal style emerges partly from a deliberate effort to become effective and comfortable in a new environment, it is also partly accidental, depending on where you happen to be in life at that moment. My being a mother was very important to my teaching style. My son was excited about my new job as teacher. He loved the campus (and all the attention he got there). He loved having student baby-sitters and eating in the college cafeteria. Students often encountered the two of us as a team, and his presence seemed to open up conversation. Bill somehow humanized my presence.

Every night I had to read and analyze a case in preparation for the next day's classes. Often I read the case aloud to him at bedtime. Bill's innocence and clarity of vision often helped me define the common denominator for a class discussion. Sometimes the first question he asked me at night became the first question I asked my students the next day.

Those questions were beautifully naive, cutting through all my adult assumptions, zeroing in on the heart of the case.

If I hadn't been the mother of a young child as I began this journey into teaching, I would never have used Dr. Seuss's story *The Sneetches* as outside reading for a case concerned with how status affects behavior.[5] Without Bill I would surely never have put scratch-and-sniff stickers on my "A" papers. If I had begun to teach ten years earlier or later, my style would not have encompassed the aspect of myself that is the mother of a young child.

After so much anxious searching for an authority that would tell me how to be an effective teacher, I began to realize the resources were close at hand. There were my previous teachers, my son, my life, my own students, the culture of my new campus. The challenge was to see, to listen, and to integrate. Maybe, just maybe, I was becoming a REAL teacher.

The Last Week of Classes

By the last week of class, I was really tired, both physically and mentally. On the next-to-last day of class, I was surprised to find the members of my morning section automatically taking on the roles of the case under discussion. The actual class deviants—the overproducer and the under-producer—were playing out the corresponding roles among the case characters. I hadn't assigned any of this. It was just happening. The section had literally turned into the case. The students analyzed and argued with the real prejudices and loyalties of the people in the case. Somehow we had leaped over the distinction between the case and ourselves. The case was no longer "out there."

In my afternoon section I felt much too tired to "make it happen." Instead of opening a case discussion, I began to lecture on small group behavior. I knew the concepts and the buzzwords, so it seemed easier just to tell the students about required behavior, emergent behavior, group norms, and so on. About fifteen minutes into this lecture, one of the students—the one who feigned being a survivor of an airplane crash during the first class—stood up and denounced me for what I was doing. Apparently furious, he said that I had forced my students to become classroom adults and now I was treating them like children. The students wanted to analyze the case and were offended that I wasn't letting them.

Whatever small "power" I may have had in that section must have been transferred. I took a deep breath, repsyched myself, and off we tore into an enjoyable (though not brilliant, not magical) case analysis.

What Is a Teacher-Student Contract?

On the last day of class, a student comment gave me new insight into the phenomenon of transferring power. Our topic was the individual and the self-concept. The case under discussion centered on E. J. Weiver, a strong woman account executive in a high-pressure consumer products firm. According to the case, she simply could not or would not delegate authority to her subordinates. The first student to speak concluded by saying that it would not be satisfying to work for E. J. "It would not be like working for you," she added, to my surprise. Flattered, I asked the student to expand. Working for E. J. would make you feel like and probably act like a child, she explained. Never given a chance to make mistakes, you probably wouldn't learn very much.

Like E. J., I had found delegation a frustrating challenge. My education taught me how to do things, but not how to let others do them. It had taken me five or ten years in business to accept the fact that I could not do everything myself. And I still was not very good at delegating. It always seemed that a task would be more efficiently completed if I did it myself—in a way that pleased me.

Maybe, I thought, what others referred to as the transfer of power was a transfer of authority and responsibility. Maybe it was delegating. Delegating the responsibility to learn. Maybe it was the transfer of adultness—a transfer impeded by the label "student," which suggests a dependent, a recipient.

Many experienced managers are skeptical of the classic pyramid structure of an organization, with the president at the top and the workers all along the bottom. The pyramid flip-flops all the time. After all, who built the pyramids in the first place? So why does the classroom still resemble the pyramid structure? Learning and gravity have never been correlated. When a manager knows how to delegate, the employees learn and the manager is not threatened by the succession of skills. He or she gives the employees room to make mistakes, room to grow, room to take the honors. Yet the manager remains ultimately responsible for the task being done. Delegation requires trust, lots of it, and personal security. It is a delicate skill, far from efficient in the short run. In the process, I think, you transfer energy, enthusiasm, insights, values, skills, esteem, and meaning. You share power.

One of my colleagues during that first year complained that I was creating arrogant students. When my students went on to other classes, they proved to be demanding, and they insisted on sharing their ideas. They were, I was told, unaccepting and difficult in advanced courses that had not yet adopted a case discussion format. I had transferred to them the recognition that the responsibility for learning can be exciting. To take it away once it has been given and accepted is to shortchange the student.

The contract between teacher and student, I thought, was much like the unwritten contract I felt I had with my customers when I was in business. The customer (student) has buying power; I have supplying power. My objective is to keep these powerful and interdependent forces in dynamic equilibrium in the classroom. Hadn't my students' comments helped me unravel the mysteries of teaching? Again and again my students provided the clues to what was happening. They were my customers, my marketplace, rich with free information.

In my catalogue company I had almost always found that the most important questions on merchandising and services were answered by the customers. At the end of every telephone order my sales staff would ask, "What else do you wish you could have purchased from us today? What were you looking for for your child that we did not have pictured in our catalogue?" The answers to these questions became the basis of the product collection of the next catalogue. And sales grew.

My students, like my customers, demanded quality, service, timeliness, and respect. They were the ultimate source of my information and, if you will, the ultimate source of my power. The more I respected these classroom customers and tried to understand them, the greater the return.

Writing a journal during my freshman year of teaching helped me keep my questions, my constant reflection, at the surface. Can my journal actually take you inside the private process that was mine? Can it transfer anything? I think there are many things that cannot be taught. But at least we know we are not alone in our uncertainties as we question and challenge ourselves.

The other night my son asked me to teach him how to blow a bubble with gum. I don't recall his ever using the word "teach" in a request to me before. I felt unprepared and a bit scared. How do you help a seven-year-old learn to blow a bubble? You can't just *show* him, because the process is rather private. Only the bubble is obvious.

NOTES

1. F. J. Roethlisberger, *The Elusive Phenomena* (Cambridge, MA: Harvard University Press, 1977), an autobiographical account of Roethlisberger's work in the field of organizational behavior.
2. Neil Postman and Charles Weingartner, *Teaching as a Subversive Activity* (New York: Dell, 1987).
3. The Head Ski Company case, like the other cases mentioned here, is copy-righted by the President and Fellows of Harvard College, and is available through the Case Clearing House, Harvard Business School, Boston, MA 02163.
4. Margery Williams, *The Velveteen Rabbit* (Philadelphia: Running Press, 1984).
5. Dr. Seuss [Theodor Seuss Geisel], *The Sneetches and Other Stories* (New York: Random House, 1961).

4

Great Beginnings

MELISSA MEAD

I LIKE BEGINNINGS, especially once they're over. The excitement and uncertainty and sense of potential that accompany the start of something new add a sharp tang to everyday life. Initiating a new adventure has always found me bounding out of bed early, my mind racing toward the day ahead. I'm frankly never certain whether I'm propelled by delighted anticipation or fear. I expect it's some of both, and my adrenal glands can't tell the difference anyway. University teaching appeals to me because it is a series of beginnings: new classes, new courses, new semesters, new students.

My introduction to teaching with cases and discussion was a beginning I will never forget. Case teaching was, for me, a new form of a known craft. I had successfully lectured for several semesters. I also was a student in a course taught exclusively via the case method. So with all this teaching and observing time logged, I expected to launch a GREAT beginning in discussion teaching. The enormousness of the gap between my expectations and the reality I encountered created a vacuum that pulled me in and swept me away without mercy. I still sigh when I recall my dismay at discovering my GREAT beginning was, in fact, a great BEGINNING.

This essay tells the story of my introduction to case teaching. It is a personal account, but I do not believe it is idiosyncratic. Humbling experiences move me off center—either into or out of my shell. Fortunately, I turned outward to colleagues and friends. Professor after professor told me stories of excitement and fear, mastery and humility. What a relief to hear variations on a theme, *my* theme. We must deal with content (what to teach), process (how to teach), preparation (how to plan ahead), control (how to realize plans), and style (making room for our own personality). These are common challenges faced by new discussion teachers, whether or not they are new to teaching.

Before the Before . . .

I knew several months in advance that I would be teaching cases to large classes. I was to teach a new required course in Management Information Systems in the Harvard Business School's MBA program. I was assigned two sections of about ninety students each. There were seven other professors teaching the same course. This was a time of delicious anticipation and excitement and preparation. Well, I thought I was preparing! I wrote a few cases, which was a way of learning from the inside out. This taught me that you have to ask a lot of questions to glean a few key insights. I watched others teach, which was a way of learning from the outside in. By observing, I found there are many good ways to arrive at the same conclusion. I also noticed it was complicated to sort out why a class went especially well or badly. This all took place in relative calm as the months passed and nonteaching activities were the focus of my work.

Then, suddenly it seemed my debut was only a couple of months off. I was asked to write a teaching plan for one of the first classes of the course. Nervousness set in—a perfect companion to the stark reality I faced. For several weeks I talked about, read about, and obsessed about teaching. For all the "preparing" I had done, when I sat down to write a teaching plan I was stumped. What would I say first? Would I talk about the case, tell a joke, ask a factual question, ask an open-ended question? What would my students say? What if they didn't say anything! All this anxiety—and I hadn't gotten past the class opening.

I thought I had found every possible thing to worry about. My teaching plan was taking shape. Luckily, an experienced colleague had pointed out that the teaching plan simply had to be plausible. I should consider all the directions a discussion might take and how I might influence this. I should also understand that I wouldn't know how good it was until I tried it in class. And I could revise it for next time; teaching plans evolve, and the first one often turns out to be a very rough draft. The main thing is to get into the game. Still I worried about questions and timing (is this a five-minute issue or a twenty-minute issue?), critical facts, and nifty little subtleties I discovered in my twelfth reading of the case. When I was done, yet another colleague thumbed through my impressive sheaf of notes once, twice, three times, then asked where the board plan was. What's going to go on the blackboard?

Blackboards! As a child I was an ardent fan of Captain Kangaroo. A key feature of his television show was the Magic Drawing Board. Given a theme or story, amazing figures would appear on the board one line at a time. As I searched my memory of the dozens of case discussions I had attended, the blackboards all shared this magical quality. At the end of the discussion there were columns of notes, calculations, and figures that captured the meaning and message of the day. But the process by which this scripture appeared was hidden. It didn't just happen; someone had planned those discussions right down to the third point on the second graph on the middle board (lower left-hand corner!) I came up with a plausible board plan to complete my plausible teaching plan. Then I panicked. It seemed the only reasonable thing to do.

Right Before . . .

I should say here that my panic and near frenzy are not universal. Colleagues said that they were unusually excited or unusually calm, but not as fearful as I was. Nobody suggested, however, that they were unaffected by their imminent entry into discussion teaching! I've come up with four reasons why teachers are either fearful or sanguine about their initiation. First, there is the relative certainty of the course to be taught. I was teaching a new course with new cases. Colleagues who taught courses with lengthy histories and long-standing teaching plans fared better. They had good road maps for their journey and guidance from those who had gone before. Second, colleagues who had no teaching experience seemed less fearful. Really. My only explanation is ignorance. Once you've been in front of a classroom you have a healthy respect for just how terribly (or how wonderfully) a class can go. Third, colleagues with spouses, near-spouses, friends, and activities outside academia had better perspectives. They had people to remind them of their strengths and that, after all, beginning discussion teaching was merely one of the all-important events in life. Finally, people are just different, and some are worrywarts. Everybody knows this—and overlooks it from time to time.

I was not so objective at the time. I lost sleep, and, most unfortunately, lost my sense of humor and with it a great deal of perspective. Having thoroughly worried about the obvious (the case, the blackboard, the talking), I went for the deeper detail. What should I wear? Where should I stand? How should I hold my hands? What sort of facial expression would be most appropriate? For each of these I had a "best" answer for ideal circumstances. Then I had a practical answer that reflected my true situation—that I was nervous and scared. So the answers were: choose clothes that don't show perspiration, concentrate on standing still, try to be as comfortable as possible. With shaky hands, have pockets . . . and set a pen down on the transparencies (to avoid a trembling shadow). Worry about your face next year. In the end I couldn't wait for the class to start; it simply couldn't be as bad as the anticipation.

Ready, Set . . .

I don't suppose I will ever forget the twenty-four hours that preceded my first discussion class. Jittery and jumpy, I pored over the case and my notes and tried to imagine what the morning would bring. In the wee hours I forced myself to go to bed. I woke up every hour like clockwork. And, worried about clocks working, got up and checked mine each time to be sure it was properly set. I slept fitfully with distorted dreams of the classroom zigzagging through my mind.

The alarm screamed and I was up like a shot. Contact lenses in sleepy eyes, ouch. Breakfast? Are you kidding? Lots of coffee and talking to myself. There are at least two dozen possible inflections for a short opening question. To the office for some last-minute preparation (I mean it) and wait. I remembered a meditative exercise I had learned years earlier. Lean back, breathe deeply. I imagined a safe place, a circle of light, where no one can stay and nothing can happen without my permission. I imagined that circle of light surrounding me, protecting me, moving with me. I was whispering the exercise even as I walked to the classroom. I was self-contained, I was safe, I was in control. I was really scared.

Go! In the Door . . .

I pulled open the door and walked in. I was the professor; I was supposed to know what was going on. I was supposed to set the tone and the pace and the expectations. This was my class. This bubble burst when a student tentatively asked whether I was the professor. Well, I was doing my best to behave in a professional manner. And I was the only one in a suit. Why did he ask? He told me I was too young to be the professor. I wanted to snap at him that I was certainly old enough to give him a grade so why didn't he just sit down. It was then I knew that in addition to all my other responsibilities, I might have to consider the feelings and needs of these students. With the weight of all this responsibility I felt sorry for myself.

Once I called the class to order, I felt better. It felt like a class and I felt like the professor and I had lots of great plans and hopes. I wanted the class to be fast-paced and interesting. I wanted all of us to learn. I wanted the students to like me. I wanted perfection but instead had to find tolerance for doing my best and trying to learn from it. By the end of the class I was exhilarated and exhausted.

Getting Smart—Caring for Myself

More classes followed and in no time, it seemed, the course was over. At times it raced by, away from me, ahead of me. Other times I thought it would surely never be over. I learned so many things. Some were little—if I didn't eat, my ears would ring and I couldn't hear my students properly. And if I didn't sleep I couldn't react very quickly in class. Relearning biological requirements is as back-to-basics as you can get. Mainly I had to remember to breathe—the course lasted too long to hold my breath the entire time. Eventually I was able to find a balance between caring for myself and caring for my teaching. The better care I took of me, the better I did in class. Win-win.

Getting Smart—Caring for Content

I also learned that my concern for class content was both universal and overblown. This was perhaps the hardest lesson for a worrying and impatient soul. The content—that is, the facts of the case and the particulars of a theory or organizing framework I tended to present with the case—was known or knowable, given enough time. The hitch was the "given enough time" part. There was never enough time for perfection. In retrospect, mastery of content was the single thing I knew how to control. So I clung to content, wanting it to be *the* major determinant of success in the classroom. Of course, the facts and frameworks are important. Then again, applying my own expertise and judgment in order to set priorities and select a manageable subset from the sea of information wasn't just smart; it was survival.

At first these choices felt arbitrary. But with practice, distinguishing the critical factual material in the cases did become easier. I found it helpful to stand back and look at levels of case analysis—a segment of a case, the whole case, a segment of the course, the whole course. Which facts were key to the lessons of a specific case? Which lessons must be covered with that case because they were not included elsewhere? Which did I think were most important.?

I began listening to how other discussion teachers limit content when they prepare for class. I heard struggle in their accounts. Some were matter-of-fact: they said, "Less is more." They said brusquely that "it's better to do a few things well than to do a lot badly." But others conjured up more vivid images. "I ask myself, if somebody held a gun to my head and told me I could pick only three key points, which would they be?" Another asked, "What do I want to write on the mirror in lipstick?" There is the temptation to select the topics we know best and can teach well. This must be weighed against the need to present a well-rounded course.

Of course, as soon as I planned to cover fewer points I began to worry about running short of material. So I would pick out my "walkaway" points—the two or three I thought were most important. Then I'd plan an additional three points. Good, I had six modules ready for discussion, two I was intent on covering and the remainder of the class content would depend on the direction of student comments. One of my colleagues told me he always carried in two transparencies about which he could talk for anywhere from five to thirty minutes. Just in case. So we plan for less, prepare for more . . . and take in a backup.

Getting Smart—Caring for Process

The more attention I paid to content, the less attention I paid to process—thinking not of the specific content, but how it would unfold . . . how to choreograph a class. Win-lose. In fairness to myself I should say that the process piece was much trickier. My early worries about blackboards and where to stand were the kernels of my awareness of process. The more I was caught up in content, the more I knew I was missing at least half of the larger picture.

Webster says that to choreograph is "to arrange the movements, progress, or details." Imagine a ballet with terrific music, story line, and dancers but no designated steps. You get the picture. Well, so did I, but I didn't know what to do about it. I've been feeling my way through. I observe others teaching and I try hard to tune out the content and tune in the ebb and flow of their process. And I simply think a great deal about the movement I'd like in my own class.

I experiment with what and how I say and do things in the classroom. For instance, I've tried volunteers to start the class, I've selected students unexpectedly, and I've tried beginning with my own overview. I've tried using the blackboards a lot and very little. I've tried overhead transparencies and handing out printed material. I've tried terse questions and a more rambling style. Afterward, I compare what happened with what I had hoped for. I sometimes ask individual students for their comments. And I check my feelings about the session. I make notes of what works for me and try not to dwell too long on the times I stub my toes. This is the invisible part of preparation—not something you *do* exactly, but which must be done.

Getting Smart—Sorting Out Style

Style is terribly important and terribly ridiculous. It has to do with what you wear. What sort of clothes, shoes, and accessories to wear. Leave the jacket on or take it off? Take it off before class or during class? I used to think these concerns were a woman thing—that men didn't have them. Ha! I began noticing the careful orchestration of braces or belts, ties (straight or bow?), and socks among my male colleagues.

It has to do with physical presence. Shall I walk, talk, change topics rapid-fire or deliberately? Should my countenance be free of judgment or shall I use it to broadcast my messages? Observers have told me much about presence—that a hand on the hip was different from a hand in the pocket and did I know which I did more often? That my model posture was admirable but imposing—why didn't I slouch now and then, or sit down? It has to do with tone and demeanor. Do I approach the class with humor or gravity, intensity or subtlety? How will I change the pace if I really can't tell jokes well? Do I want to be hard-nosed and hard-driving or gentle and facilitating? Is it possible to be loved and respected simultaneously? Are these reasonable questions to ponder when there is so much content and process to be mastered?

This concern is terribly important because the professor's style is a salient feature of the teaching environment. If you doubt this, talk to students. They absorb details of style and pass uncompromising judgment. Professorial style, for better or worse, becomes a structural element of the class that reduces uncertainty. It is important because students notice, indeed come to depend on, consistency of style. It is important because it defines what kind of person you are in the classroom.

Style can also become terribly ridiculous precisely because it is important. It goes something like this: style is important so we think about it (a lot) and try to think up an *effective* style (we want to choose the *best* style). This is where it gets ridiculous. There simply is no one best style. Many times I thought of stylistic changes that were theoretically possible but completely missed the demands of my own personality. Many times I wished I could be like one or another colleague. Many times I tried to be.

What I began to sort out was a personal style. Yes, I thought about my appearance, my presence, my tone. But I limited myself to a range of behaviors and experiments that fit *me*. I found my own pace, my own brand of humor, my own way of challenging students, my own way to connect with them. I discovered my own style when I began considering how I felt when I was at my best. What did I say, how did I move, what did I wear at those times?

When I looked at the me I'd known for years I realized I'm more laid-back than frenetic. I admire professors who buzz around the room; I think that style is really neat. But I feel nervous and silly when I do it. My energy needs a more contained expression. I found I truly love the sharp, dry, spontaneous humor that can spring up in class. I'm good at catching those moments, but terrible at planned jokes. I had been so busy lamenting my disastrous attempts at canned humor that I was taken aback when one student told me she envied my knack for creating humor unexpectedly with a look, a well-timed laugh, or the tweak of an innocent statement. I had to learn to play to this kind of strength.

Another personal quirk: I like to ask a lot of questions. I suspect my friends think I am developmentally stuck at age five. I always want to know why. While my questions aren't great at a cocktail party, they serve me quite well in the classroom. Some are planned and others come in response to students' comments. All these things help me feel comfortable in the classroom. And I've discovered that when I am comfortable my classes go much better. Finding my own style was important; bending myself into an idealized form of what a professor should be was ridiculous.

Getting in Control—Well, No

In retrospect, I believe much of my concern for content, process, and style was really a longing for control. I wanted the certainty that control would bring. Certainty about what I needed to be prepared for, about what would happen in class, about what my students would learn. I thought if I worked hard enough and worried long enough and was clever enough, I could control all these things. I had the foolish notion that I was 100 percent responsible for my students' learning experience. I understood the concept that discussion teaching opened up vistas of opportunity because control and responsibility were shared between students and teacher. And I thought this would be terrific and exciting if only I knew what to expect. Remembering this wish still brings a sigh and a smile.

One day after a particularly difficult class (one in which I felt especially out of control) I stopped, exhausted, in the office of a friend and fellow teacher. What I wanted was sympathy. What I got was five minutes of commiseration and thirty minutes of a new point of view. My friend helped me think through a wide variety of elements that influenced my class. The list grew to include events in the world and at school, which had nothing to do with my class (for example, the class had a term paper for another course due today), what might have happened in the class just before mine, how students responded to the case, events in the personal life of the student I called to open the class. . . . How many of these elements could I reasonably expect to control? Not many. But I could become better informed about them. And things I couldn't control I might be able to influence by acknowledging them while refocusing on the class at hand. The final suggestion was that I might relax a little and see what happened. I discovered that control was one of those perverse things that eludes those who grasp for it. For me this meant doing my job and trusting that my students would do theirs. Taking a leap of faith and believing that they, too, wanted the classes to be fast-paced and interesting, wanted to learn, and wanted us to like each other.

I had success with this approach later. After a few days of flat classes I decided to approch the students and ask whether they noticed this and what they thought the problem was. As it turned out they were caught up in the search for summer jobs and were worried and distracted. This had nothing to do with my class and I couldn't fix the problem. But once we had talked about it there was renewed energy in class. I think we got back on track because my students were gently reminded of their responsibility and supported by my interest in them.

Getting Help

I was often desperate for improvement in my teaching. I took constructive steps in addition to indulging in copious amounts of worry. The chief form of assistance was observation by my colleagues. Over time I found I got really terrific feedback when either my observer was an experienced evaluator of teaching or I asked that he or she specifically watch a narrow set of class features. For instance, would the observer keep track of my pattern of calling students from the left, center, and right of the room. Or notice the demeanor and nonverbal responses of students: Were they distracted, attentive, bored, confused, angry, and when? I wanted an objective opinion to compare to my own. I also wanted ideas about what I might do differently or new things I might try.

The very best feedback I got was notable because it touched on every issue I was worried about and because it was honest. My colleague focused on questions in my class. Every question I asked that day was noted. I was amazed to see that many of my questions were vague, or invited monosyllabic answers, or rambled on endlessly, or failed to pick up interesting student comments. This discovery was both painful and wonderful. No wonder I wasn't getting stellar responses in class—my students were too busy trying to figure out the question or squelch their frustration. Questions are a way of incorporating content, influencing process, and exerting control in the classroom. What's more, the way I chose and phrased questions was a way of defining and asserting my personal style.

So for me questions became my bridge to getting better. I could plan my class by planning the questions. There were the mainstream questions and the contingency questions and the humorous, tongue-in-cheek questions. I could write the most important ones out in advance to ensure clarity. I could practice them out loud. It was a practical beginning— precisely what I needed. Others find a bridge in prepared lecturettes, or prepared audiovisual material, or prepared jokes. These are all structures that provide the beginning of a portfolio of teaching tools. They are our starting point.

Getting Perspective

This is an essay about a beginning. Which means it could also be about an ending. When I lived out this story I strained to find an ending. As a result I almost lost sight of the beginning and failed to understand that what lay before me was a long journey. I saw the course as a closed entity rather than as a gateway. I held my breath. I wanted a short, steep learning curve—to emerge at the end of a single teaching of this course a polished discussion teacher. A dear friend tells me I am like the king of Syracuse. What? The king of Syracuse hired Archimedes to give him instruction in geometry. To the king's displeasure, the lessons were arduous and long, progress slow. Weary, the king implored Archimedes to relieve him of this burden and deliver directly to him the knowledge and insight he craved. To which Archimedes replied, "Sir, there is no royal road to geometry." Just because the parable fits doesn't mean it's comfortable. My struggle has been getting perspective. I must remind myself that the unfolding experience of developing a skill and learning a craft, with all its frustrations and imperfections, may be a valuable and enjoyable one. As I enjoy watching my students progress, so too must I learn to notice and take pleasure in my own progress.

One day recently a secretary on campus asked if I got nervous when I taught. "Well, yes," I confessed with a nervous laugh for punctuation. She told me the professor she works for, after twenty years of teaching experience, still wants half an hour of undisturbed time before class to review the material and collect thoughts. I smiled and thought of my ritual of brief meditation before teaching. Maybe my beginning was a *great* beginning after all.

It's Not Over 'til It's Over

Time has passed—since beginning case teaching, since I wrote this essay—and I am now teaching the course for the third time. I feel uncomfortable seeing my hopes and fears written down. I hope that other beginners will read the essay and do things differently. But what do I think I might have done differently?

First, I would spend some time before the course begins *developing reasonable expectations*. I would distill into one or two sentences the primary purpose for the course, write it down, and tack it over my desk. Then I would carefully review the syllabus with this kernel of purpose in mind. My goal would be to create for myself a picture of how the course hangs together. I think of this as a road map with clear starting and ending points (what you expect students to know at the beginning and end of the course). Each case is a meaningful landmark along the way. With this kind of context I would have a head start on my day-to-day case preparation. If I hit a rough patch in midcourse I would still be able to get my bearings. Although great attention is paid to the purpose of the course as well as individual cases when a course is developed, I believe an explicit review shortly before teaching is of key importance.

I would also think ahead about reasonable expectations of performance. What should I expect of myself and how will I know when I've achieved it? Talking with other teachers might be a way to get some benchmarks. Once classes begin I would keep notes each day of what goes well or goes poorly. It's easy to lose track of the trends over several weeks. Futher, notes help later with course redesign or when you teach cases again.

As it turned out, I expected too much of myself and too little of my students. So the second thing I would do differently is *share responsibility with students*. When I reread my essay I find almost no mention of students. I viewed them as passive recipients of my teaching rather than as active participants. I also needed a sign that said, "Students are people, too." I have learned that students have strengths and weaknesses and that I should expect both to influence classes. I can invite my students to join with me in creating a class rather than assuming (usurping?) sole responsibility.

A third suggestion is: *Ask for what you need* to do a good job. Ask colleagues for assistance when it's needed. Are there recent real-life examples they can share to update a case? Perhaps you need them to tell more of their past experience teaching a particular case. Ask if you can prepare a case informally with a colleague to learn some of his or her skills and approaches. If you need someone to observe a class and give feedback, ask. On the other hand, if you need less input, less scrutiny, ask for that.

On the personal side, as a beginning teacher today I would *commit to good health* and *commit to real life*. We all know the benefits of a well-balanced diet, adequate sleep, and reduced caffeine intake. The demands of a new teaching experience, however, have ended with many of us consuming coffee and junk food, sometimes late into the night. Since that first course, the key for me has been keeping a personal "center" so that teaching is merely one of many important aspects of my life. I make a point to get together with friends on the weekend. I plan nonteaching work activities, such as editing papers, that are flexible and lead to visible accomplishment in other areas. I focus on more than teaching and enjoy visible progress on important projects.

Finally, I would *strive to listen*. Feeling tired, uncertain, and alone made it hard for me to listen to the good advice and encouragement offered by my colleagues. It made it almost impossible to listen to my students outside the limits of a case discussion. I also didn't listen to myself; the guiding voices inside were noise rather than signal. In each instance, I would have had a better experience if I had been a better listener.

These are the things I would change if I had it to do again. On reflection, I believe they are listed in order of difficulty for me. Developing reasonable expectations and sharing responsibility, once identified, are matters of effort and some risk. I find asking for what I need harder to do. Somehow struggling along seemed the safer course; maybe nobody would notice. And making the commitment to good health, a fuller life and careful listening . . . Well, at the time these seemed like expendable luxuries. Today I view physical well-being and a balanced perspective as two cornerstones of effective teaching.

5

Changing Ground: A Medical School Lecturer Turns to Discussion Teaching

DANIEL A. GOODENOUGH

THIS IS THE STORY of how a fourteen-year veteran of teaching histology forsook the pedagogical high road of lecturing to help blaze a trail in the (to me) uncharted wilderness of discussion teaching. Two years ago I began leading intensive eight-week discussion courses in basic medical science as part of the Harvard Medical School's experimental program known as the New Pathways in General Medical Education. Despite the mistakes and false starts that attend all new ventures, the results are exciting. I have felt renewed by participating in a process that develops students' self-confidence, cooperation, and mastery faster and more effectively than I would have thought possible.

Why would anyone willingly trade the security of well-received lectures for the uncertainties of discussion teaching? In my case, a combination of personal and institutional forces virtually compelled me to accept the challenge, yet my participation was ultimately a leap of faith. Intellectually, it seemed crucial to confront the disturbing problems in modern medical education such as the absence of values from most curricula and the long-term inadequacy of rote memorization as a means for coping with the information explosion.

On the personal side, having given very similar histology (microscopic anatomy) lectures for fourteen years, I was growing bored—and, I feared, boring. In addition, a medical crisis in my own family had brought me face-to-face with what seemed a dangerous failing in the medical system: a lack of community among physicians that creates isolation and reluctance to seek help from colleagues.

All these factors influenced my decision to join the administrators and teachers who developed the New Pathways, as an attempt to prepare physicians for medical practice in the late twentieth century and beyond.

The program uses small-group case discussions to teach medical sciences such as cell biology, histology, and anatomy, although students also experience traditional laboratory and clinical work, standardized formal testing, supplementary lectures, and computer-assisted learning. Perhaps the best way to present my change of ground is to portray my old lecture style, show how my education conditioned my teaching, describe the events that triggered my decision to change, and, finally, give an idea of how the content that I used to expound from the podium now emerges in discussion.

Traditional Medical Education and Its Shortcomings

Medical education is usually divided into two years of preclinical class-room and laboratory work, and two years of clinical work with patients in hospitals, under doctors' tutelage and supervision. Although most grades are pass/fail, all students must master a large body of knowledge in order to pass the standardized medical exams. But the process by which students learn can have powerful implications, and that process is the focus of our new approach. In the classical curriculum, beginning students sit through four to six hours of lectures each day, trying to assimilate detailed information about anatomy, biochemistry, physiology, immunology, microbiology, genetics, and pathology in the same year. Traditional lecture courses involve highly organized lecture notes and textbook assignments that specify exactly what to learn at each point. Most instructors stick to these notes, and some even read them in class. As a lecturer in histology, I tried to engage students' intellects and emotions with humor and a certain human perspective. My goal was to cover the material in the required lecture notes, but not necessarily in the conventional order. In some sense, perhaps, my journey to discussion-based teaching began with this predilection to get my students to think with me and feel momentum, suspense, and drama as I showed them visually exciting slides and drawings of microstructures of cells.

Each year, in my first histology lecture, "An Introduction to the Cell," I would describe the anatomy of a typical cell, name its constituent parts, and explain how it synthesizes proteins. My illustrations included forty to fifty slides, chosen for beauty and clarity and assembled in an inductive sequence to give students the sense of exploring a realm of mystery. Leading my students on an active sleuthing expedition, I posed questions about organic form and, in answering them, evoked—I hoped—a silent "aha" reaction. For example: in microscopic terms, a skeletal muscle cell is enormous. Projected at high magnification on a screen during lecture, it seems miles long. I would show slides of such a cell, highlighting a complex apparatus deep inside it, and ask, "How can this whole vast, complicated structure contract in a microsecond when the stimulus to contract is so far away, at the surface of the cell?" After a dramatic pause, we would "discover" the T-system, an infolding of the surface membrane that surrounds the muscle cell and carries the electrical impulse deep into its enormous bulk. If my strategy worked, the students would have anticipated the existence of this structure and felt satisfaction at seeing it.

No elaborate philosophy of learning led me to teach this way, just experience distilled from lectures I had attended, good and bad, and an intuition that people learn better when they are intrigued. Even the beauty of my slides was part of a strategy to get students to participate in my lectures, with their minds, if not their voices. Part of my first lecture had to do with pancreas cells, which synthesize enormous amounts of protein for digestion of food. Darkening the room, I would show a series of slides of these cells. As the magnification increased, their microanatomy became visible, revealing a complex and magnificent system of internal structure. When my lecturer's instincts told me the students were intrigued, I would turn on the lights and ask, "So what does all this have to do with protein synthesis?" Then, at the blackboard, I would chalk a series of diagrams worked out years earlier and so often replicated that my drawing appeared effortless. The drawings showed the flow of information through the cell from DNA to proteins. Talking fast, I paced back and forth, trying not to focus my attention on a single person, because one chuckle at a joke didn't mean everyone was amused, nor did one scowl or yawn mean I had lost the whole group. My energy level stayed high because I feared that if a lecture sagged in the middle it would die.

Over the years, lecturing brought a variety of payoffs: gratifying teaching evaluations and a string of teaching prizes. Also, as I repeated my lectures, teaching preparation took less and less time, freeing more hours for my research. But I began to tire of lecturing on the same material. Exciting new ideas about almost every piece of tissue in the syllabus filled the journals, but my lectures still had to cover the basics. So I began talking faster, trying to present an ever more intricately faceted jewel of knowledge—basics for the students, recent advances for me—without burning out. This was impossible, but it took me a while to face the fact, partly because my own educational background included little but lectures.

I graduated from Harvard College in the mid-1960s, having studied architecture, but, after a late-adolescent identity crisis, switched to biology in my senior year. Many of my lecturers were world-famous scholars or scientists, and some were remote star performers who dazzled their undergraduate audiences, which numbered in the hundreds. Most were forgettable, but some quite memorable—though not always for the right reasons. In a chemistry lecture, for example, Professor George Kistiakowsky built a glass "rocket" on the lecture table one day. The contraption had two fuel chambers, one containing liquid oxygen, the other kerosene. From my second-row seat, I saw the two liquids empty into a glass reaction chamber and form a swirling, swelling puddle as "Kisty" slowly retreated to the other side of the room and said, "It's going to explode." I don't recall the explosion, only a sense of shock, a high ringing in my ears, and a girl in the front row weeping. No one was hurt by the accident, but as we left the lecture room, I felt tiny bits of glass in my hair and heard Kisty comment, "Now you know why there are occasional problems on the launch pads at Cape Canaveral." I remember these impressions, but not the valance states of manganese and oxygen, which I think I memorized.

In those days, large undergraduate lecture courses often included discussion sections: groups of ten or fifteen students who met with a graduate student every week. Unfortunately, section leaders often took these sessions as opportunities to practice their lecture styles. In retrospect, it seems we were all terrified of each other—especially the graduate students. They weren't much older than we and had received no training in discussion leading. How could they know what to do with us? We rarely learned our fellow students' names, much less felt we were working with them. Whatever these meetings were, they weren't real discussions.

In graduate school I "zoned out" in better than half the lectures, having become pretty good at figuring out what I had to learn. All of my lecturers knew their subjects, but most were distant, formal, or obviously nervous when they talked. They would darken the lecture hall, show a slide (perhaps depicting a slice of kidney), and drone through a list of names while training a light-pointer on various indiscernible spots on the screen. The next slide might show an immensely complex table of data, with writing so small and faded it was impossible to read. After a perfunctory apology for the poor slide, the lecturer would launch into a ten-minute talk about one of the numbers on the table, which had to do with his own research. These lectures conveyed information, but no enthusiasm. Still, the subject of histology fascinated me, and I realized that, if I wanted to make a career of studying it, lecturing would be part of my job. It was time to find a role model.

One of the best lecturers I encountered was Jean-Paul Revel, a professor of anatomy who taught me histology, science, and much about beauty in the world. His lectures were interesting and fun. For one thing, he didn't keep the lights out during the whole lecture, and his repertoire of illustrations extended beyond slides. He used drawings—often several views of a structure from different perspectives—and his own expressive gestures. Jean-Paul didn't just talk about a cell, he *became* that cell for us. Portraying a heart cell, he slid along the top of the big lecturer's desk clutching his jacket to show how his membrane (the jacket) had to wrinkle up as he (the cell) contracted. He came across as warm and safe, almost as if he were speaking directly to me. It was Jean-Paul who told me that lymphocytes, like pajamas, come in small, medium, and large. And he knew how to explain the kidney in terms of sieves and heating pipes, which I could conceptualize and recall when tackling the complex textbooks full of unpronounceable names. Furthermore, Jean-Paul was about the only lecturer who honed his metaphors and paused to explain difficult concepts in a variety of terms. Rather than exposing us to a long list of facts, he seemed more concerned to be sure that we clearly understood at least one point on which to build our knowledge. I remember thinking, "This is the way I want to lecture."

Later an indelible personal experience made me question traditional medical education and my part in it. In 1975, in the week after the cesarian birth of our second daughter, my wife developed serious medical complications. During her month-long hospitalization, I hovered in the background, helpless, taking care of our children. My wife recovered, but the ordeal baffled, terrified, and frustrated me. During the crisis, none of the hospital shift doctors had considered my struggle as part of my wife's illness. None had asked, "You have a new baby—how're you doing?" I had heard only brush-offs. It occurred to me that my kind of teaching was partially responsible for what had happened to my family. I was helping to train doctors so narrowly specialized that they had difficulty seeing beyond their own areas of expertise. The experience made me think about the whole system of medical education, not just histology. If the students were good, and I and my colleagues were doing our jobs well, why weren't things turning out better? As the trombone player lamented, "How come when I blow in so sweet it comes out so sour?"

I felt compelled to speak to students about this deficiency in their education. Shortly after my wife's medical crisis, I stepped around the podium and—scared to death—added a brief coda about "feelings" to the last lecture of my histology course. As far as I knew, there was no institutional precedent for my message, but it seemed essential to talk about loss of feeling, danger, and the terror of responsibility—all unofficially taboo subjects in the basic science part of the medical curriculum. Normally there are all sorts of background noise during a lecture. This time there was utter silence. I finished my brief speech feeling like a fool, but, to my surprise, after a moment there was applause. Later a group of students asked me to sponsor a forum for them to discuss their feelings. They wanted it structured like a course. How ironic, I thought: I ask them to acknowledge the emotional element in becoming a responsible physician, and they think they can find it in a reading list. I agreed to meet with them, and that was the beginning of my first peer support group. Not long afterward, the dean for student affairs asked me to join her program of peer groups, which is open to all Harvard medical students. Normally, about half of them sign up, and six faculty members lead weekly groups of about fourteen students throughout the academic year. In leading these sessions, I try to help the student assimilate the kaleidoscope of emotions—pride, fear, excitement, awe, alienation—involved in becoming medical doctors. Regular, honest contact with their fellow students helps them explore their own feelings and grow as people within the context of professionalization. As a side benefit, the process helps them feel comfortable with colleagues and begin to develop a network of peers.

In running such groups for the past eleven years, I learned how to cede control to the students and refrain from protective intervention during the occasional uncomfortable silences. Listening to students and talking with them—not merely speaking in their presence—turned out to be excellent preparation for discussion teaching.

The New Pathways Program

Rumblings about a change in the Harvard medical curriculum started in 1982, in tune with a general spirit of reform throughout the country. Our dean collaborated with other medical educators on an official report, which called for a thorough overhaul of medical education to meet the needs of future physicians. We should focus more on concepts and less on facts, the report argued, and help students learn to build their own data bases. The educators also expressed strong concern about the humanness of teaching and the integration of values and attitudes in the education of physicians. At Harvard the dean and faculty undertook the enormous task of revamping our curriculum to address these deficiencies. The new curriculum would replace the traditional large lecture courses with a sequence of new discussion courses to be led by qualified faculty.

Skeptical at first, I soon realized I was trapped into participation. The director of the new program asked whether I—an instructor who publicly urged students to confront their own vulnerability—intended to practice what I preached. My reservations about medical training centered on narrowness, reluctance to admit ignorance, and the creation of emotional distance—first among students, then between lecturer and student, and finally between doctor and patient. Case discussion teaching seemed to address all three concerns. I accepted the director's offer.

To implement the institutional shift to case teaching, the director and the dean organized a Core Committee to oversee the development of the pilot program that came to be known as the New Pathways. Supplementing the Core Committee's work, each member assembled an independent Curriculum Development Group (CDG), composed of research scientists and clinicians who would teach in the new program. The CDGs then rolled up their sleeves and began to sculpt a new curriculum, fitting the old materials into a series of blocks—The Human Body, Metabolism, Matter and Energy, Identity and Defense, Life Cycle, Information Processing, and Behavior—organized to correspond to the ways in which human beings are put together. I headed the CDG that developed the Human Body course, incorporating the material previously taught in cell biology, histology, gross anatomy, and, to a lesser extent, radiology. My colleagues included professors of gross anatomy, physiology, radiology, pediatric surgery, and cell biology. Each CDG was free to choose the size of its discussion groups, frequency of class meetings, cases, and details of teaching style—but we knew we would have to defend every choice before the Core Committee.

After a few CDG meetings, I noticed our group forming patterns of affiliation similar to those I had seen in the students' peer support groups. A sense of excitement, mutual respect, and task orientation came to our discussions as we produced a new course more expeditiously than any one of us could have managed alone. Our strategy called for discussion leaders to pose provocative questions as they guided students through a diagnostic scrutiny of details in real medical cases, which our clinical colleagues would supply (appropriately disguised to protect patients' privacy). Teachers were to guard against dominating classes by slipping into the lecture mode. Our pedagogical purpose was both to bring out key content through questioning and to model the learning process itself. We agreed to measure our success by students' performance on written examinations and the degree to which they learned to formulate fruitful questions on their own.

One of our aims was to create an environment in which the students could succeed only through teamwork. We selected cases that could lead deep into the content of our course by stimulating straightforward questions that could not be answered without rigorous scientific inquiry and study. For example, in a case involving chest pain and "shortness of breath," several questions arise. What can cause shortness of breath? How do we breathe? When we exhale, how do we expel air without deliberately pushing it out of our lungs? When we strain to lift a weight, why does breakfast stay in our stomachs? How do we blow up a balloon? Such questions would, we hoped, rapidly immerse the students in textbooks of anatomy, physiology, and internal medicine. Their groups would either build a collective raft of knowledge or founder and sink in a sea of information.

Another goal of my CDG was to teach biological structure and function at all levels of magnification, so our students could learn to move comfortably between gross and microscopic structure. Knowing that this would require the students to develop a conceptual framework—a set of structural rules for living systems—our CDG went through a similar process. We asked ourselves: What is a system; how do we see one? What are the boundaries of systems, and what are their properties? When our discussions really got going, we discovered that we ourselves were a system. Social groups, like cells, have structural and functional rules; our personalities and their interaction influenced the content of our discussions. This was the sort of insight we hoped students would find in similar sessions and carry into their professional lives.

During one CDG meeting we roughly planned the first day's discussion: we would ask a student to read the first page of the case aloud while the group checked it for unfamiliar vocabulary or concepts. Drawing on the group's collective experience, we would then examine these words and ideas so the students could begin to see what they needed to learn to understand the case. We further agreed to add a visual dimension to discussions by inviting students to the blackboard to draw the structures under discussion, guided by their colleagues' suggestions and criticisms.

Finally, we would list the group's questions and issues as a rough agenda for the next day's meeting.

Though I had had no formal preparation for discussion teaching, my experience leading peer support groups gave me some confidence, and my wife, a family therapist, suggested a theoretical model for group dynamics conceived by David Kantor and William Lehr.[1] The model perceives four basic roles in any social system—leader, follower, opposer, and bystander. These roles are exchangeable in a healthy group. With this model in mind, I planned to stimulate a classroom dialectic in which people could slip from role to role at different points. My idea was to try to include the bystander, get the opposer to follow now and then, and unseat the leader—even if the leader happened to be me.

Investigating a Case

Our opening case, which corresponds to my opening lecture on cell biology and protein synthesis, is a good example of the many levels on which case discussion moves. As a leader, I wanted to introduce some unfamiliar concepts and help my students begin to know each other, work together, and learn how to define and organize their own learning agenda. On the first day of classes I entered a small conference room to meet six students seated around a table. I had read a list of their names, colleges, majors, and maybe some interests and hobbies, but all this fled my memory as I smiled, took a seat, and began: "Hi, I'm Daniel Goodenough. Please start by introducing yourselves and saying, briefly, how you'd like to label yourself—biologist, social scientist, historian, or whatever."

One fellow volunteered, "My name is John C. I was a biochemistry–molecular biology major, and I wrote a master's thesis—in addition to an undergraduate honor's thesis—on the protein-RNA interactions in the Signal Recognition Particle (SRP)." The woman on my right paled somewhat, and the room became very still. Oblivious, John continued his recitation with some nonscientific hobbies, including white-water canoeing and photography. The woman looked down at her notebook. After finishing off the fingernail on his left ring finger, another fellow gave a nervous laugh and said, "I'm George D., and I must be in the wrong room. I only understood every other word that John C. just said about his theses. I majored in philosophy and only took the bare minimum of pre-med and science courses, most of which I don't remember. I'm clearly going to be a stone around everyone's neck in here."

The woman beside me blurted out, "Oh no, you're not," and blushed. Then she continued, "I'm Martha M. I majored in biology but spent most of my time on a project in the South Bronx doing fieldwork for an epidemiology research team. I took cell biology and biochemistry, but I don't remember much. I guess I'll have to begin again from scratch."

Another young man spoke up. "I'm Roger S., and I majored in physical chemistry. I remember that there are secreted and nonsecreted proteins made by cells and that the SRP is involved somehow, but I can't give any more information than that."

"At least you've heard of SRP," Martha said.

John C. said, "You guys are making me out to be some kind of freak. Come on, I don't know anything about medicine."

At the end of the table sat a very withdrawn-looking Oriental student. I looked at him, hoping he would speak, but he remained silent. I smiled and finally said, "And what about you?" He looked uncomfortable and said, "I am Su-Yin Chang. I majored in biology also." There was silence. We waited for him to say more, but he remained silent.

"Well, that leaves me," said the other woman in the group. "I'm Ella R. I majored in art history, but took biology as a second major."

When Ella finished I said, "One of our main goals is for each of us to discover that all of the others have really important information and viewpoints to add to a group discussion. Some people think it's enough to learn biology and molecular biology, but that's not what it means to be a doctor. We all need to be each other's teachers. You're not in here to impress anyone. As soon as you start reciting merely to show that you know information, I'm going to make you stop because that won't help anybody else in the group. You must talk to each other." (The students knew that their grades would all be pass/fail, but I would be writing paragraphs of evaluation on their performances for use within our program.)

Then, following our CDG's general plan, I said, "Will one of you please read the first page of the case?" They looked at each other anxiously, until George, the philosopher, volunteered. The case told the story of Georgi Markov, a Bulgarian who defected to the West and worked as a writer and television commentator in England. Someone jabbed Markov in the back of the thigh with an umbrella point while he waited for a bus at the Waterloo Bridge. Within twenty-four hours, Markov ran a high fever, with vomiting, and died in heart failure. The case imparts its information bit by bit, like clues in pulp detective fiction.

In our discussion, I played Watson to the students' Holmes. At first we knew only that Markov had defected, been stabbed, fallen sick, and died. (Later in the case one learns that the pathologist found a small poison pellet under Markov's skin, but the students hadn't received this information yet.) I asked, "Are there any vocabulary words that you don't know?" (A medical dictionary is always available in the room.) They all shook their heads. So I asked, "Are there any groups of words that carry a concept we need to define before we can understand why Markov died?" John C., the biochemist, said, "Well, I would want to know why Markov had a fever and why he vomited." George quoted the phrase, "irregular rhythms of the heart" from the case, and said, "I'd like to know more about them and what could cause them." Ella said, "What we really need to know is, was Markov murdered? If he wasn't, why the cloak-and-dagger stuff?" Then George jumped in: "We can't decide that because there's not enough information here—innuendo, but nothing direct."

"Right," I said. "We can't make this decision yet. Maybe we should go back, as an exercise of how to do a case, and be more critical about the words. Someone mentioned fever and vomiting. Do we all agree we know what those are? Why do you get a fever? When? Do you always get one for the same reason? How, when, and why do you vomit? Let's see if our collective experience can define all the ways you get a fever." John said, "You can get a fever with the flu." George recalled that his uncle got a fever after eating shellfish. Martha mentioned bee-sting. John remembered that his grandfather had fevers with cancer of the large bowel. George told us that a first cousin had regular fevers every morning for a while, but they went away. Roger mentioned that an uncle with something called Whipple's disease had fevers, but nobody in the family ever figured out what was going on.

I noted that they had collectively listed most of the circumstances of fever, which none of them could have done alone. "Let's talk about why Markov vomits," I continued. "Why do people vomit?" Roger, John, George, and Martha came up with experiences including flu, car-sickness, rotten clams, anxiety, pregnancy, overdoing exercise, bulemia, and the same grandfather with bowel cancer. As the four started getting used to discussing medical subject matter together, I tried to make eye contact with Ella and Su-Yin, hoping to get them to relax and participate on this simple level. Neither said a word.

"Who will read the second page of the case?" I asked. George obliged, introducing the pathology report that tells of a hollow metal pellet in Markov's thigh.

"What could be inside the pellet?" Martha asked. "A poison?" Roger said, "A bacterium, maybe, or a virus that could multiply?" I asked, "How does the poison or bacterium get to the heart?" John said, "Through the blood." George said, "Through the lymph." Martha said, "By swimming."

At the end of the hour I left the students with a question. "John, George, Roger, and Martha have talked a lot, but Ella and Su-Yin haven't said anything. Are you happy with that? How would you like to deal with it?"

At our next meeting on the Markov case, the students came back loaded with information and questions. John asked, "The pellet is under the skin. What is skin?" Martha said, "We have to talk about the blood vessels that carry the poison out of the pellet." I commented that some of the answers to these questions were in the histology text and asked, "What is the structure of a blood vessel?" After we had talked about that for a while, I mentioned that we would also be going to the histology lab to look at blood, blood vessels, and skin in the light microscope—and there the students would see a lymphocyte. Martha said, "Oh, you mean lymphocytes can travel through the blood vessel wall, back and forth between blood and tissues? Why can they go through blood vessel walls while red blood cells can't?" I looked around. John volunteered material he remembered from several lectures in a college cell biology course. His presentation was a liturgy about things like "actin, myosin, phosphorylation, calmodulin, and actin-binding proteins." The others looked confused and scared. Martha sighed. John closed a book and glanced at his watch. It was time for me to intervene with a wrap-up and a call for the next day's agenda.

Details in the Markov case can readily be used to direct the students to elements in the curriculum. The article from which I adapted the case gives the dimensions of the hollow poison pellet that was found under Markov's skin. With first-year chemistry and a calculator, students can determine roughly how many poison molecules could be contained in the chamber. Obviously this number sufficed to kill a person. Then, how much poison must it take to destroy a cell? Comparing the number of cells in the human body (information in our texts) with the number of poison molecules in the pellet, students find a ratio of about 1:1, so each molecule must have destroyed a whole cell. How? By blocking protein synthesis, without which the body cannot survive. Thus we reach one of the topics of my old first histology lecture: protein synthesis. But we come to it organically, so to speak, in a human context, through the students' inquiries.

As our first semester progressed, the instructors in my unit began to meet—informally, at first, over lunch—and work through each case before teaching it. Although we never defined a formal process, we ended by developing a rather effective mechanism for teaching preparation. By testing the cases, we could not only gauge the relative effectiveness of various lines of inquiry, but also supplement our individual (sometimes fairly irrelevant) expertise with pertinent information from colleagues. Just as important was the empathy we gained from probing the cases with our peers in a process not so very different from the one our students would experience under our guidance.

During that first year, I often made a serious error: I tried to keep control of the group of six students, stressing those questions about the case that interested me and, far too frequently, answering them myself. At the back of my mind were "learning issues" I thought the students should cover. These derived directly from my old histology course. Since our first discussion cases were in the areas of cell biology and histology— subjects about which I knew a great deal, with very definite ideas about what was "important"—I simply talked all the time, playing lecturer-in-discussion-leader's-clothing. And the students sensed my game. They talked to me, not each other. It was like a replay of my undergraduate discussion sections.

But when our cases moved outside my area of expertise, my inept discussion-leading technique met its nemesis in the form of a knee. More precisely, a set of crescent-shaped cartilages in the knee joint, the lateral and medial menisci, undid me. I simply didn't understand them. As the students discussed the cartilages, I peered over their shoulders at our anatomy text, growing tenser and tenser as I tried to follow their comments and understand the illustrations along with them. Suddenly it all seemed clear to me.

"Yes, well," I began, "the menisci are situated thus and so in the joint cavity"—I leaned back in my chair—"and you can see how they are attached here and there by the appropriate mechanisms." I continued my explanation, relaxing as the group listened, nodded, took notes on my lucid explanation. But they had tasted a little too much independence to remain completely passive. As they wrote, they continued to inspect the illustrations in the anatomy book. Finally John said, "If what you say is true, how do you explain this drawing, which clearly shows the menisci attached over here, not in the location you pointed out?"

I looked at the picture. Both my adrenal glands emptied themselves into my bloodstream. My mouth went dry. My heart rate soared, and I felt as if I were eight years old again, making my stage debut in the Foote

School Christmas pageant, as an elephant. After clearing my throat, I conceded my error and unfamiliarity with this particular structure and admitted that they had caught me in a moment of pretension that I would try not to repeat. The episode cleared the air, teaching my students that it was safe not to know answers in a discussion class. Identifying ignorance is the first step to remedying it. We were all learning together.

The group's energy picked up after this episode. The students began talking to each other, rather than to me, and I began to listen, watch, and learn. For me, it was a vivid lesson in trusting the discussion process. I don't mean to recommend ignorance as a qualification for discussion teaching. On the contrary, as a scientist, I have learned how to think about structure, formulate fruitful questions, sift evidence, and form hypotheses. And these skills combine with my knowledge of histology to condition the kinds of questions I ask in class. But at some level, what we are modeling in the New Pathways curriculum is the scientific method, and I find it both appropriate and exhilarating to function occasionally as my students' fellow-learner. Our tightrope walk into discussion teaching is not without its safety nets. The program offers one or two lectures each week, either because the material doesn't lend itself to discussion—the extremely delicate structure of the peripheral nervous system is one example—or because students request further briefing on some subject. And our daily, supervised laboratory sessions remain essentially unchanged from the old curriculum. All the students in the program work at the microscope and at the cadaver with lab manuals and slides, and there are many instructors available for help, advice, explanations, and support.

As a discussion teacher, I have developed new standards for evaluating classes. In lecturing, success meant that students paid attention, laughed at my jokes, and applauded me. I told them what to learn, and they learned it. Now one measure of a good class is the gleam in students' eyes as they head for the library or the lab to answer some of the questions the group has hammered out. And after case discussions I often reflect on whether I have learned, and whether good, provocative questions have emerged with little or no prodding. Even more exciting, sometimes I have heard questions proliferate so rapidly and efficiently that the group has worked through a series of complex biological structures with speed, coherence, and enthusiasm. When I teach now I worry about such questions as whether everyone in the group has participated. Have questions generated energetic (but respectful) controversy? Has the group really pried the case open, created an agenda for further study, and developed a strategy for addressing its own questions? My initial fears about motivating students to cover the material have evaporated. Beginning medical students are responsible people, and the group discussion process tends to generate its own motivations.

For example, one of our cases mentioned that the patient experienced difficulty micturating. Martha asked, "What does 'micturate' mean?" John thumbed through the medical dictionary and said, "It means urinate." I asked, "Well, how does one micturate?" George said, "You need a full bladder, and then you have to relax some muscles." Roger broke in: "Which muscles?" "I don't know," said George, "but it feels like one of those complicated muscles in the pelvic floor we looked at yesterday." Ella, who had been inspecting a gross anatomy atlas, volunteered, "In this picture there's a urethral sphincter that seems perfectly positioned to regulate urine flow." I asked, "What kind of muscle is it, voluntary or involuntary?" George said, "It must be voluntary, since you can make it relax when you want to urinate." Martha objected, "That can't be right, or you'd always have to think about keeping it contracted when you didn't want to urinate." This brought us to an impasse. I said, "It seems we need to study this more before we can have a clear discussion." The students noted all the unanswered questions they had generated, and we adjourned.

The next day, the group was full of information. Roger had made a schematic drawing of the urination pathways, including the brain, spinal cord, and bladder with its associated muscles and complicated nerves. There was lively discussion about these structures, with Roger and Martha getting into an argument about whether the external or internal sphincter controls urination. When, at length they hauled out their textbooks and began quoting at each other, it became obvious that the texts had contradictory information. George said, "I'm beginning to think nobody knows how urination is controlled." Then Su-Yin put his hand up—an unusual gesture for him. I looked at him with raised eyebrows, and he said, "I asked Professor R. about this problem. He said the physiology texts are incorrect. Their authors have used laboratory animals to study the physiology and anatomy of urination, and humans are very different." Ella asked, "How did Professor R. explain the human anatomy and physiology?" Su-Yin then presented a beautiful description of pelvic geometry that elucidated the function of several muscles in the control of human urination. I was delighted, not only because Su-Yin had joined us at such a critical juncture, but also because the physiology text I had read had left me as confused as the others in the group.

Moments like this, when the process works for the benefit of all concerned, allay my old worries about the unhealthy separation of intellect and emotion in medical education. Roger and Martha's argument and Su-Yin's promising triumph over his shyness were as integral to the learning process as the research any of us had done—much of which turned out to be wrong anyway. Such exchanges are a rich reward for taking a chance on discussion teaching (though there have also been moments of panic, indecision, frustration, and discouragement). After three years of leading discussions, I am beginning to learn how to manage this complex, dynamic process. But the satisfaction of watching groups of beginning medical students forge solid working relationships while mastering huge amounts of difficult technical material encourages me to say that I will never go back to the didactic lecture model. The verve with which my students tackle complex questions delights and impresses me as much as their ultimate success. Even the blind alleys and wrong turns our discussions sometimes take have value. If nothing else, they help our students learn to cope with the inevitable uncertainties and frustrations of their profession. And it has been a pleasure to hear several students—speaking of colleagues from widely disparate socioeconomic, cultural, or racial backgrounds—say, "So-and-so is my best friend, and I never would have gotten to know him [or her] if we hadn't worked together in a group like this." The impact of the process on future health care delivery is still unclear, but our goal of helping medical students blend the competent self-confidence of researchers with the cooperative consulting skills of team workers seems to be within reach. In a profession where today's state of the art is tomorrow's obsolescence, active problem-solving is an indispensable skill.

The power of group discussion in medical teaching suggests that the method is broadly applicable to other disciplines. This power has nothing to do with self-aggrandizement or adulation by students and peers. Rather, it is the power of meaningful interconnection among the students and teachers as they all learn and, in a very real sense, transcend themselves, adding a vital new layer to the growing coral reef of human understanding.

NOTE

1. D. Kantor and W. Lehr, *Inside the Family* (San Francisco: Jossey-Bass, 1975).

6

Every Student Teaches and Every Teacher Learns: The Reciprocal Gift of Discussion Teaching

C. ROLAND CHRISTENSEN

IT HAS BEEN SAID that we live life forward but understand it backward. Looking back over years of discussion teaching, I see how intensely its process has intrigued, baffled, and intellectually nourished this practitioner—and the fascination shows no signs of abating. At its core lies a fundamental insight: teaching and learning are inseparable, parts of a single continuum—more Möbius strip than circle—of reciprocal giving and receiving. In discussion pedagogy students share the teaching task with the instructor and one another. All teach, and all learn. This view of the dynamic has implications for every aspect of discussion teaching, from fundamental assumptions to the finest points of classroom behavior. I make no claim to understand them all. But looking at teaching through the prism of reciprocity has allowed me to discern certain components of the process that can be named, described, studied, and communicated.

The reader should not be surprised to find "what I know," and, in particular, my descriptions of how I think while teaching, in the form of questions rather than statements. Four decades of discussion teaching leave their mark—in my case, an aversion to divorcing knowledge from challenge, dialogue, emotional engagement, and personal development. The quest for wisdom, as distinct from knowledge, will always remain open-ended.

This essay will present insights I have collected about the discussion teaching process with some details about the context that allowed me to see them. It will begin in the past, with my very first discussion class and fledgling efforts to learn how to learn about its mysteries. It will then continue with hypotheses about the nature of the process and the very powerful role students play in sharing its leadership with their instructors. And it will conclude in the present, with overarching "lessons learned" about values and the essential ingredient in all good teaching: faith.

Early Years: How I Learned to Learn about Discussion Teaching

Exploring the discussion process has been a wondrous adventure, a long journey within the confines of classroom walls. Like any productive educational enterprise, mine was aided by a fortunate synergy between instructor and institution. My colleagues on the faculty of the Harvard Business School, honored teaching as a legitimate subject to be studied, as well as an action to be performed—an attitude that affected my perspective on everything that I saw, heard, and sensed as I taught, and my decisions on the best investment of my own intellectual resources.

My personal chain of discovery began with the first discussion class I ever taught: Tuesday, February 14, 1947. Yesterday. Remembered painfully, it was a bit like a session with a dental surgeon, sans novocaine. I was to teach an eighty-student section of the required second-year Business Policy course. The course mission was complex: to help students learn the functions, roles, and knowledge requirements of a general manager, with emphasis on the qualitative intricacies of strategic decision making. Underlying all this was the more basic goal of promoting the development of essential personal qualities: judgment, wisdom, and ethics.

Promptly at 8:30 A.M., having sweated through the weekend and Monday, I opened the door to Baker Library 101. It was a thin, cold room, with windows that rattled in the northeast wind and metal blinds stuck in various positions of closure. A slightly curved amphitheater format barely allowed space at the front for a platform, replete with brass rail and curtain that but partially hid the instructor's chair and desk. My suit coat over one arm—army exercise had changed my body frame and Harvard's salary did not allow for wardrobe refurbishment—and a folder of class notes in the other, I walked to the small platform, started up the three steps, tripped, and fell.

I blushed a bright red and knelt to gather my scattered papers. The room was quiet, except for an embarrassed half-laugh from the right, so brief it must have been squelched. I took a deep breath and, finally, stood up to look around at "them": scores of almost indistinguishable faces. A few smiled at me, thank heavens. My opening question—"Mr. Adams [you can imagine my reason for selecting him to start off], what is your diagnosis of the Consolidated Vultee situation?"—went well. But the remainder of the eighty minutes was a blur. My carefully prepared teaching plan, crafted to direct the group through an efficient analysis of the case that would reveal both the principles of Business Policy and my own indispensability to the discussion process, had minimal impact.

We were discussing a case about a company organizing for rapidly expanded military production during wartime, a topic still of high interest in 1947. The students wanted to pursue their own concerns and questions in ways that were meaningful to them. They agreed, disagreed, expressed confidence in (or incredulity at the naiveté of) their associates' suggestions. Infrequently, someone would admit confusion—a predicament appreciated and shared by the instructor. A few seemed bored, but most were deeply involved in the case, both intellectually and with their guts. There was no antagonism—all were polite—but the group permitted neither plan nor professor to get in its way.

When the class was over, I had heard hundreds and hundreds of words—verbal exchanges between and among the students, a multiplicity of conclusions, and an explosion of suggestions as to what the president of Consolidated Vultee should do. For me, it had been an academic Tower of Babel, a throw of conversational confetti. Most puzzling, however, was the reaction of the students. Seemingly, the class had made sense to them. Small groups stayed in the classroom after the discussion. Others left still carrying on their dialogue with an intensity that would have been difficult to contrive. Several commented, "Good class, professor." I thought, "Good class? Come on!"

The few steps back to my office felt like a stroll through a sandstorm. All I could remember of what had happened but minutes before were a few major themes and some dramatic statements. Students' comments fused; I couldn't recall who had said what or the responses those comments had triggered. A psychologist might have diagnosed my condition as cognitive overload: too much information to process too fast. How could I lead such a confusing process as this discussion had been? "It can't be done," I thought. "It simply can't be done!"

The only sensible course of action was to get help. Our faculty was the best, artists of the classroom, the teaching equivalents of Monet, Miró, and Jasper Johns. I asked senior colleagues to explain the discussion teaching process to me. Unfortunately, mastery of a creative activity does not guarantee the ability to explain it or help another master it. "Play it by ear, just play it by ear," was a typical response. For all their classroom genius, my colleagues treated teaching like the proverbial "black box": a container full of powerful mechanisms, but sealed.

During that first year of teaching, succeeding classes continued to listen much like the first one. The weeks marched by: dozens of class meetings, three times a week, with two eighty-person class groups. The discussions were spirited—decibels galore, dialogue, orations, even disquisitions. Crisp comments and pauses, murmurs, and mumbles. Themes did emerge in class, and the group often obtained reasonable consensus by the end of the session. Assumptions were tested and points proved. I had a good notion that cooperation powered the process, but even so, its dynamic eluded me. It was still a noisy mystery "out there." I felt like a stranger in the midst of the familiar. Nietzsche somewhere notes that all that is profound wears a mask. I wanted to look behind the mask that the learning process wore every day in the classroom.

Getting help became a puzzle, a pedagogical Rubik's cube. By now I had guessed that the students were responsible for my survival, thus far, in the classroom. Slowly this realization became a clue to learning about the mysterious process of discussion teaching. If colleagues couldn't "give" me the answer, perhaps I might find it with the students. After all, they were the reason it was working. I wondered if, somehow, those whom I supposedly led could help me learn how to lead. Perhaps I could work out a way to study what we all did in discussions and discover order in the apparent chaos. This would mean observing other teachers' classes and, as far as possible, my own.

I soon learned that mastery of course content wasn't the key. At the very beginning, I had, like most instructors, assumed that my job was to devise the clearest, most insightful analysis of the material possible, compose a list of questions to elicit that analysis in class, and then lead the students through my list in a courteous but authoritative manner. How starkly that assumption clashed with what I observed in class! When I tried to figure out what distinguished higher- from lower-quality discussion classes, I noticed that the better discussions were those in which the students asked particularly good questions—questions that often eclipsed those I had prepared. And the best discussions often modified or completely abandoned my neatly sequenced teaching plans. I was intrigued to realize that this aspect of good classes lay largely beyond my control, as did another common feature of productive discussions: students' listening to one another with attention and care. Good discussions frequently took paths that the group found reasonable but I had not foreseen. It seemed increasingly obvious that I neither could nor should try to control the discussion process. The students were my co-teachers.

Over time, such glimmers of insight brightened to beams of light that illuminated at least a portion of the contents of the black box of the discussion process. My early, overwhelmed conclusion, "It can't be done," evolved to, "It *can* be done, but not alone." But if the students were teaching, what was my job? To help them teach better. This meant that I needed not only to master the skills of leading the discussion process but also to devise ways to describe and explain the process to others.

Self-knowledge is the beginning of all knowledge. I had to find the teacher in myself before I could find the teacher in my students and gain understanding of how we all taught one another. Slowly, I learned to make my classroom observations more productive by focusing them. I started to try out tiny experiments. Instead of waiting for the class to assemble before making my appearance, for example, I tried arriving early to see what that might teach me about my students. The exercise proved valuable. Talking with students and watching them enter the room revealed much about their lives and interests—who played sports before class, who was under the weather or visibly fatigued that day, who had special interest in the day's topic (or, conversely, an apparent desire to hide). Coming to class early also allowed me to prepare a genial, cooperative atmosphere by welcoming students by name, and it gave me an opportunity to note students' subgroups.

Some other early experiments: I dropped my initial practice of calling opening speakers in alphabetical order and made choices based on some knowledge of students' backgrounds and interests. And I took a tip from a student who noted a preponderance of "whats" among my questions and tried more "whys." Simple, simple steps, rooted in practicality. But these were my first glimpses of the workings of the black box.

Finding time to reflect on the discussion as it unfolded in class was still like trying to meditate on a speeding fire engine. The after-class reprise was equally difficult. But I now had some ideas about why certain classes seemed more productive than others. Much of what we teachers do in the classroom seems intuitive. My task was to examine this apparently automatic behavior, show its workings, and identify areas in which judgment might play a part. "Process," whatever it might be, was clearly going to be the major focus of my attention.

Like most academics, I assumed that abstract principles of some sort would be my best guides. But my initial attempts, directed at understanding "process" in its purest sense, brought little practical reward. It seemed that the farther down the "abstraction ladder" I climbed, the closer I came to my real goal, an ever-deeper understanding of process. Near the bottom of the ladder, on the operational (how to) level, I began to make observations that truly dispelled confusion. When I came to class with a simple, practical teaching experiment in mind—something like evaluating the effect of calling on students seated in different parts of the room—I got results. Sometimes I focused on the art of questioning. What happens when I ask the same question of two students in succession? What is the effect of asking a delayed question—one to be answered after a moment of reflection—compared with asking the same question "cold"? Sometimes I concentrated on phrasing. What is the difference between using a student's name and simply gesturing? Or I concentrated on timing: How long can a silence last before restlessness sets in? I repeated these experiments from class to class, year to year, trying, like any researcher, to hold as many things constant as possible each time in order to evaluate the variable element.

Once I learned to focus on what a teacher says and does in the classroom, possibilities for experimentation and learning began to proliferate. The classroom proved to be a perfect laboratory for my nuts-and-bolts experiments with the discussion process. As an observer, of myself and other instructors in action, I truly began to learn. My experimental approach to the discussion process revealed that all participants, instructor included, spent most of their time either asking questions, listening to people's answers, or making some sort of response to those answers. I began to appreciate that these activities—questioning, listening, and response—were the most basic "stuff" of process. I also realized that every discussion produced rehearsals of data, analysis, questions, challenges, and syntheses, but not necessarily in a predictable sequence. This insight suggested that one of the instructor's most crucial tasks is linking—explicitly relating, and helping the students to relate, current points of argument to others that may have appeared earlier that day or in a previous discussion. This point, I realized, had important implications for teaching preparation as well as discussion management.

What I found inside the black box of the discussion process was an ever-changing flow of activities that resisted abstract analysis but yielded to disciplined observation and the application of very specific skills. To some extent, all of the essays in the present book examine aspects of these skills from the points of view of experienced practitioners, teachers at work. And what is our work? To create a favorable learning climate, to set a teaching/learning contract, to ask and respond to questions, listen to contributions, and promote the formation of groups in which students can teach themselves and one another. All these are practical approaches to a process that cannot be abstracted without substantial loss of identity, for the discussion process is a true slice of life. Guiding it takes skill, patience, and a basic faith that one may learn, with time and effort, to preside over disorder without disorientation.

Some Insights about Process and Students' Role in Its Leadership

Seen in retrospect, my attempts to understand the workings of the discussion teaching process have much in common with the process itself. Both exhibit the disorderliness of discovery: even the most steadfast explorer cannot march straight through a jungle. Most attempts to capture the essence of the discussion process produce frustrations as well as insights. The very meaning of the phrase, for example, still teases our profession. The totality of a discussion includes the intellectual and emotional experiences of a whole roomful of people: material to occupy psychologists, neurologists, sociologists, anthropologists, and philosophers for years to come. My own quest for an enlightening definition produced little to help me choose which of ten vigorously waving hands to recognize. All processes are flows, either of activities or thoughts, but this basic definition gives one no handle on why some opening questions inspire lively debate while others trigger alienation or apathy, or why the comments of "student experts" sometimes help and sometimes hinder a discussion. Nor does it distinguish what happens in a discussion classroom from what happens on an assembly line.

I found the exercise of drawing distinctions more fruitful. Contrasting process with content provided practical help. Confusing mastery of material with mastery of the discussion process produces a common error: a controlling teaching style that creates bilateral frustration when students inevitably try to go their own ways. This lesson became clear to me as my students continued to offer polite, but stubborn resistance to my attempts to shepherd them through the meticulous analyses that had cost me so many hours of preparation. And when I examined my own initial inclination to choose opening speakers alphabetically from my class list, I found that it showed another typical novice's confusion: the failure to distinguish process from procedure. Procedures are logical and rigid sequences of actions, indispensable in making an arrest, performing an appendectomy, or accessing a computer file—but fatal to leading a meaningful group discussion. Discussions are liquid. They do not move in straight lines; they undulate.

Over the years, I have found the use of metaphor enriching to my understanding of the discussion process. What is a discussion, if not a voyage of exploration, with the leader as both captain and crew member? To appreciate the frequent reversals and indirections of the process, one may imagine a discussion class as a mountain climb, where even apparent reversals produce ascent. In the discussion process, "wrong" can be more helpful than "right"; an obtuse statement can spark a charged, enlightening debate that straightforward analysis could never provoke.

Discussion teaching is noisy. Messy, too. It greets an observer with a verbal cacophony—an unnerving scene for teachers unprepared for its energy. Good discussions unfold in unexpected ways that modify the programmed logic of a teaching plan. They pose new questions, uncover and gnaw away at sanctified assumptions, rejuvenate old topics with fresh insights, broaden perspectives, and create new paths of inquiry. But focused observation and systematic analysis can reveal meaning in the noise and logic in the disorder. The rough-and-tumble of classroom interchange contains opportunities that enhance the learning of both students and instructors. What unsettles a teacher may energize the students: less disorder, then new order. Discussion teaching demands a milieu of freedom, an openness that encourages students to share power over, and responsibility for, the leadership and conduct of a class.

In discussion teaching, tidiness can tyrannize. Messiness can work miracles. To succeed, the enterprise requires the active contribution, not merely cooperation, of the discussion group. Mutual collaboration—reciprocity of effort—is not only engaging and exciting for students, it is also imperative for the discussion leader. However impressive your experience or skills, you will have difficulty in questioning, listening, and responding while simultaneously observing, synthesizing, reflecting, and evaluating the discussion dialogue, and planning for the rest of the class. A teacher would need more than one pair of eyes and ears to carry out such a task—it really *can't* be done alone!

This realization suggests a further point: a great deal of essential information—factors that condition the instructional choices of the moment—emerges only in action as the process unfolds. Should an idea be explored in greater depth or overviewed in a hurry? Should the class move on to another topic? Would it be helpful to raise or lower the abstraction level of the argument? What does the group understand? What is missing? What topics need to be covered again? What questions are bothering or intriguing the group? What new avenues of exploration should we investigate now? It helps to remember that the teacher does not bear the sole responsibility for answering these questions. Students control a surprisingly large part of the turf of discussion leadership. They participate in critical "framework" decisions by influencing the agenda, sequence of topics, and allocation of time to various topics. They help determine the minute-by-minute direction of the discussion process and the quality of the dialogue. They contribute to the creation of a class culture, accept responsibility for their own involvement, and teach their peers. They develop and practice the skills of leading and following. Without their co-leadership, there is no true discussion.

I have found it helpful to consider students' contribution to the leadership of the discussion process under six broad categories. First, when responsibility is collective, the students play a significant role in constructing the agenda of the day. The instructor may find his or her preclass teaching plan influenced by the addition of new topics of interest to students, suggestions for restating issues in ways that provoke different questions, or requests that materials from previous discussions be combined with the dialogue of the day. Sometimes the class will simply reject the instructor's program. In these cases capitulation is advisable, if not inevitable. Teaching is difficult enough when students want to learn, virtually impossible if they are uninterested. Given these circumstances, discussion teachers do not, like lecturers, set the agenda; they manage its emergence, direction, and evolution.

Second, the students affect the sequence in which topics of the day are discussed. Teachers and students prepare differently. Instructors' plans exploit a flow of inquiry that seems logical to them, consistent with course objectives, and built on past experience with the material and students. But the instructor's teaching logic may not match the students' learning logic. In discussion leadership, efficiency does not always equal effectiveness. Last year's—or last hour's—discussion of a particular topic will never exactly predict the one that's about to begin. Even very experienced instructors, who have been teaching longer than their students have been studying (sometimes longer than their students have been alive), have an inferior command of one essential topic: their students' agendas and learning styles. As a result, questions that an instructor may wish to consider early may well be out of sync with the students' wishes and needs.

Accordingly, a wise instructor prepares twice: both from his or her point of view and, more important, from the students' point of view. How will participants be likely to approach the material? What paths of inquiry might they follow? When the instructor's approach differs from that of the students, the discussion may well tilt in the students' direction. The professor proposes, but the class disposes.

The third aspect of the discussion that students influence is timing. When their involvement in a question or topic is intense, it will be difficult for an instructor to redirect their energy. One can force a shift in topic, but students' interests, though denied, do not disappear. They reemerge, deftly inserted into their responses to the instructor's new questions. The sensitive instructor will "hear" the discontinuity and act accordingly.

Fourth, the types of questions students ask of one another and of the instructor play a critical role in directing the minute-by-minute flow of dialogue. Their questions may be directionally neutral—"Where do we go next?"—or may shift the discussion to another topic. The phrasing, tone, and delivery of their questions and comments influence the mood and tempo of the class, encourage conflict, excitement, resolution, or reflection. The astute instructor will listen carefully, and on several levels, to students' questions and also respectfully note the directive power in the students' choice of which individual or subgroup to address. This choice is another, crucial contribution students make to determining both the style and content of discussion.

Working and playing together over a period of time, students get to know their associates better than the instructor can—their itches and ouches, blind spots, areas of experience and wisdom, cares and concerns. And students possess current information about their peers to augment this background information. They are familiar with Rosa's or Juan's circumstances today, this minute. They know Herman's special interest in the topic and his mood. Was he worked over in an earlier class today? Is there a family crisis going on? This sort of student intelligence (in the military sense) lies mainly beyond an instructor's reach. But its power to maintain continuity or produce radical change in the direction of dialogue will show up in the classroom.

Such information can improve the quality of the group's communication. Effective communication—in which words encourage and advance understanding for others as well as the speaker—is difficult to achieve under the best of circumstances. Indeed, as the late Fritz Roethlisberger observed, the first law of communication is to expect miscommunication. Communication is even more complex in crowded classrooms, where dialogue is rapid-fire, personal commitment—even passion— accompanies many comments, and reflection time is limited. In such situations, students' intelligence does more to influence the flow of dialogue than the instructor's directions can.

Fifth, because students relate to one another as peers, they can often communicate more effectively than the instructor in class. Why? Not because they are more rigorous in thought, skilled in semantics and phonetics, or expert in their artistry of explanation. Rather, because they possess rough and ready emotional profiles of one another. In what fields does Ms. Peterson feel confident, have the knack of explaining, and the interest, patience, and ingenuity to state her message in a variety of ways? What are the barriers, the ignorance, bias, lack of interest, that limit Mr. Ripley's understanding and ability to listen?

Students also tend to share the language system of their generation, a common idiom of "go" and "no go" words and relevant metaphors ("needle in a haystack" might resonate less well than "contact lens in a swimming pool," for example). This, plus their knowledge of fellow students, brings them swiftly to the core of effective communication, speaking *to*, not *at*, one another.

Equally important, it is simpler and less threatening for participants to check and recheck each other's meaning than for the instructor to do so. They can accept "I don't understand what you said" more easily from a friend than a potential judge. Correction of the inevitable miscommunication is less complicated when it comes from a classmate than a teacher. When a fellow student says, "You didn't read me right. I meant this," or "Give me that again, Bill. Your assumptions are off base," the remark is less likely to be perceived as an accusation of ignorance or error, and more likely to be seen as a low-key request for help.

Finally, the sixth aspect of the discussion process that students influence heavily is class culture. Discussion groups derive tone and character from the way students work together in the daily routines of class. What is to be the balance between cooperation and competition? Where are the boundaries? What is acceptable and nonacceptable behavior? What are the responsibilities of a class member to himself or herself and the group? Obviously, all students should prepare, attend, and participate. It is difficult to experience a discussion in absentia. But what more? How will these particular participants work out the fundamental challenges of a member of a discussion group—when to stand out, when to blend in, when to lead, when to follow? How members of the group help one another through these complexities affects the context in which the discussions take place. The resolution of these problems contributes to the quality of the learning milieu.

The apparent disorder of a discussion class is, then, but a mask for a complicated teaching and learning process in which students play a vital, but far from obvious role in leadership. Only appreciation of, and attention to, process can help us teachers understand students' essential teaching contribution—a key understanding for effective educational discussions. Most important, the mask blinds us, as teachers, to a fundamental fact: we not only teach a course, but also simultaneously help the students learn how to teach one another. It is not enough to ask "good questions"; we must understand the art of questioning, listening, and responding constructively; model those skills in class for our students and, by so doing, demonstrate our respect for their importance.

Lessons Learned

Years after that first disorienting class, I still regard the mysterious power of discussion teaching with awe. I have shed the youthful naiveté that led me to search for "the answer," but I still work away at pedagogical questions. Accommodation is the order of the years, but the decades have brought a measure of understanding. My belief in the essential magnificence of teaching grows ever stronger. What I have learned about the abiding conundrums of discussion pedagogy makes me even more certain that teaching is a great learning experience. And for the study of teaching, what better research laboratory than the classroom, where the teacher can experiment with the real "stuff" and test, modify, and retest all hypotheses? I have stressed the rewards of this pursuit, but I am also aware of its price. The gains in depth and specificity that come from "knowing more" increase the pressure for yet higher standards. As hands-on classroom knowledge builds, one can no longer turn to easy excuses—the students just didn't like the material; another course had a long report due this week; or (most common of all) I just had a bad day. None of these explanations works when one grasps the dynamics of classroom process. Higher standards are a constant reminder to do better.

In working up a "wish I had learned this earlier" list, I asked myself: Does my experience suggest one quintessential lesson? Perhaps the answer is yes. Teaching is a human activity. Intellect does not teach intellect; people teach people. No matter how factually accurate and time-tested our data, how clear cut and disciplined our analytical methods, or how practiced and skillful our pedagogical techniques, true learning emerges only when we honor the human factor. One measure of pedagogical maturity is the ability to augment technical expertise with attention to people.

Given this overarching proposition, I would like to offer some lessons learned from students, colleagues, and day-to-day classroom practice. Some of these lessons have been purchased at substantial personal cost. Many lessons had to be both learned and relearned. On reflection, I find none of them surprising. Why didn't I think of them earlier? No one reason. But is a lifetime in the classroom really long enough to figure out what effective teaching is all about?

1. *A teacher's openness and caring increase the students' learning opportunities.* When students perceive the instructor at the front of the room as distant and impersonal—a figurehead, not a friend—their learning opportunities suffer. "He lives in another world, guys; I don't know what turns his flame up. . . . I'm just line twelve on the class list." Enduring learning needs a human context, an emotional matrix, in which to grow. The teacher who provides that context and encourages it in the learning group must let students know him or her as more than an intellectual resource or mobile data base.

Our educational conventions put distance between teachers and students. Without sacrificing propriety or relinquishing our role as guides, we teachers need to open our worlds to students. Far too many people in public view become, as Dr. Grete Bibring put it, "individuals with faces that have never been lived in." Our students want and need to know what we stand for. The opposite side of this coin is our need to understand students as people. What are their ambitions, uncertainties, blind spots, and areas of excellence? When we open our wider worlds and appear "in the round," we also maximize our possibilities for learning about them. Openness brings mutual advantage because it permits mutual learning.

But openness is not enough. We must combine it with caring. Teachers must do more than feel concerned; we must actively look after and provide for the welfare of students. We must not only appreciate, but also become personally involved in, their progress. By so doing, we measurably enhance the potential for learning on both sides. One experienced associate noted that most students want to know how much you care before they care how much you know. His judgment, though paradoxical, makes sense to me. Caring converts impersonal offers of academic assistance into gifts, and every gift of learning enriches the giver as much as the recipient. Students sense the difference between perfunctory offers of help and true personal willingness to teach and learn with them. Openness increases a discussion leader's opportunities to help students. Caring makes the process work.

2. *Effective discussions require the classroom to become a learning space.* As a novice instructor I would have defined "learning space" physically, as the classroom. Baker 101 was an adequate room—satisfactory acoustics, lights in working order, enough chairs. I looked for nothing more. Over the years, however, my view of the classroom has grown metaphorical and far more demanding. A true learning space is psychological, not physical, and the teacher bears the primary responsibility for creating it.

I now view the discussion classroom as a joining ground where students, instructor, and ideas meet and commingle; a space where, as Henri Nouwen suggests, "students and teachers can enter into a fearless communication with each other and allow their respective life experiences to be their primary and most valuable source of growth and maturation."[1] The creation of such space requires a mutual trust in which teachers and learners (those shifting roles) can present themselves as colleagues in a common quest for truth. A genuine learning space is more than a container for this quest; it is a place where all feel free to question one another constructively and where an aggregation of competitive individuals, dedicated to personal goals, can become a learning group.

When we teachers create and support an atmosphere of intellectual hospitality, we help students believe that they have something of value to contribute. This belief, in turn, encourages them to risk trying out ideas—the risk that makes learning possible. Perhaps most important, it is only within a welcoming classroom space that we can obtain students' active involvement in discussions. Discussions that take place in true learning spaces engage students verbally and reflectively, intellectually and emotionally.

Above all, such spaces make risk-taking safe—as safe as it can be, that is. And safety—students' anticipation of aid and comfort in tough situations—is the greatest antidote to the discussion leader's ever-present, always unsettling challenge: silence. Joe isn't contributing very much anymore. What's going on? Is he reflecting on points made earlier, contemplating new questions to ask, wrestling with uncertainty, just feeling turned off—or is he scared? We teachers sometimes forget how difficult it is for students to develop the capacity for what Donald Schön calls cognitive risk-taking. A glance backward at our own student days may help us remember. Didn't we use silence to protect ourselves from questions—by peers, instructors, or ourselves (these last often the most painful)? In a safe space, members of a group with especially complex needs and concerns (that includes most of us, doesn't it?) can reveal their sensitivities and needs. When this happens, community is strengthened, and all benefit.

The creation and maintenance of a safe space is not very arduous, and its rewards are bountiful. David Riesman's metaphor of the teacher as host, or welcomer of guests, may serve as a useful guide. There is little cost but great value in learning something about students' backgrounds and current circumstances in time to welcome them personally to the upcoming dialogue. Similarly, the few moments we instructors devote to weaving "safety nets"—techniques for supporting students who run into trouble by taking on complex or unpopular points of argument—are well spent. Safety nets enable participants to walk the high wire of adventuresome thought and argument with daring bolstered by a sense of security.

When the instructor fosters the creation of a learning space in the classroom, everyone gains. The class becomes a community. A working partnership emerges between teacher and students, and risk-taking increases on both sides. We sometimes forget that instructors are as risk-averse as students. We hesitate to reveal our own uncertainties and areas of ignorance. We hold back from presenting positions in their early stages of development. We resist challenging popular points of view. But in a safe learning space, we can reveal what we know and need to know, and also what we are and would like to be.

3. *Modest expectations are the most powerful of all.* Teachers select their life's work for complex reasons, unique in every case. But one basic circumstance of our vocation unites us all: our work simultaneously allows us to serve the wider community and make significant contributions to the lives of the individual students entrusted to our care. Stories about master teachers give us pictures of what the great can do. Each of us has had some personal experience of the impact a teacher can make on a life by stimulating interest in a topic or field of study, providing a role model, or molding our basic values and beliefs. Teachers can ac-

complish so much of importance. But the contemplation of that accomplishment can overwhelm as well as inspire.

As my years in the classroom have multiplied, I have made the paradoxical discovery that modest expectations, particularly in the realm of content, trigger more effective learning than ambitious ones. Material learned in depth—with heart as well as head—stays with students, but broad-based lists of facts, techniques, and theories tend to fade. J. D. Salinger noted that the mark of immaturity is a desire to die nobly for a cause, but maturity brings the willingness to live humbly for one. Our colleague Abby Hansen suggests that discussion leaders' best songs are anthems of modest expectations. I have found that teaching practice improves when I fit my expectations about how much the group should cover in a given period to a quite modest standard. Thoroughness and depth compensate abundantly for the sacrifice of breadth. Retention of a few crucial things over time brings far more benefit than superficial mastery.

There are few tasks more difficult than evaluating the effect of our teaching. Trying to gauge success is like tossing coins into the Grand Canyon and waiting to hear the clink. How can we ever know just what we have contributed to a student's education? Teachers have much in common with performing artists, but our applause (or boos and hisses) may not come for years, if ever. Who knows what students retain a day, week, year, or decade after a seminar? It is chastening to be thanked by an alumnus for all you taught him only to realize, as the conversation continues, that he is praising a colleague, not you.

Gradually I have abandoned my interest in final outcomes—whatever they may be—and begun to derive satisfaction from the act of teaching itself. When I consider the innumerable gradations that intervene between success and failure, the complex natures of the parties involved, and the magnitude of the daily efforts that go unevaluated, I marvel at the imponderability of long-term effects. I have learned that wisdom and effectiveness lie in a constant struggle for improvement, rather than a quest for final results. Like virtue, teaching is its own reward. For me this means that if I practice and hone my skills, welcome observation and constructive criticism, and experiment and grow, my efforts may very well have an impact. Minor miracles do happen—often enough, in fact, to justify this hope.

4. *Instructors' patience promotes students' learning.* Patience, though a virtue of restraint, has the effect of energizing students. Inquiry, growth,

and learning flourish under low pressure. Concepts and ideas are difficult to plant in our intellectual garden. They have erratic, individualized growing cycles, and harvesting is always under the student's control—exam schedules to the contrary notwithstanding. Yet I found this simple lesson difficult to learn. Patience is not readily acquired.

Impatience comes more easily. Having worked through the process of understanding the applicability and limits of the ideas under study, we feel we know our subjects. The material is ours, and we forget the missteps we took on the way to this possession. But discussion teaching is not a straightforward dispensing of knowledge. Students have their own missteps to make; their journeys will not necessarily parallel ours. Discussion leaders who fail to appreciate the constructiveness of inefficiency make a serious error. Efficient teaching does not always equate with effective learning. On the contrary, students often discover valuable lessons at the ends of blind alleys—lessons that we teachers cannot anticipate before they unfold in the discussion. What seems like a digression may link the challenge of the moment to prior explorations. Apparent tangents examine questions of the students' creation, not because of any obvious link to the assignment of the day, but because they hold high, continuing intellectual interest for the students.

The syllabi we develop contribute to our impatience. There is always more to be taught than time to teach. A rigid, daily roster of material to cover pressures us to ignore crucial elements of context—school events, local and national circumstances, and personal matters. A colleague tells of a friend, a Civil War historian, who puts the point well: "In my class Grant has to arrive at Richmond before Thanksgiving, no matter what!"

The costs of such rigidity can be high, even cruel. As an unknown poet once said, "All the flowers of all the tomorrows are planted in the seeds of today." We need to nurture, tend, and let them mature at their own pace. Forcing can kill. Nikos Kazantzakis makes the point tellingly in *Zorba the Greek*:

> I remembered one morning when I discovered a cocoon in the bark of a tree, just as a butterfly was making a hole in its case and preparing to come out. I waited awhile, but it was too long appearing and I was impatient. I bent over it and breathed on it to warm it. I warmed it as quickly as I could and the miracle began to happen before my eyes, faster than life. The case opened, the butterfly started slowly crawling out and I shall never forget my horror when I saw how its wings were folded back and crumpled; the wretched butterfly tried with its whole trembling body to unfold them. Bending over it, I tried to help it breathe. In vain.

It needed to be hatched out patiently and the unfolding of the wings should be a gradual process in the sun. Now it was too late. My breath had forced the butterfly to appear, all crumpled before its time. It struggled desperately and a few seconds later, died in the palm of my hand.

That little body is, I do believe, the greatest weight I have on my conscience. For I realize today that it is a mortal sin to violate the great laws of nature. We should not hurry, we should not be impatient, but we should confidently obey the eternal rhythm.[2]

This lesson has special meaning for teachers. We must bring to each class infinite patience, and moderate our critical judgments about students' progress. Walter Jackson Bate reminds us, in his biography of Samuel Johnson, how difficult it is to appreciate "the actual process and daily crawl of other people's experience."[3] But it is precisely this "daily crawl" that we must respect, protect, and honor. And we must, I submit, do it in a context of positive belief in students.

5. *Faith is the most essential ingredient in good teaching practice.* Thus far I have discussed in depth two essentials of discussion teaching: knowledge of pedagogical concepts and mastery of process skills. It is now time to consider the third essential: faith. Faith in the fundamental worth of our vocation, in the values that govern our relations with individual students and classes, and in the likelihood that at least some of the results we desire will be achieved. To me, faith is the indispensable dimension of teaching life. Why, then, is it so rarely mentioned? Perhaps because academicians may feel more comfortable with hard facts, logical analysis, and readily observable skills than with intangibles like belief. But without these intangibles—the "soul," if you will, that animates that mechanism inside the black box of discussion teaching—technique becomes mechanical, skills manipulative, and attitudes suspect.

Can faith be codified? I have found that certain insights have not only endured but assumed increasing significance for my teaching practice while other observations and theoretical constructs have faded or been replaced. I offer these articles of faith—so meaningful to me—not as prescriptions or dogma, but as a purely personal testament: *credo*, after all, means "I believe."

• I believe that the profession of teaching is crucial to the maintenance and advancement of civilization. Only our most talented—master craftspeople who perform to the highest possible standards—should undertake it. As Theodore Roethke put it in "Words for Young Writers," we need "more people that specialize in the impossible,"[4] and that is what teachers do. To me, teaching carries an awesome responsibility to encourage students to want to know, to show them how to know, and to insist that they ask and answer the question "For what purpose do *I* need to know?"

• I believe in the teachability of teaching. For the past two decades my pedagogical research, statements, and teaching objectives have centered on this fundamental conviction: good teachers are made, not born. We can observe, analyze, and communicate the artistry of discussion leadership to other practitioners. Effective teachers both practice and constantly search and research their own activities; their classrooms are both instructional arenas and laboratories.

• I believe that active involvement is critical to enduring learning. In discussion classes, students and teachers alike must give of themselves. Without involvement, the discussion of the day is but noise and its leadership a charade. There's a world of difference between a lackadaisical game of "Simon Says" and the muscle-building that takes place when a committed coach leads an eager team through a workout. Involvement transforms passive, received knowledge into the active ability to apply that knowledge effectively.

• I believe that discussion leaders need to master both process skills as well as the substantive knowledge of their course. Without knowledge of process, instructors are limited in their effort to help students discover, assimilate, and retain course content. It is through command of process that the primacy of content is realized.

• I believe that teaching is a moral act. Ethical commitment must temper the balance we strike in selecting materials and working with them in class. Morality must shape our treatment of students—David Riesman calls teaching "power, with sympathy"—and the values we develop for the classroom community. As the late Professor Lon Fuller suggested, we must distinguish between a morality of duty—that which is formally and/or legally appropriate—and a morality of aspiration—a striving for excellence and idealism. The latter must govern.

• I believe that what my students become is as important as what they learn. The endpoint of teaching is as much human as intellectual growth. Where qualities of person are as central as qualities of mind—as is true in all professional education—we must engage the whole being of students so that they become open and receptive to multiple levels of understanding. And we must engage our whole selves as well. I teach not only what I know, but what I am.

• I believe that, in the words of Professor Charles Gragg, "teachers must also learn!"[5] We cannot truly teach unless we let ourselves experience the vicissitudes and exhilaration of exploration—the mastery and communication of ideas, coupled with the reception of new insights, and the never-ending desire to know more. Teaching and learning are inseparable; the process of education is a reciprocal gift.

• I believe that fun has a critical place in teaching. Great classes include multiple moods—verbal pyrotechnics, moments of stillness, measured, cadenced analyses, and flights of fancy—but always in a context of celebration. Fun permits breakouts from routine. It enlivens the humdrum and sustains generosity as all participants give and receive enjoyment along with wisdom. And fun can heal: it is difficult to dislike someone with whom you share a laugh. Humor can broaden the scope of the possible, but, as Samuel Johnson noted, "Nothing is more hopeless than a scheme of merriment."[6] In a context of good nature, fun will emerge unplanned from the inevitable incongruities of all extended conversations: the extrapolations that take comments to maximum exaggeration and the implosions that carry words and images to absurdity.

• I believe that the teacher's challenge in evaluating students is less to separate the gifted from the ordinary than to find the gifts of the ordinary. And I believe that we must communicate our evaluations in a manner that helps students understand their competence, or lack thereof, without destroying their confidence. Robert Frost said it well: "No figure [or letter] has ever caught the whole of it." At best, grades are imprecise measures even of academic achievement. They do not weigh the worth of a student as a person, now or in the future.

• I believe in the unlimited potential of every student. At first glance they range, like instructors, from mediocre to magnificent. But potential is invisible to the superficial gaze. It takes faith to discern it, but I have witnessed too many academic miracles to doubt its existence. I now view each student as "material for a work of art." If I have faith, deep faith, in students' capacities for creativity and growth, how very much we can accomplish together. If, on the other hand, I fail to believe in that potential, my failure sows seeds of doubt. Students read our negative signals, however carefully cloaked, and retreat from creative risk to the "just possible." When this happens, everyone loses.

One student—call him Andy—was tottering between Low Pass and Unsatisfactory in my Business Policy course. Together we devised a remedial program. He would write five "dry run" exams before a "make-or-break" final that could determine whether he would graduate with his class. After each remedial exam, we would meet to discuss what he had written. Andy worked hard, but progress came slowly. At our last meeting, somewhat discouraged, I asked, "Andy, do you think you can handle the exam tomorrow?" He looked at me and said, oh so softly, "Professor Christensen, Professor Christensen, that's not it. The question is, do *you* think I can handle the exam? *Do you believe in me?*" His comment hit home—helped me. It reminded me of his strengths and the gains he had made. "Andy," I said, "would I spend this much time on a hopeless cause? Yes, I think you can pass this exam and take your degree. What's more, I know you will have a wonderful career. *I believe in you.*"

My words affected him visibly. He smiled, and I thought I could see his back straighten a bit as he left my office. He passed the final exam, graduated with his class, and went on to great success, in both business and civic affairs. Many people have benefited from Andy's capability and generosity—his family, our school, his community, and society in general.

We learn so much from our students. Andy and others like him taught me that if I round out my knowledge of Business Policy and skill at discussion management with faith in them, they can accomplish the improbable and enable me to do the same. For the reciprocity of teaching and learning—their inseparability—makes us share in our students' successes, just as we share in their failures. To give up on students is to give up on ourselves, and that I have never done.

NOTES

1. Henri J. M. Nouwen, *Reaching Out* (Garden City, NY: Image Books, 1986), p. 85.
2. Nikos Kazantzakis, *Zorba the Greek*, tr. Carl Wildman (New York: Simon & Schuster, 1952), p. 120.
3. Walter Jackson Bate, *Samuel Johnson* (New York: Harcourt Brace Jovanovich, 1977), p. 233.
4. Theodore Roethke, *Straw for the Fire: From the Notebooks of Theodore Roethke, 1943–63*, selected and arranged by David Wagoner (Garden City, NY: Doubleday, 1972), p. 185.
5. Charles I. Gragg, "Teachers Also Must Learn," *Harvard Educational Review*, vol. 10 (1940), pp. 30–47.
6. Samuel Johnson, "The Idler," in vol. 2, no. 58, *The Works of Samuel Johnson*, ed. Robert Lynam (London: George Cowre, 1825).

PART III
Building Blocks

7

Establishing a
Teaching/Learning Contract

ABBY J. HANSEN

A discussion course is a little like a group sky dive: exhilarating to look back on—if the parachutes worked. I offer what follows as parachute cloth.

Introduction: What Is a Teaching/Learning Contract?

MOST PEOPLE THINK OF parchment, fancy seals, and signatures when they hear the word "contract," and they're right, up to a point. In general, contracts are formal documents, but unwritten, implied agreements also govern human relationships. I will argue that a complex contract, with both explicit and implicit aspects, structures every educational enterprise, but has particular importance in discussion pedagogy. This "teaching/learning contract" is a matrix of reciprocal agreements that determine the ground rules of behavior for instructor and students alike. In discussion teaching, the contract can become extremely intricate. Taken as a whole, it defines the classroom culture by setting boundaries for conduct, encouraging some sorts of participation and discouraging others, labeling certain styles of action and language as taboo and others as desirable. Instructors who acknowledge the existence of a teaching/learning contract and appreciate its complex nature can gain some leverage over the unspoken rules that condition how they and their students deal with one another.

The explicit and implicit components of the teaching/learning contract often coexist uneasily. Sometimes they even clash. When they do, the implicit contract tends to prevail. By explicit contract I mean the routine administrative details published in the course syllabus and proclaimed in class. The explicit contract usually covers such matters as the precise subject of the course, time and place of class meetings, texts, assignments, format (lecture, seminar, group discussion, or some mixture), instructor's office hours, and grading policy. The implicit contract includes subtler agreements about values, assumptions, and ideals. These are set by behavior. Into this category fall such crucial details as the way people speak with each other (with kindness or cruelty), the manner in which the instructor poses questions (as a friend, perhaps, or an interrogator?), the thoroughness of students' preparation for class and, in general, the emotional feel of the course.

The unspoken rules of conduct hold enormous power in discussion classes, where the relationship of teacher to students changes constantly. Lecturers address one conglomerate entity, but discussion leaders frequently switch roles in class. At times, they conduct dialogues with individuals; at times, they make small speeches or summaries to the class as a whole; at times, they simply call on speakers; and at times, they stand aside and let students direct the flow of discussion. The lecturer's best asset may be a silver tongue, but the discussion leader's is a quicksilver adaptability. A strong, creative contract can prevent this adaptability from deteriorating into anarchy.

We all have our sense of what makes a good or bad discussion class, a good or bad course. A teaching/learning contract that prevents (or at least contains) attacks, monopolies, intimidation, and conflict produces the trust that in turn encourages enthusiasm, responsible preparation, active participation, risk-taking, courtesy, and cooperation. These powerful intangibles, which color the discussion process and create the emotional climate of a course, play an enormous role in the ultimate value of the discussion process.

Before proceeding further, I would like to suggest a caveat: the concept of contract is a useful metaphor to help one appreciate the power of ground rules for classroom process. Like any metaphor, however, it has limitations. Many factors combine to make Professor A's discussion class in real estate law stimulating and Professor B's a stupefying bore. Contract is only one of them. Moreover, the uniqueness of human perception guarantees that few teachers will agree on what elements should be explicit, what implicit, and precisely how to distinguish among them. One teacher's innuendo may be another's proclamation, and vice versa. Still, the underlying idea—that a set of procedural agreements conditions classroom culture and that only some of these agreements are openly stated—can greatly enhance teacher's awareness, understanding, and power to direct what goes on in the classroom.

Why Are Teaching/Learning Contracts Important? (And Why Don't Instructors Spend More Time Thinking about Them?)

Especially in a discussion setting, conscious attention to the teaching/ learning contract can tip the scale from chaos toward cooperation and minimize the potential for unpleasant surprises. But most discussion teachers pay little or no attention to their pedagogical contracts with students. Why? I would say the answer lies in our educational system. After a few decades of taking and giving lecture courses, most teachers internalize one basic ground rule: teachers do the work. In the lecture mode, the students participate actively *after* they leave the teacher's presence, when they study, do research, and write papers. Lecture classes provide more exercise for students' finger muscles than their brains. Instructors who have functioned primarily in settings like this have little cause to ponder subtleties of contract. As a consequence, they find themselves completely unprepared for the delicate agreements that govern discussion teaching.

To illustrate the dangers of this lack of preparation, let us consider a hypothetical Everyteacher, Dr. Jane Smith, about to sail into these strange waters. A well-published scholar with ten years' experience as a lecturer, Jane assumes, like most teachers in her position, that command of the course content will serve her needs as a discussion leader. Still, as she walks—in tailored blazer, starched shirt, and conservative skirt— to the classroom to confront her first large group after a long night's preparation and two extra cups of morning coffee, her palms are moist and the butterflies behind her solar plexus seem to be playing rugby.

As Jane strides to the teacher's place, "center stage," she holds her head high and squares her shoulders, anxious to project confidence. The classroom is well populated and quiet, for this collection of strangers has not yet formed the familiar relationships that produce a low, gossipy buzz. Jane organizes her notes and papers, and raises a hand for silence. Then she announces the course name and her own (with full academic title) in a clear, firm voice, and rattles off some policy announcements about attendance, written work, and grades before plunging into a witty synopsis of the course material. No chairs squeak, nobody yawns audibly. Jane's jokes get laughs. She takes an easier breath, rubs her palms drier, and calls a name, at random, from her class list. Fortunately, the student is both present and alert-looking. Jane poses a snappy, fairly difficult question to show the group who's boss and demonstrate the level at which she expects this class to function. As the student speaks—articulately, Jane notes with relief—she focuses on formulating another trenchant question. What she catches of the student's remarks seems sensible. Jane smiles as she notices that the students are taking notes. This is beginning to feel like a good class.

From the point of view of contract-setting, however, it isn't. Jane Smith is courting several kinds of disaster with this discussion group. First, her clipped reading of academic policy probably fell on deaf ears; many of the students were absorbing her manner and style more than her content, and they were also sizing one another up. Second, if Jane's opening speech was as polished as she hoped, she may have irritated the competitive students and intimidated the shy. And who can tell what silent alarm bells rang in students' psyches as they noticed how superficially she listened to their classmate's answer to her first question? Who can guess how badly her brisk pace, born of nervousness, exacerbated *their* first-day jitters? Perhaps many began to see Jane as a sort of solo performer looking for an appreciative audience. If so, she unwittingly squelched their inclination to independent inquiry.

Jane's behavior may have begun to set a contract that could produce mistrust, alienation, cold-blooded attempts to ascertain and reproduce her "party line," at the cost of whatever boldness the more hesitant students may have been struggling to muster. Her lack of awareness of the overtones of behavior—in other words, of the implicit teaching/learning contract—may launch the course on the path to boredom and frustration. No discussion class can thrive if the teacher does most of the discussing.

Jane's problem stems from unfamiliarity with the discussion mode. Lecturers may fairly assess the quality of the classes by their own performance because they are the stars of the show. Discussion teachers, however, must judge their classes by the quality of their students' performances. They do not "run" their classes any more than a steering wheel runs a car. But no one warned Jane Smith that reciprocity is the most salient factor in the process. She doesn't know that she must encourage her students to learn, teach one another, and teach her as well. The unique interplay of influence between instructor and students in discussion teaching always creates a de facto behavioral contract. Like Molière's *bourgeois gentilhomme*, who discovered with amazement that he had been speaking prose all his life, discussion leaders always operate by tacit contracts with students. Jane Smith's tense behavior set a one-sided contract that unintentionally implied many undesirable rules of the game. Had her written syllabus included generous invitations to partici-pate, these would have paled by comparison with her behavior in class.

In teaching, as everywhere else, actions speak louder than words. If Jane's syllabus states "no late paper," for example, but she grants a few—and then more than a few—extensions, her contract has changed. Simi-larly, if she tells the class, "There's no penalty if you occasionally can't prepare a class assignment; just let me know before the discussion," but conveys annoyance or hostility toward unprepared students, how seri-ously will students take her invitation? It is surprisingly common for teachers to violate their own explicit contracts. And when they do, their implied contracts come into full force. Confusion is the customary result.

Emotional atmosphere and ethical values, always crucial in educa-tion, are never more so than in discussion teaching. Attention to the implicit contract offers a means to gain some power over these elusive overtones of behavior. Take trust, for example. Many discussion leaders state that it is acceptable to make mistakes in class—desirable, in fact, because an error can provide a beautiful opportunity for the group to thrash through a problem. But most students prefer silence to the risk of seeming stupid. All the explicit statements and written documents in the world won't create trust in a classroom where the instructor greets errone-ous comments with sarcasm or permits students to do so. On the other hand, a kindly reception coupled with a sincere invitation for the group to examine, and—gently—correct, the error will show the teacher's will-ingness to incorporate blind alleys in the group's intellectual itinerary. The teacher models values as part of the contract-setting process.

If an instructor consistently behaves with empathy, the students will react with trust. Their contract will promote cooperation, not only be-tween teacher and student, but among the students as a group. An in-structor's behavior implies certain rules of procedure, sets a tone, and triggers expectations that the rules will stay in force. In general, contempt breeds contempt, and courtesy, courtesy. Many of the disasters that befall teachers in class, from late-semester apathy to unnerving emotional out-bursts, spring from underlying flaws in the implicit contract.

Critical Characteristics of the Contract

The reciprocity of the teaching/learning contract deserves further empha-sis. Although the instructor has greater leverage over the contract than the students do, there is no such thing as a purely unilateral contract in discussion pedagogy. Teaching and learning are aspects of a single process. Even in a lecture hall, if the students don't pay attention or grasp what they hear and write down, the instructor is performing, not teaching. In discussion classes, the inseparability of the teacher's and students' roles is even more striking. Both contribute to setting the contract and putting it to work—if not, the result is likely to be conflict. Jane Smith's approach was dangerous because it stemmed from a basically unilateral concept of the teaching/learning contract.

To whom does a course belong? Most teachers refer to "my French History class" or "my eight-thirty class," for example, but their students use the same proprietary terms. They think the class is *theirs*. Who's right? Looking at classroom process in terms of bilateral contract, one can see ownership on both sides, although not in perfectly equal shares. In the final analysis, the educational experience belongs more to students than teachers. Their active learning is the primary measure of its success. But the teacher's leadership is crucial. It's difficult to imagine a good course—particularly a discussion course—led by a maladroit, hostile, or confused teacher. At its best, the educational process is synergistic; through active cooperation, teacher and students achieve insights none of them would have attained alone.

Syllabi and course descriptions are important documents for setting the explicit contract. Circulated in written form, they usually outline the protocols of the course: subject matter, number and times of class meetings, titles of texts and readings, grading policy, written and oral assignments, office hours, and the like. But further aspects of the explicit contract may be communicated orally, either at the outset of the course or as it progresses. Public statement makes an element of a teaching/learning contract explicit. Even seemingly informal remarks like "If I notice people skipping class a lot, I'm going to start taking attendance," or "Please remind me of your names for the first few weeks" are explicit contractual statements. So are students' suggestions. For example, "If we have a problem speaking in public, could we substitute two written reports for the oral presentation?" Even simple proposals set norms and precedents, thus contributing to the rules that condition the classroom culture. In general, explicit elements are easy to grasp and change because they are in plain sight.

Implicit components of the teaching/learning contract are, by contrast, both harder to pin down and more influential. Nuances, overtones, implications, and inferences accumulate to create the unspoken agreements by which the class conducts itself. Set by behavior, the implicit contract is both powerful and complex. Subtle aspects of teaching, like style, pace, body language, tone of voice, and emotional overtone belong to its province. The implicit contract that Jane Smith unwittingly presented to her students seems destined to create alienation, despite her good intentions. Why? Because her self-protective body language is unlikely to inspire confidence. Because she launched her first question with no warning (terrifying to many students). And because she greeted the first speaker's answer with her attention focused on her own next move. Students can usually tell when a teacher is listening only superficially. In other words, Jane communicated self-absorption and insecurity—not qualities that inspire trust. However impressive her opening speech may have been in content, its subtext—the emotional message she sent by posture, pace, and tone of voice—probably swamped it.

The implicit contract compromises all the behavioral agreements that are understood rather than enunciated. For example, the teacher who gives students class time to prepare answers to tough questions conveys several messages—considered opinions are more desirable than snap judgments; no one will be put on the spot; in this class you may collect your thoughts and marshal your self-confidence before "going public" with statements that may provoke criticism. Each of these small communiqués is a piece of the implicit behavioral contract that helps determine the quality of the discussion process. Similarly, the teacher who listens to students' comments respectfully, perhaps with head cocked in the speaker's direction, noting a few key points, conveys another complex message: I, the teacher, take both your comments and you seriously; this class is not very likely to deteriorate into a bull session, so prepare accordingly.

The implicit contract may be set and modified in a potentially infinite number of ways. Its terms begin to be understood from the moment the teacher and students gather together, and are continually refined until the course is over. Although students must implicitly ratify the contract, the teacher tends to wield greater power to set its terms, and this is nowhere more apparent than in the early class meetings, when significant events occur for the first time. For example, when a teacher first deflects a student's comment by gesturing to another student rather than answering directly, the implication is that the class discussion process will not center exclusively on the instructor. Students are to learn from each other. This message is especially important, because the teaching/learning contract exists not only between teacher and students, but also between each student and the rest of the learning group. When a class cooperates to support the weak and encourage the strong, all know they are working within a humane contract that includes respect for one another in class.

The implicit contract helps determine how students will challenge one another's logic (with mortal combat or tactful disagreement?), what sort of language they will use in class (formal, colloquial, proper, profane?), whether they will behave like a collection of warring egos or a cooperative unit, how thoroughly they will prepare for class discussions, and how they will deal with extremes, whether of proficiency or weakness.

I have stressed the elusive nature of the behavioral, almost unconscious, component of all teaching/learning contracts. How, then, may teachers know what sort of contract they are setting, especially if much of it exists in students' individual and collective inferences? It is difficult, but worthwhile, for teachers to learn to "read" their students. Note their behavior. Is the discussion group acting as if it has absorbed the procedural rules and values you most desire to promote? When students repeatedly deprecate or interrupt one another, or generally behave in unhelpful ways, the teacher may call attention to this counterproductive behavior, and instigate change—by precept and example. Teachers may also invite sympathetic colleagues to their classes to observe their own and students' behavior, see how the contract seems to be evolving, and make suggestions. After several class meetings—perhaps a week's worth—it may be reasonable to devote some class time to a discussion of values and procedures. The purpose of a contract is to promote a healthy classroom process; efficiency is not the crucial issue.

The teaching/learning contract is organic. Like any living thing, it changes over time. Just as the course progresses from simpler to more complex material, and the social structure of the learning group matures throughout the semester, the contract that underlies these complex relationships undergoes myriad subtle changes, some predictable, others not. The predictable changes will probably include a progression from something like parental support to more comradely collegiality on the part of the teacher. For example, the discussion leader may pose very specific questions in the early part of the course, then progress to less directive requests for contributions, and finally—when the discussion group has developed solid expertise and a reliable commitment to the process—offer general, almost casual, invitations to participants to join the discussion. When an instructor has overseen the development of a truly strong, productive contract, he or she can step back from the discussion process without relinquishing either leadership or influence.

Among the less predictable changes lurk joys and sorrows. An apparently untalented group may suddenly catch on, and its discussions begin to soar. On the other hand, a promising group may turn lackadaisical or sullen. If students' preparation nosedives, the teacher may realize that he or she has fallen into the habit of wrapping up each discussion with an overly neat summary on the blackboard—inadvertently cheating students of the opportunity to make their own assessments about the significance of each discussion and creating dependency. If previously confident students are growing shy and hesitant in class, perhaps the teacher has pushed them toward independence too quickly. When these, or any other indications of deteriorating contracts occur, only bilateral action, clearly understood by all, teacher and students, can instigate a beneficial change. Either side may initiate the efforts, but both sides must agree on terms.

It is more than misleading—it is dangerous—to suppose that, once set, contracts stand, immutable, for the rest of the course. In most discussion courses the teacher can expect to nurture the student group less and less overtly as time goes by. It may be appropriate to "spoon-feed" students in class—lead them through unfamiliar arguments, supply data for their assertions—during the infancy of their dealings with new material or a new discipline. But, once the initial unfamiliarity has worn off, the contract should change to permit the students to exercise and cultivate their growing mastery, or revolution may be the result.

When contracts change for the worse, both teacher and students usually notice that the course is foundering. Often unintentional implications or misunderstandings turn out to be the cause of the deterioration. Then the instructor might do well to try to isolate the source of malfunction, perhaps by taking class time to discuss the matter, quite openly, and ask the students for help. (The best opportunities are provided by the natural breaks of the course—at the end of a unit of study, after a holiday or vacation, after an examination.) In the best of all possible worlds, the contract's explicit and implicit elements mesh so perfectly that open discussion is unnecessary. But in the real world, open discussions of contract often reveal surprising discrepancies between participants' understandings of what they expect from each other and themselves. In assessing the success of a contract one should probably think in terms of "critical mass." A single disgruntled student may be a crank, and two may be two cranks. But ten suggest that something is really wrong with the contract.

In general, a working contract achieves four purposes: it details individual and joint responsibilities—for the instructor, each student, and the students as a group; it clarifies roles; it establishes boundaries for subject matter and appropriate classroom behavior; and it sets procedural rituals that eliminate anarchy in discussion, turning potential bull sessions into disciplined inquiry.

Setting and Maintaining the Contract

The explicit contract may appear in writing, more or less fully formed, on the first day of a course. But the implicit teaching/learning contract grows by accretion. Especially in the early days, teachers and students observe, interpret, and often unconsciously predict each other's behavior. Thus, significant actions tend to acquire the force of precedents, and the values they embody become the values the contract reinforces and promotes. Especially in a discussion class, where the group knows it must develop a unique relationship and set of social norms, overtones of behavior are particularly important in the early class meetings because they create expectations and assumptions that will swiftly harden into policy unless the process is consciously stopped. The teacher—who has the greatest opportunity to create policies by modeling, or acting them out in class—should prepare for this responsibility before the first class meeting. Matters like pacing, tone, and emotional style, for example, will settle themselves in class. Instructors who give thought to these issues and consider how their initial presentations may affect the group will make good progress toward building a productive contract.

I have noted that even the tiniest details of behavior can carry contractual implications. If Dr. Jane Smith smiles at a particular comment, students will be likely to attempt to produce that type of comment again. Everybody likes positive reinforcement. By the same token, nobody likes negative reinforcement, so Jane's reaction to the first appearance of inappropriate behavior will be equally significant in establishing the teaching/learning contract. For example, if she wants a genial, cooperative atmosphere, she should intervene immediately if a student calls another's remark stupid. If she wants to convey the message that students should address one another's points, she should deflect the very first comment a student addresses directly to her for approval. If she wants to ban profanity from the classroom, she should do so, politely but firmly, as soon as it surfaces. This is not to say that Jane, or any teacher, need interrupt a discussion for a sermon on manners. A courteous request ("Intriguing comment, Bill; could you rephrase it for us in more appropriate language?") can deliver this contract-setting message with minimal embarrassment. If a student ignores subtle but repeated statements of this sort, a telephone call or private note may be in order. But promptness is essential. Policies are best set and acted upon swiftly. It's easier to establish than change a behavioral norm.

A teacher has great freedom to set policy in the early days of a class. When a student does something marvelous—introduces a lively and appropriate bit of privileged information, makes a provocative connection between pieces of disparate data, supports a fellow student with noteworthy skill, poses a truly intriguing question—the teacher can endorse and encourage this sort of behavior in various ways. A smile, an upward tilt of the head, an appreciative "mm hmm," a bright look around the class as if to invite other students to share the pleasure—these nuances of behavior can powerfully influence the ways in which students will participate. Similarly, if a student propounds some infuriatingly vague generalization, it isn't necessary to stop the class for a speech on rigor. All that is needed is a question to the rest of the group—"We'll need some data to support a statement like this; can anyone help?" The tacit assumptions here—we (the *whole* group) need (*require*) data (*supporting facts*)—set the contract.

Something about group psychology in classroom situations seems to turn early events into precedents. A brisk initial discussion triggers general expectations of a fast-paced course. If Jane Smith had arrived in a sweatsuit, with a stained backpack instead of a briefcase, what would her students have inferred about her expectations for their subsequent classroom attire? The instructor's dress and behavior in the initial class meetings are usually taken as models, and models are implicit statements of policy, whether the instructor intends this or not. When one instructor noticed that his students were blocking one another's attempts to present valuable personal experiences in class, he recalled that the first time personal experience came up in the discussion he had smiled sardonically and apologized for not having included the student's biography in the reading for the day. But the class missed the humor and incorporated the underlying principle—no personal experiences; stick to the readings—into their implicit contract.

Instructors' words and actions always carry implications of policy, prompting students to make inferences and form expectations. Of course, teachers cannot predict all the possible inferences students may draw from every scrap of their behavior, but it is important to strive for sensitivity to overtones. How? As I have mentioned, by inviting a friend to observe your teaching, by "reading" the class's reactions in progress, and by including attention to contract in your routine preparation.

All group contracts have an element of compromise; they tend to slight individual needs. To what extent should an instructor make special contracts with individual students? What about foreign students with language difficulties? What about the handicapped? What about students with pressing personal problems? What about students with unusual strengths? Should an instructor expect more of the talented or hardworking? It's a rare, perhaps nonexistent teacher who makes no exceptions. In dealing with a Chinese student who has missed a week's class to fly home for his father's funeral, a student who has plagiarized under pressure from a tyrannical parent, or a depressed student who could clearly try much harder, the teacher will probably have to fine-tune the general contract and come up with something similar in spirit and values, but unique in details.

Conclusion

When it really clicks, discussion teaching sets off sparks that warm as well as illumine. A group of strangers meet and blend both strengths and weaknesses to achieve greater enlightenment for all. I have posited a complex contract at the heart of this complex, powerful process, a contract that shapes every aspect of classroom culture, from gross to gossamer. Though largely tacit, the teaching/learning contract is as real as the unstated code that makes us, for example, put business momentarily aside to help dear ones in crisis—and expect the same from those who hold us dear. Our *bourgeois gentilhomme* analogy (teachers have always had contracts with their students, whether they have realized it or not) suggests one of the most persuasive reasons for paying serious attention to the contract: How can you create a good one, or fix a bad one, if you don't even know it's there?

There are, of course, instructors who practice their craft successfully, oblivious to the implied and inferred rules of conduct that create their relationships with students. Like riveting stage performers, they often teach by intuition without analyzing their feeling for the best way to act and react in class. (After a particularly searing dramatic performance, Sir Laurence Olivier reportedly mused, "Yes, I was superb, *but how did I do it?*") Even accomplished pros run the risk of forgetting how to perform. Acknowledging the existence of the teaching/learning contract is a first step toward analyzing good teaching and making it a learnable art. Equally important, appreciating the reciprocity of the contract can help instructors strike and keep a productive balance of power with their students. Education cannot be inflicted. Especially in discussion classes, learning emerges in a living process that breathes and constantly changes. The by-products of the discussion process—intellectual growth, enthusiasm, and enhanced self-confidence for instructors and students alike— perpetuate its energy. Like a supple spine, the teaching/learning contract can permit learning to run, leap, dance, and stretch to its fullest height.

8

With Open Ears: Listening and the Art of Discussion Leading

HERMAN B. LEONARD

The Discussion Leader and the Art of Listening

LONG BEFORE WE LEARN how to speak, we have begun to learn how to listen. From our earliest hours as human beings, we are bombarded by sounds of varying volume, tone, and texture. As infants, we learn to separate background noise from more important messages and to concentrate our listening on narrow ranges of the audio spectrum. We hear the wind and we hear voices, identifying each with certain needs and learning when to focus on which kind of sound. Only gradually do we develop the ability to project our own messages as accurately as we distinguish those we hear.

To a large extent, the rudiments of listening and interpreting other sensory perceptions (sight, smell, taste, and touch) are self-taught. We develop these skills at a time when the world can still communicate much more subtly to us than we can to it. Even an infant can express strong feelings (hunger, pain), but with very little precision. By contrast, we can distinguish between a rose and a dandelion by sight, smell, and touch long before we have words for any flower. Perhaps because we learn the rudiments of basic sensory skills on our own, little formal educational attention is ever given to refining these abilities.

Adults are generally very poor observers. Our habits for collecting, storing, and retrieving sensory messages are poorly developed and generally sloppy. We work at learning how to project complex and subtle nuances of thought in speech and writing—but neglect to strengthen our skills in recognizing these nuances in the speech of others. Children are educated to focus on the substantive content of speech and receive virtually no guidance in distinguishing, remembering, and learning from variations in tone, texture, emotional force, and other less objective aspects of spoken language. Consequently, much of what we see and hear does not really register.

Nowhere is this problem more obvious than in classroom discussions. Instructors are often frustrated by how little of what seems important is perceived and retained by students. People who review tape recordings of discussions are routinely amazed at how much participants missed—how many good ideas went unnoticed or were abandoned in the tumultuous process of oral exchange.

Active listening is a vital component of learning by the discussion method. If a class is a discussion, there must be an exchange of ideas, with messages received as well as sent. There can be great excitement in a classroom where ideas are merely presented—but there can be no discussion unless students are encouraged to absorb and reflect as well as to speak. Then ideas can be expanded, criticized, and sharpened. For such discussion, the capacity to listen is a precious resource. At any given moment, after all, all members of the group but one are engaged in listening. Discussion leaders need to make it clear that attentive, critical listening is a fundamental part of the group's work.

By "listening," I mean not only hearing, but also integrating other perceptions—of gestures, facial expression, and so on. Moreover, listening is useless without a modicum of retention. We must be able to organize the ideas we hear into a form of knowledge that we can retrieve at the right time. Codifying and storing perceptions is an integral part of the listening process.

The classical educational process does little to develop listening beyond attending to objective content, facts, and information. Our students have been taught largely in a lecture format, and so have we. They expect their teachers to tell them what they need to know, and they have been conditioned to learn this material and repeat it when asked. Students typically listen to instructors only along a limited dimension—largely for facts and theories—and to each other hardly at all. Starting a real discussion requires a major transformation of the sociology of the classroom. Both students and teachers need to open their range of hearing to capture signals they have largely tuned out, at least in the educational process.

Good Listening

Good listening nourishes our ability to communicate the subtle nuances of our own thoughts. Human interaction—speaking and listening—has great power. There is ample evidence that learning is more compelling when the communication is personal (that is, given from person to person) than, for example, when a book is read or a lecture is viewed on videotape. Gestures and vocal tone greatly expand the range and subtlety of human communication. But such variations are communicated only to the listener capable of distinguishing them. Speech can support a rich variety and texture of meaning, but it is our capacity to listen that unlocks the power and efficiency of the language.

Spoken communication encourages the listener to engage ideas actively. Concepts articulated in discussion become a sort of leitmotiv around which the listener's views on the subject—sometimes conflicting, and sometimes consonant—can be spun. It is not easy to develop the self-discipline required to keep one's own thoughts from becoming the centerpiece and to focus on engaging the speaker's views, particularly when some members of the group do not respect the contributions of others. But when we achieve reflective engagement of ideas, the mental energy focused through discussion has a startling potential.

Good listening enables us to appreciate complex and subtle ideas. It requires, first, that the listener focus carefully on what is being said—and *how*. This kind of listening, requiring simultaneous focus on a number of different channels, is a demanding challenge for most. Good listening is also critical listening. It is not simply a process of absorbing and storing what is said, but of thoughtfully reviewing and editing the ideas presented.

And listening is comprehensive: it attends to the full range of spoken communication. Substantive content is only the most obvious, often the most important, component of oral messages. The tone and music of the speaker's voice, the perspective from which she speaks, the degree of authority or confidence invoked or projected, the speaker's emotional attachment to the ideas, and the emotional force of the ideas on the listener—all these elements are integral to the full meaning of a message. Overlooking any component reduces the overall impact of the message and may distort its meaning.

Finally, good listening requires a continuing stream of strategic decisions. At any given moment, the listener must decide (consciously or not), whether to concentrate listening energy on hearing the next words, processing the last message, reflecting on the ideas being communicated, evaluating their validity, deriving implications from them, pursuing some other thought they inspire, writing them down, or writing down a related (or unrelated!) thought. And all those decisions must be made without knowing what will come next.

Good listening—focused, critical, comprehensive, and strategic—requires discipline. A wide spectrum of messages can be conveyed through spoken communication, and the shades of meaning can be very subtle. Great concentration is needed to absorb, organize, and store verbal communication in a form that makes later retrieval both possible and useful. But if true discussion is to take place in the classroom, then all participants—leaders and students alike—must acquire perceptive listening skills.

Diagnosis and Treatment of Listening Pathologies

Our capacity for critical listening is often undermined in the classroom by particular habits of bad listening. There are many ways to listen poorly, and often it is difficult to tell why someone failed to hear. Sometimes the group as a whole is confused, perhaps because of ambiguity or confusion in what the speaker said. But often poor listening is due to a recognizable pathology. You probably already have your own list of these classroom problems. I would not be surprised if you encountered at least a few of my favorites.

1. *The Mortar Lob.* This student has prepared a single point that he found in the materials for the day's discussion and is ready to discuss it in detail. The mortar is loaded with one round, to be fired when the discussion moves within range. Throughout the session, the student is trying to decide when the conversation has moved as close to the point of impact as it is likely to get. Whenever the cue arrives, he will fire off the prepared set of comments.

Obviously, this behavior does not often build on the contributions of others. As an instructor, you want to reward preparation for class, but you don't want to encourage unconnected observations. At a minimum, each speaker should be expected to provide a link between the new observation and the preceding discussion. "That's an interesting analysis, Rick," you might comment. "But I'm not sure how it relates to what

Sharon was just saying. Can you help us to see the connection?" Such a response will at least convey the requirement that "contributions" fit into the flow of the overall conversation.

2. *The Mongoose's Strike.* The mongoose survives by striking swiftly when it sees an opening in its opponent's defenses. Much of what passes for listening is really only (barely polite) attention as students wait for the speaker to finish so that they can make their own point. Often the pounce will be highly selective, concentrating on a minor weakness in some part of the last speaker's statement rather than engaging her whole set of ideas. When hands go up while a student is still talking, suspect a mongoose problem. One of my colleagues stops the class whenever someone starts waving a hand before the speaker has finished. "Put your hand down," he says; "you can't be listening if you already know what you are going to say."

Simply waiting for someone to stop talking is not true listening, of course, and this behavior pattern can result in a disjointed series of comments. A good remedy is to require the speaker to relate his or her comments to those of the last speaker. "Well, Cheryl, I guess you disagreed with John about one small piece of what he was saying—how do you respond to the rest of his statement?"

3. *The Spartan's Shield.* Warriors in ancient times believed that Spartans carried shields that could not be penetrated by ordinary arrows or swords. Though untrue, the story was useful to the Spartans, and they may have started it themselves. Some students seem to have similar armor. When asked a question, they turn it aside with a deft parry, and go on to make whatever observation they had in mind. A good poke will reveal that the shield is not really impervious. Ask the student to return to your question and answer it; this reinforces the necessity to keep comments in context.

4. *The Pit Bull.* Pit bulls have a reputation for always pursuing the same line of attack and for hanging on tenaciously once engaged. Some students evidently believe that this kind of single-mindedness is a great virtue. They seize on a particular issue and pursue it relentlessly; often, they will pick similar issues in every discussion. One will always emphasize goals, and another tactics. One will always serve up the libertarian perspective, another the Marxist view, and yet another the feminist approach. Of course, it is often useful to have a variety of different views represented in the classroom, but when a particular perspective becomes

identified with a given student, the class (and the leader) may stop listening because the points seem automated. This pathology leads to two disagreeable syndromes: first, the pit bull listens only for the right opening in which to raise his or her familiar issue; second, the rest of the class stops listening to the pit bull at all. One possible solution is systematically to require nonbulldogs to present different points of view. Encourage other members of the class to explore the issues presented from a perspective different from their own. This may lead to a more original and less predictable presentation.

These four pathologies are variations on the same theme: students often want to make independent observations rather than relate them to what others have said. It is harder to comment on the ongoing conversation than to introduce wholly independent thought; because it does not require careful attention or listening, the latter procedure is considerably less taxing. For many, it is also more comfortable; many students need to feel well prepared before they speak in a group, and are not comfortable thinking on their feet in the midst of a fast-moving conversation. These pathologies, which threaten the integrity of the discussion structure, come in many forms. Fortunately, most of them can be cleared away by exposure. Discussing these problems explicitly when they occur is a good way to redirect energy toward the productive parts of class discussion.

5. *The Tune-Out, Type A: I Don't Need to Know This.* Students' attention often wavers during a conversation, frustrating the instructor, who senses that they do not recognize the relevance and importance of the points being made. Discussion-based teaching provides an opportunity for motivated learning spurred by an understanding of relevance— but it doesn't guarantee success. I find this pathology is best addressed by a frontal assault. Rather than pontificate about why I think the material is important, I ask the class to identify why the points under discussion are relevant. When they have focused on the issue and persuaded themselves, we can move on.

A particularly pernicious form of the Type A tune-out is active disrespect for other students' contributions. Some members of the group sit waiting in sullen boredom while another student is talking, ready to rejoin the discussion only when the instructor starts speaking again. I try to ask students who are having this problem (the nonlisteners, not the speaker!) to think out loud about what their classmate has just said and why it may be important.

6. *The Tune-Out, Type B: I Already Know This.* Nothing shuts students' ears more surely than the feeling that they have already learned this material. Sometimes they are right. More frequently, they have overestimated their command of these ideas, and the instructor is deliberately encouraging the class to dwell on them. Often, though, the students do not pick up the difference between what they already know and what is being discussed now. This failure comes from bad listening, but the listening it generates is even worse. All learning will cease until this veil is pierced. Here again, I usually attempt a frontal attack by posing a problem designed to highlight the limit of their existing knowledge.

Discussion leaders have their own pathological listening patterns. Here are a few that I find myself falling into:

1. *The Teacher's Express.* Too often the classroom program billed as a discussion is a lecture or a fully planned exploration of the subject in an order determined by the leader. In many situations, of course, the class needs help from the leader in developing a structure for the discussion and in sensing when to move and where to go next. Such help is a two-edged sword, however. If it becomes obvious that the instructor is driving the class through a preordained discussion —and if this happens, it will nearly always be obvious—then the "participants" are likely to lose interest. Students will show little eagerness to answer questions when they sense they are merely being asked to fill in the blanks, not to be creative.

This problem is at least in part a pathology of listening, because the instructor's agenda does not depend very much on what the students are saying, and there is no need to listen to their contributions very carefully. When the teacher's express pulls out of the station, very few class members are likely to be on board.

2. *Hiding the Ball.* A variant of the teacher's express occurs when the instructor has in mind a preferred answer to the questions he or she asks. Students quickly realize that the instructor is merely waiting for the desired response and will then move with it to the next point on the agenda. (This pathology is so common that students often think it is happpening even when it isn't.) Discussion learning is at its best when a conversation moves from one point to the next naturally, because a response provides a useful opening or points in a fruitful direction. When transitions are forced, or completely preplanned, they may be artificial

and destructive. Students feel they are just being asked to guess what the instructor is thinking, and the game quickly becomes sterile. It is a pathology of listening because the instructor is waiting to hear only the desired response; the rest is hardly heard at all.

3. *Everything Goes.* In this pathology, the instructor and class operate in the mode of false affirmation, approving of each comment or observation. Any remark is treated as intelligent, interesting, insightful, even profound. This is an easy mode to slip into because it makes things more comfortable for everyone. If it doesn't matter what you say, you have no need to listen actively—nor does anyone else need to listen to you. The class may be quite happy (everything is very easy), and so may the instructor (participation is often quite lively). Though the conversation is flapping like a dying fish on the dock, there is a polite agreement not to notice. The classroom resounds with an active, happy babble—but very little learning.

This pathology is particularly pernicious because it often grows out of an attempt—sometimes quite necessary and important—to make class members feel less threatened, more at ease. Students will not contribute voluntarily or comfortably unless they feel confident that they won't be savaged. But, if everything goes, bad observations will drive out good, and there won't be anything worth listening to.

To avoid "everything goes" without suppressing critical thought and comment, I try to make the distinction between ideas and people, between intellectual toughness and personal harshness. All of us are in the class to try out new ideas. Some will be good, others won't. We won't ever be able to tell which ideas are worthwhile and which should be discarded unless we subject them to rigorous intellectual scrutiny. It is a delicate—but vital—task to help the class distinguish between attacking ideas and attacking their authors as people. The instructor must foster an attitude that all ideas are tentative and are offered for examination, that wrong observations can be helpful because they provide clarifying insights and because others may be harboring the same errors, and that people are not at risk just because their ideas are challenged. This attitude helps produce a classroom atmosphere in which much will be said that is worth listening to.

These instructor-listening pathologies ultimately reflect a lack of faith that the class can carry its part of the discussion. They convey a strong message—"I don't trust you"—that the class is usually quick to pick up. Prevention (or cure) requires that the instructor trust the class and behave accordingly. The most compelling demonstration of trust is real listening. If the instructor really hears what students say, and reacts to it, it will be obvious that trust has developed.

Listening pathologies can be a great roadblock to better classroom discussions. But the mere absence of listening problems is not enough. The instructor who wants a true discussion learning environment must go further and attempt to build up underlying listening skills.

Building Classroom Listening for Discussion

A serious program to build listening skills and enrich discussion will require considerable time and effort from both instructor and class. You should be fully aware of the investment you are making—is it what you really want? Many teachers say that they want discussion classes, but their actions often suggest otherwise. They behave as though their real objective were to instill their ideas in the minds of their students. Many would like a discussion, but reserve half of it for themselves, so that students are involved in sequential one-on-one discussions with the instructor. If this is what you want in your classroom—and for some classes and some material it may well be the most appropriate pedagogic style—then building listening skills is less essential than if you intend to foster true discussion.

Many discussion classes follow a simple format: first a question, then a response. The leader (or a participant) makes a comment or raises a question, and one or more participants (possibly including the leader) respond. Teachers concerned with improving the quality of classroom discussion often focus on crafting questions that will elicit the kinds of responses they want. But this approach directs the leader's attention to what is said, in the instructor's questions and the participants' responses. The critical role of listening is overlooked. A true discussion is not a question-and-answer session but a connected series of spoken ideas. Listening is the glue that holds together the whole process of questions, answers, and comments.

Developing good listening skills—both your own and your students'—will release a tremendous potential for creativity and idea development. In the more common one-on-one sequential discussion format, much of the mental energy of a group is unfocused. Good listening directs the power of the participant intellects to the same problem. Just as mental discipline allows an individual to focus energy on thinking through a problem alone, effective listening and concentration enable a group to wield its mental energy collectively. Group concentration is difficult to attain, but can be enormously powerful.

Consider what happens when this power is systematically diffused. For example, when time is short and many members of a committee still want to speak, the chair often proceeds by calling on people in the order in which they raised their hands. This approach virtually guarantees that each comment will have little to do with the preceding one. Such "conversations" are "efficient" in the sense that they are orderly and comments are generally short. But true discussion grinds to a halt. There in no debate and no valid exchange of ideas. Since each comment is independent, participants need pay only minimal attention to what others are saying and there is no opportunity to follow up on useful points.

Real discussion is an enriching exchange of related thoughts and discerning insights that build on each other. To foster the active listening that makes such discussion possible, you must first be a good listener yourself. Concentrating your attention on what is happening in the discussion will have three important effects. First, it keeps you close to what is going on. Second, you become a role model for your students—a clear demonstration of the value of listening. Finally, your attentiveness affirms students' participation and the value of their contributions. You show them, by example, that discussion is predicated on respect for all contributions. Joining in a discussion means respecting what other participants offer—and the most obvious token of respect is attentive listening.

Respect does not mean an absence of criticism. Quite the contrary, good listening is always critical. It is a sign of respect to take a participant's ideas seriously enough to review and critique them carefully. Respect and personal supportiveness are components of good listening and building blocks for effective discussion. But an obsequious affirmation of every comment systematically destroys the foundation of the discussion, for it is a thin veneer that participants will quickly penetrate—and it is ultimately only a form of contempt.

Aside from developing your own listening skills and concentrating on listening carefully, there are several things you can do to encourage the class to listen better.

Get Off on the Right Foot

If you are to have real discussion in your classroom, it must begin right away. A colleague with years of teaching experience once told me that if you don't get students talking in the first week of the course, you never will. Students quickly form impressions about how a class will be conducted, what is expected, how much and in what form they will be asked to speak, how carefully they have to listen. Get started in the right direction in the first two class sessions and half the battle will be won. Students will themselves be listening very carefully at the outset to discern the rules of the game. If you set the right tone at the beginning— convince them that they have to continue to listen as carefully as they do in the first sessions—your (and their) task for the remainder of the course will be much easier.

Discuss Listening Explicitly

Talk with the class about how hard it is to listen carefully, and how important it is. Discussion classes can begin with the observation that their pedagogic style creates a problem for the students. "Listen here," you might say, "this is a different way to learn. There is more here, available to be learned, because of the discussion. But it is never as neatly organized as you may be used to; you have to build your own framework for it. And to do that, both to absorb what others are saying and to be able to contribute effectively, you will have to concentrate on listening very carefully."

Learning from discussion is in some respects more "natural" than learning in lectures, since it more closely resembles most of the learning we do in life, where we must draw lessons and observations from a stream of information that was not explicitly designed or controlled to emphasize particular points or views. In this rich vein lies an ore of great value, but that ore must be refined to extract its salient lessons. Listening is a key component of the extraction process, and explicit discussions can make students more aware of its role and value.

Some students seem to misinterpret the task they are given. They seem to believe—and we too often seem to tell them—that their main tasks are to *think* and to *speak*. When students are graded on classroom performance, it is almost always on the basis of what they say. But, if there is to be a true discussion, students will spend most of their time listening actively while others speak, then building on their classmates' contributions. Explaining the students' responsibility in this way can help them to understand the importance of listening carefully.

Develop Exercises to Build Listening

Simple exercises can help (force?) participants to listen carefully. The key is to find techniques that do not become an issue in themselves, disrupting the flow of the discussion. You can experiment with devices that require students to reflect, in their own words, what they have just heard. It will soon become clear whether they have really been listening or have heard only what they expected to hear.

You might, for example, ask students to rephrase in their own words the question you have asked before answering it. Only after you agree that the question you asked is the one the student is about to answer should he or she proceed with a response. (Note how carefully this will require you to listen to the student's formulation of your question.) Similarly, you could ask each student to recapitulate the previous speaker's main point before proceeding to make another. You might even require the last speaker to agree that the point has been understood correctly before the conversation can move on. Alternatively, you can ask that each speaker show comprehension of what the last one has said by developing an implication of the point. At a minimum, you are forcing people to listen carefully to what is being said (particularly if you choose who will speak next rather than taking volunteers). But you also create an opportunity to explore misunderstanding. If a point is not recapitulated correctly, is that because it was poorly stated in the first place or because it was poorly listened to? If more than one person misunderstands the point, or if different observers understand it in different ways, the speaker and the rest of the class will learn something about precision in communication. Listening, articulation, and thinking will all be sharpened. Not a bad expenditure of class time, all things considered.

A still more challenging approach is to ask for a short analysis of the point made by the last speaker. This could be a brief restatement, a comment on whether the point seems correct, and an observation about its relevance. After such an assessment, the speaker can proceed with his or her own point, to be followed by a similar set of comments by the next speaker. This procedure raises rather substantially the stakes for clear thinking, expression, and listening. Used sparingly, it can help to build good listening (and other) habits.

Good listening may also be encouraged by effective note-taking. Taking notes in class may help participants to focus on what they have learned. Discussing what good notes might look like, or examining and critiquing examples of notes taken by various participants, may provide additional encouragement for careful listening and codification. Finally, you might occasionally ask students to hand in the notes they have taken on a given discussion so that you can comment on their form and substance.

Reinforce Continuity in Discussion

To facilitate a good discussion, in which contributions build upon one another, support statements that advance the trend of the conversation. Many teachers tend to affirm intelligent remarks ("good" observations), whether or not they are relevant to the current discussion. While you do not wish to discourage insightful comments, you would prefer that they be contributed at appropriate times. Thus, while affirming the value of an observation, you may indicate that it should not be pursued for the moment. (Note, once again, how carefully this will require you to listen and to think ahead during the discussion.) This approach will reinforce the value of both good observations and continuity, for both are important in true discussion. If you grade on classroom performance, continuity should be a criterion for evaluation—students should get credit not only for the intellectual content and clarity of their remarks, but also for how well their contributions fit into the flow of conversation.

Pose Open but Approachable Questions

Truly active participation and listening involve having the ears open far enough to permit the entry of new ideas that change existing perceptions. People are most attentive when they understand their lack of knowledge and their need for it. When they perceive that the question at hand is sufficiently complex that their own view is not a certainty, they are likely to listen more attentively. They may also be *less* inclined to speak, because they are unsure or because they want to reflect. It may be relatively easy to get an active discussion by focusing on a topic on which students are deeply divided but have clearly made up their own minds—but there will probably be little learning. It is better to seek issues on which minds are still open and the questions will bend to careful analysis.

Create a Physical Space That Supports the Message

Few teachers have much choice about the physical arrangement of the rooms in which they teach, but even small adjustments can make a difference. To accentuate the importance of listening and make the process easier, remove background noise, arrange chairs (or students among chairs) appropriately (for example, in a circle or semicircle to encourage face-to-face interaction), and position yourself and your notes so you don't obstruct discussion. When students see only the instructor facing them (and perhaps the backs of other students' heads), the arrangement signals that each interaction should be a one-on-one exchange between a student and the instructor. Make subtle changes that support a comfortable sharing classroom environment and reinforce listening as a key component. Being conscious of the physical surroundings—and perhaps discussing them explicitly with the class—can provide another opportunity for emphasizing your priorities.

The size of the class itself makes a difference. Large and small groups carry on discussions of very different types. In an intimate group of eight, each participant can join in a major way in every discussion; in a group of ninety, only a small fraction can say anything lengthy in a sixty- or ninety-minute session. But within the limits imposed by class size, the way the space is arranged to accommodate students can have a major impact on the way the discussions flow.

Conclusion

Listening, in the comprehensive sense discussed here, is a profoundly human activity. It requires that we be sensitive to various strands of the messages we hear. It requires that we be conscious of the multiple dimensions of what people have to say. It affirms our respect for others as people, and for their ideas and contributions.

In the discussion classroom, good listening is a vitally important responsibility of all participants—and it helps to build responsibility in the group. Responsible comment. Responsible discussion. Responsible contribution.

Careful listening binds the group together and to the task at hand. It focuses participants' energy on a single target. It fosters group cohesion and intimacy. It creates a garden where intellectual creativity can bloom amidst respect, personal support, and constructive criticism. A potent obstacle to creative expression is fear—but a powerful antidote to fear is group intimacy born of a respect nurtured and expressed through careful listening.

Good listening skills do not come easily. An atmosphere of careful attention has to be built and continually nourished. Emphasis on these skills takes precious time and energy away from other aspects of class activity, from substantive ideas that could be pursued, from additional material that could be covered. But it is not a luxury expenditure—it is an investment in basic infrastructure that, if made well, will be repaid many times.

An early investment in building good listening will improve the precision of discussion, making later class sessions more effective and more efficient. The productivity of class time will be enhanced. Moreover, good listening skills will benefit students throughout their lives. The ability to concentrate on, to sort out, to learn more effectively from the constant stream of information we receive aurally is a vital set of skills. It is hard to imagine any specific set of substantive ideas of greater value to students. If we take seriously their overall educational advancement, then time devoted to helping them become better listeners is well spent. Finally, the character and content of the conversations that take place in your classroom will change as students become better listeners. Build an atmosphere in which subtle thoughts can be heard and handled with care, and you will be surprised at how much more will be said.

9

The Discussion Teacher in Action: Questioning, Listening, and Response

C. ROLAND CHRISTENSEN

IT WOULD BE HARD to name a more valuable pedagogical accomplishment than the mastery of questioning, listening, and response: three teaching skills as linked, though distinct, as the panels of a triptych. Difficult enough to appreciate and analyze separately, these activities become even more complex as they work together, sequentially and simultaneously, in practice. Just as the aspiring swimmer isolates breathing, kicking, and stroke before reintegrating those skills and just swimming again, discussion teachers will find it helpful to unravel the intricacies of questioning, listening, and response before reweaving them.

The following discussion of this basic triad takes the form of a self-portrait rather than a manual because the spontaneity of discussion teaching will always resist prescription. My intention is to depict something of how I think during a discussion—the values I apply and options and potential consequences I weigh as I teach. Experience has made the process so automatic that it feels almost like instinct. But this feeling can mislead; sophisticated teaching is the product of study and practice—seasoned with a liberal dash of trial and error.

From my earliest attempts to analyze what discussion teachers, myself included, actually do, I have observed that we spend the bulk of our classroom time posing questions to students, listening to their replies, and making some sort of response—not always a further question. The time we invest in these activities would, by itself, recommend studying them, but I discern a further stimulus: teachers who treat questioning, listening, and responding as skills to master with reasoned care also gain the ability to influence aspects of the discussion process—mood, tone, pace, culture, and abstraction level—that otherwise seem untouchable.

Lest my assertions appear to border on the mystical, let me locate these skills in the realm of applied art, not magic. Like singing or orchestral conducting, they can be observed, described, analyzed, studied, consciously practiced, and stamped with each practitioner's style. I urge instructors to make their own studies and tailor their own practices to fit the circumstances of their teaching. Ralph Waldo Emerson noted his disappointment when the glistening beach pebbles he had gathered at the shore seemed to be lifeless when separated from their native sand, spray, and sunlight. My suggestions about questioning, listening, and response may share the same property: they shine best in their natural home, the classroom.

One further note: I shall summarize my thought processes in various teaching situations by presenting the sorts of questions I ask myself before making instructional choices. The questions I give are samples, approximations of what runs through my mind. But they are not merely rhetorical exercises. To avoid them is to answer them by default. To wrestle with them is to gain sensitivity and, eventually, skill.

How does one develop knowledge of a skill? My method here will be to distinguish what I consider to be significant constituent parts, analyze them, discuss their use, and recommend appropriate practices. Mastery of questioning does not begin and end with framing incisive queries about the day's material. It requires asking the right question of the right student at the right time. By the same token, true listening involves more than close attention to words: it means trying to grasp the overtones and implications of each participant's contribution with empathy and respect. Response, probably the least understood of the three skills, means taking constructive action—action that benefits each student and the group— based on the understanding that one's listening has produced. None of these three activities can be completely prepared before a discussion class, but teachers can lay some groundwork for questioning and achieve at least a modest feeling of confidence by sketching potential queries before class. Without listening, however, it will be impossible to know when and how to use them. And how can any teacher determine in advance when to toss a prepared question list aside and follow the students' lead?

Expert discussion leadership requires—and rewards—flexibility. Instructors who lead group discussions have the opportunity to appreciate multiple viewpoints, insights, levels of understanding, and creativity. It is a familiar paradox that we often discover what we know only in conversation with others. In discussion, we may uncover forgotten knowledge and free imprisoned ideas as participants frame their own questions, negotiate with other minds and personalities, and reflect. As one discussion group member put it, "The operations of many minds on a subject can be far more illuminating than a single taught point of view."

Questioning, listening, and response enable the instructor to orchestrate the operations of these "many minds." Communicating what knowledge we possess about these skills presents difficulties since we discussion teachers have no common professional language in which to talk with one another about the hands-on techniques of our practice. Even veteran instructors often can provide little practical enlightenment. As a young teacher, I once spoke with an experienced colleague whose confidence matched his competence. "I'm very good with student dialogue," he said. "I probe and read their every meaning. I can't tell you how to do it, though. But don't worry; I'm sure you'll figure it out for yourself—over time."

My colleague's nonchalance reflected a common implicit assumption: teachers simply develop good teaching practice, as infants cut teeth. A variation of this theme is the notion that masterful teaching is itself unteachable—a gift. Both attitudes exact substantial costs, particularly for beginning instructors. (A wise academic once noted that universities do not murder their young instructors; they just induce suicide.) Assigning a novice teacher to a freshman seminar with no practical coaching is a bit like asking a surgical intern to perform a triple bypass on the first day in the operating room. Even experienced instructors need help; if artistry remains on a completely intuitive level, core skills can calcify into routine or deteriorate into anarchy. And magic has a nasty habit of wearing off.

One distinguished educator, for example, who chose early retirement because he felt his classroom magic had disappeared, said, "The students would just sit there and answer my questions politely, but I couldn't get them stirred up anymore. No zip!" A colleague of his saw the situation from a more detached perspective: "'Why' questions had disappeared from his repertoire and 'what do you think?' was replaced by 'don't you think?' It was as if he had forgotten to listen." Artists, it is said, die twice.

Mastering the skills of questioning, listening, and response is a lifelong process for discussion teachers, but the gains are enduring and substantial. If we teachers deepen our knowledge and systematize our practice of these skills—if we find better ways to communicate the "what" and "why" of our practice to others—we will serve both our colleagues and ourselves. We can help one another by talking over mutual problems, and we can observe our colleagues' classroom practice and offer focused analyses and suggestions. Such collaborations inevitably suggest new teaching techniques to try and new ways to improve one's own day-to-day practice.

Skills as complex as questioning, listening, and response are learned step-by-step; mastery is a climb up a ladder, not a pole vault. When the president of one of our nation's largest companies was asked how any mortal could manage such a huge, complex organization, he replied, "How do you eat an elephant? One bite at a time." I invite readers to share my efforts to learn about questioning, listening, and response "one bite at a time." But caveat emptor! The familiarity of these activities makes them seem deceptively simple. My professional experience in teaching management practice will certainly color the content and affect the slant of my observations. And much remains to be learned.

Developing Competency in Questioning

Whether the setting be home, place of work, or classroom, questions initiate learning. They can excite, disturb, discipline, or comfort, but they always stimulate inquiry. And good questions, as John Ciardi reminds us, are infinitely generative:

> A good question is never answered.
> It is not a bolt to be tightened into place.
> But a seed to be planted and to bear more seed.
> Toward the hope of greening the landscape of ideas.[1]

Questioning unites the known and unknown, past and present, teacher and student, youth and age. Socrates, when asked his greatest accomplishment, replied, "I taught men to question." In the past several hours, as I sat at my desk overlooking a peaceful New Hampshire lake, two precious grandsons have asked dozens of questions. "Why does moss grow at the bottom of the tree? Who taught the fish to swim? How does the airplane stay in the sky? If we eat these M&M's now, will Mother be angry?" Simple and powerful queries from the very young. How will the coming years of formal education affect their natural ability and inclination to wonder? The answer will depend in large measure upon how their teachers handle the activity of questioning.

For a teacher, the question is a symbol of authority and power. It can be a shepherd's staff or a billy club. For a discussion participant, questioning is a way to explore the intellectual content of a topic and contribute to a group's developing dialogue. For both, questions are the entry point to the discovery of knowledge, the key to intellectual growth. As Neil Postman and Charles Weingartner tell us:

> Knowledge is produced in response to questions. And new knowledge results from the asking of questions; quite often new questions about old questions. . . . Once you have learned how to ask questions—relevant and appropriate and substantial questions—you have learned how to learn and no one can keep you from learning whatever you want or need to know.[2]

Discussion teachers ask questions under all kinds of conditions. In the heat of an energetic debate, some questions work exactly as one had expected, but others boomerang or trigger explosions. Particularly in fast-paced discussions, the art of questioning will always remain partly intuitive. But disciplined observation and focused analysis can highlight some graspable, technical aspects of the art. As James Austin reminds us elsewhere in this volume, observers can help instructors appreciate and, potentially, improve their styles of asking questions.

On a very fundamental level, questions permit a lecturer or discussion leader to stimulate students to think about and analyze the day's assignment. They also provide means for testing and exploring the validity of students' comments. In discussion classes, however, they have other special properties. They make it possible for the teacher to guide the discussion process along paths that balance the instructor's desire for rigor and thorough coverage of the material with the students' need to explore course content freely, in ways meaningful to them.

By tailoring questions to individual students' needs and interests, and to the needs of the whole group, instructors can manage the levels of student involvement. In this context, I assess my own teaching questions by asking myself what kind of dialogue is desirable at this point in the class. Should it be restricted to an analysis of technical facts or an extension of a line of reasoning? Or might it be useful to bring matters of emotion and value to the fore? How do I want the students to engage with the material at this point—with detachment, mild involvement, intense passion? Questions help create and maintain the culture of a class; they can promote competition or cooperation.

To integrate the diverse and sometimes contradictory contributions of the class as a whole, discussion teachers need to move beyond thinking in terms of individual questions. How? By considering patterns of questioning—and this means taking a mental step back to link the question of the instant to upcoming, as well as prior, questions. I have found that patterns do usually emerge when I, as instructor, listen for them. Often, the questions I ponder silently in the heat of discussion give me valuable perspective on the class in progress. I ask myself what the questions of the past few minutes have in common. Are they predominately informational, analytical, speculative, or something else? What is their emotional tone? As instructors begin to see questions in clusters, we can build a broad frame of inquiry that provides context for contributions to subsequent discussions as well as today's assignment.

Teachers who appreciate the power of questions to influence the intellectual and emotional tone of the discussion process will be encouraged to construct each question with care, giving special attention to phrasing, choice of words—especially adjectives and metaphors—and to the embedded directions, whether explicit or implicit, that questions usually carry. For example, the teacher may ask a respondent to refer his or her answer to another student in the room—perhaps one who has previously made a point relevant to the question of the moment. Or one might ask two students to give their reactions to a colleague's comment in sequence. The instructor can guide the discussion by specifically asking a speaker to build on a previous comment, by calling for role-playing, or by asking for a devil's advocate rebuttal. The construction of a question can influence the style, content, and emotional character of the response it triggers. Consider, for example, the difference between asking, "What strategic problems attend the reunification of Germany?" and "What policies should the countries of Europe take as they deal with a neighbor that brutally attacked and occupied them earlier in this century?" Both questions cover roughly the same material. But what vastly different emotional responses they would elicit!

Recognizing the emotional dimension of questions means that the instructor should be sensitive to the manner in which a question is put as well as to its design. The effects of a question depend on tone, voice level, speed of delivery, facial expression, bodily stance, and eye contact as well as content. One may pose questions on an emotional spectrum that ranges from the steely blue of distant, even hostile, formality to the warm, rich orangey-reds of geniality. "What do you think?" can communicate many different meanings, depending on the questioner's inflection, emphasis, and demeanor. And there is all the difference in the world between a smile and a smirk. An instructor can pose a question as a request for a contribution—with outstretched, open hands—or a demand enclosed in a clenched fist. Tone will always outweigh words.

I have found it enormously useful to develop a typology or inventory of questions, if only to appreciate their extraordinary, many-layered power. Most teachers who construct such a list come up with eight or ten basic types plus dozens of ancillary questions that often prove difficult to pigeonhole. The trick is not to construct the world's longest, most exhaustive list, but to compile a usable set that can cover most teaching circumstances and still remain short enough to remember.

Here is a typology of questions that I find helpful in teaching a course in the formulation of corporate strategy:

Open-ended questions:	"What are your reactions to the General Motors case?" "What aspects of this problem were of greatest interest to you?" "Where should we begin?"
Diagnostic questions:	"What is your analysis of the problem?" "What conclusions did you draw from these data?"
Information-seeking questions:	"What was the gross national product of France last year?"
Challenge (testing) questions:	"Why do you believe that?" "What evidence supports your conclusion?" "What arguments might be developed to counter that point of view?"
Action questions:	"What needs to be done to implement the government's antidrug campaign?"
Questions on priority and sequence:	"Given the state's limited resources, what is the first step to be taken? The second? And the third?"
Prediction questions:	"If your conclusions are correct, what might be the reaction of the Japanese auto industry?"
Hypothetical questions:	"What would have happened to the company if a strike had not been called by the union?"
Questions of extension:	"What are the implications of your conclusions about the causes of the Boston bottling plant strike for executives in plants in other large cities?"

Questions of generalization: "Based on your study of the com-
                                            puter and telecommunications in-
                                            dustries, what do you consider to
                                            be the major forces that enhance
                                            technological innovation?"

The exercise of developing a typology of questions typically expands
one's repertoire, and the advantages of a larger "tool kit" will soon become apparent. (As Mark Twain put it, "If your only tool is a hammer,
pretty soon all the world appears to be a nail.") A daily teaching plan
can assume unsuspected subtleties when one considers what types of
questions might best serve particular segments of the upcoming discussion. If the objective is to highlight integration of new concepts with
previously covered materials, the instructor may wish to stress questions
of extension and generalization. If student involvement needs to be
heightened, challenge questions should come to the fore. If reflection is
in order, hypothetical or predictive questions may serve the purpose. As
a class unfolds, the typology becomes a "back of the mind" template—a
sort of overlay for listening—that helps the instructor match a specific
question to the instructional need of the moment.

Developing a typology is a ground-breaking step toward mining the
riches of the art of questioning. Further steps bring further rewards. All
questions, for example, have operational as well as structural aspects.
They influence class process. Opening questions merit particular attention, since classes rarely recover from a poor beginning. I think of every
opening question as having three components. First, it should be linked
to the instructor's introductory comments—and, more specifically, to
the signals these comments send to the class. What do we need to accomplish today? What is to be our operational mode? Second, the instructor
must decide what type of question to employ. For openings, I prefer a
general rather than directed queries; these give the group leeway as to just
where to begin and show me what topics interest—or don't interest—this
particular class. This knowledge, in turn, lets me adapt my teaching plan
accordingly. I also think about the relationship between my opening
question and the study questions listed on the assignment sheet. Finally,
I think about giving instructions or assigning a role to the student who
will handle the opening question. Suggesting that a student summarize
his or her opening comments in two or three minutes minimizes the
risks of a long-winded disquisition. How the teacher words the question
also determines whether the respondent feels free to decline the invitation

to speak, without risking loss of face. "Give us your conclusion, please," offers little choice, but, "Would you be willing to start?" leaves some maneuver room.

Another key decision: Which student shall begin the discussion? I tend to give priority to a student who has experience or special interest in the topic (and sufficient self-restraint to avoid a harangue), to a student who might especially benefit from opening a discussion, to one who would gain from articulating his or her views on the matter under consideration, to a shy student, or to one who handles solo commentary better than dialogue.

Of the many other operational challenges that merit an instructor's serious attention, I shall note but two. The first involves using questions to change the abstraction level of the ongoing dialogue. To ask, for example, "What performance standards are appropriate for bank officials?" is to operate high on the abstraction ladder. To ask "Should this bank president lose his job?" is to move from generalization and theory down to specific example. I tend to lower the abstraction level of questions—work with specifics—to increase the personal involvement of participants or emphasize an applied "this needs to be done" line of discussion. Conversely, I tend to raise the abstraction level of questions to encourage students to broaden their perspectives, summarize, generalize, or redirect focus to an important area as yet untouched in this particular discussion. Abstractions run to coolness, specifics, to heat. If the goal is to defuse an emotional discussion, it is probably wiser to ask "What political, economic, and ethical factors affect the current national debate on abortion?" than "Do you believe in abortion in cases of rape and incest?"

Other challenges are posed by personalizing a question. ("Alma, we all know you have thought a great deal about the telecommunications industry; what observations would you like to make?") The benefits of personalization can be substantial. The student enters the discussion at a point of strength, with an opportunity to "star"; the class gains from the student's expertise. And individualizing the question demonstrates respect for the student in two ways: it shows that the instructor remembers the student's special qualities and has confidence in his or her ability to make a contribution to the dialogue of the moment.

But personalizing carries risks as well as benefits. Alma may know a great deal about telecommunications, but can she match her knowledge with the current needs of the class? What if she happens to be unprepared that day? It can be devastating to introduce a star performance that turns into a flop. Others in the class, unbeknownst to the instructor, may be equally interested in or competent to speak about this particular topic. Why, they may ask themselves, was Alma singled out to speak while I was overlooked? Favoritism? One simple way of handling this risk is to follow Alma's comment immediately with a group-directed question: "Are there other members of the class who find this topic of particular interest? Would you give us a hand?" Or at the conclusion of the class the instructor might return to that part of the discussion and mention how valuable it is when members of the class share their personal experience and expertise with the group.

After every class I make notes on the success (or lack thereof) of that day's tactics (for example, "This worked today but was a disaster last year—why the difference in outcomes?"). I try to sift my daily classroom experiences, and those of my colleagues, to "pan out" the useful. I have learned, for example, to avoid asking a substantial number of challenge questions early in a class. Students often read this behavior as antagonistic. I am wary of asking hypothetical (subjective) questions before the class has probed the hard facts available in the written material in depth. If I am going to ask a particularly difficult question later in the class, I give an early alert to allow reflection time. Or I preface the question with a "wriggle out" clause: "This is a tough one, Fred—at least it is for me—but could you get us started? What's the first item we need to consider?" If I have used directive questions for an extended period of time, I give the class a chance to take over. "Given the points just made, Sam, what is the next question that we need to work on?"

And, of course, I have a "shalt not" list too. I avoid, "Don't you think?" because it is an answer disguised as a question. The authority implicit in this phrase implies that any disagreement must be mistaken—hardly a message to stimulate free inquiry. I have also forbidden myself the use of, "Who doesn't understand this?" and its close cousin, "Does everyone see how I reached that conclusion?" It takes a brave or foolish student to accept these noninvitations.

Questioning lies at the core of any academic activity, from mastering a field of study to planning a research project to organizing a semester course or a daily teaching plan or working out a relationship with one's students. But questions through which a teacher guides a discussion reflect, and encourage, a certain "attitude of mind" (to borrow Charles Gragg's phrase). To promote a spirit of eager inquiry, the discussion leader should encourage students to question themselves, their peers, the instructor, the organization of the course, and the presented facts in general. As a Pirandello character put it, "A fact is like an empty sack, it won't stand up 'till you've put something in it."[3] Students need to appreciate this.

A pervasive spirit of inquiry—something far more profound than a predilection for asking numerous questions—can turn the barrenness and "endingness" of answers into the richness and openness of exploring the yet-to-be-known. Answers often simply aren't! They are merely launching pads for further exploration, places to prepare for the creation of new and more insightful questions. Yet much of our education system reinforces "getting the answer" as the ultimate goal of learning. Students have so often been trained to memorize and feed answers back to teachers for approval (read "grades"). Rarely does an examination ask students to list questions that the course has posed for them. We are, as Paolo Freire noted, working within a pedagogy of answers rather than questions. "We meet students, we teach biology, philosophy, and linguistics, and we start giving answers to them before they have the questions."[4] The sequence needs to be reversed.

While no instructor can revolutionize the academy singlehandedly, each of us can improve his or her own practice. We can all invest time and emotional resources in studying the art and science of asking questions—"the most important intellectual ability man has yet developed,"[5] as Postman and Weingartner put it. Moving beyond increased knowledge and improved skill, we can embrace inquiry as the essence of our practice. We need to learn, as Rilke suggests, "to love the questions":

> I want to beg you, as much as I can, . . . to be patient toward all that is unsolved . . . try to love the *questions themselves*. Do not now seek the answers which cannot be given you because you would not be able to live them. . . . *Live* the questions now. Perhaps you will then gradually, without noticing it, live along some distant day into the answer.[6]

Listening: A Critical Imperative

Society honors distinguished speakers. Boston abounds with statuary recognizing their achievements, but no monument, to my knowledge, has ever paid tribute to an accomplished and sensitive listener. Wise observers, however, have long recognized the importance of this skill. Ben Franklin suggested that the Lord gave us two ears and one mouth so we could listen twice as much as we talked. Good advice, but rarely followed. Essential to most professional activities, listening assumes crucial importance in teaching. Charles Gragg reminds us that "teaching is not only the art of thinking and speaking. It is also the art of listening and understanding. Nor by listening is meant just the act of keeping still. Keeping still is a technique; listening is an art."[7]

The artistry of listening holds rewards for any teacher. But when education aims not only to transfer knowledge but to prepare students to apply that knowledge in action and develop qualities of character and mind—and when classroom patterns shift from a teacher-student Socratic dialogue to a group learning mode—listening assumes even greater significance. The discussion leader needs to listen to each comment with at least two objectives in mind: to gauge the individual student's command of substantive material and the logic of his or her argument, and to assess the potential contribution of the comment to the group's continuing dialogue. This second dimension has major operational implications.

I listen for continuity: the relationship of the speaker's point of the moment to previous and expected dialogue. Does the point build on what has preceded it, strengthen the flow of discussion? If the comment deviates from the common path of inquiry that seems to be emerging, has the student given a reason for such redirection? Has he suggested, for the benefit of succeeding speakers what steps need to be taken next, what questions merit prompt consideration?

I also attempt to gauge the speaker's involvement. Does she sound detached, like someone merely performing a classroom obligation to comment on the issue under consideration? Or is she speaking as a player in the drama, showing personal feelings about the problem as well as intellectual grasp? I try to capture what Carl Rogers and Richard Farson call "total meaning": both the technical dimension of the student's argument and the deeply felt convictions she expresses—explicitly or implicitly—about the subject.

Another aspect of dialogue that disciplined listening can detect is certitude of judgment. Has the student presented points as "chiseled in stone," or just "best current conclusions," with which others of good judgment may understandably disagree? In this context, the instructor can listen for the student's sensitivity to the strengths and weaknesses of his own presentation. Does he indicate the points at which he believes his position to be most secure and those where it might well be questioned? What can the instructor learn about his willingness to welcome such queries?

Listening is an audiovisual exercise. An old Swiss proverb (are there any new proverbs?) puts it well: "If you shut one eye, you do not hear everything." The instructor can learn a great deal by watching the mechanics of presentation. Can the student be heard clearly? Is the comment delivered with animation? Hushed tones and funereal expressions sometimes betray uncertainty. To whom is the student directing his attention—his classmates or the instructor? It seems to be a universal desire of students to place the instructor at the center.

Discussion teachers share a common challenge with the conductor of any musical group. As Douglas Hofstadter put it, in *The Mind's I*, the conductor "must follow the paths of individual voices and at the same time hear the whole effect."[8] Listening to each student and to the whole class simultaneously is artistry of high order. Is the class listening en masse, or, as typically happens, are there pockets of attention and areas where subgroups appear to have tuned out? What lies on the other side of their silence?

As the dialogue unfolds, I listen not only for the content of students' comments, but for their ability to listen to others and their sensitivity to their own filters. And I try, while listening to others, to listen to my own listening. Where are my barriers? Where do my own firmly held convictions interfere with my understanding? With so much to share with their students, teachers sometimes overpack the teaching plan of the day. Typically, we succeed in bringing to the forefront the material we strongly want the students to consider—but our success can block our own ability to hear what the students are trying to communicate to us. Moreover, in attempting to cover a certain territory, we may inadvertently hurry the class by assuming that the whole group comprehends a point that has really been grasped by only two or three participants. Speeding up a dialogue—hothouse learning—impedes the teacher's capacity to listen and typically produces an unpalatable educational salad. Learning takes time!

As a rule, one's listening abilities are improved through a marriage of self-education and self-discipline. The education is long term and programmed; the discipline is "of the moment," and occurs as the teacher consciously grants total attention to each classroom speaker. On the operational level, one must know and understand students in depth. Moreover, the instructor who wishes to improve his or her listening must learn the class's current language system. New words, phrases, and metaphors move into the classroom from the wider worlds of campus, entertainment, sports, and of politics, and "old," seemingly familiar words take on new meanings in the current context.

The key to listening is selectivity. The lesson is illustrated delightfully in the following story, perhaps apocryphal, told about Robert Frost in his later years. A reporter went to Frost's New Hampshire house, knocked on the screen door, identified himself, and asked for an interview. Frost, a bit of a curmudgeon, glared at the visitor a minute and then asked. "You got one of those machines—those recorders?" "No sir," the reporter responded. "Well, all right," Frost replied. "Come on in. Those people who take down every word never get anything right."

Frost's wisdom surely applies to the discussion classroom. If an average person speaks about one hundred words per minute, and a discussion class ranges in size from twenty or thirty to nearly a hundred, the sheer volume of words to be processed is overwhelming. One deals with this impossibility by listening selectively for what seems to be critical to the day's teaching and learning targets. I listen not only for the accuracy of key facts, but also for value-laden words ("The company murdered those customers," for example). I listen for critical judgments, stated and unstated assumptions, and conclusions. I listen not only for points made by an individual speaker, but also for the patterns that emerge as several students make their contributions.

In conducting my continued self-education in pedagogy, I have found it extremely useful to invite a colleague, on a reciprocal basis, to observe the quality of my listening. We meet before and after each class and plan for a series of visits with observational targets that change as the course progresses. Almost invariably, the arrangement benefits both parties.

Response: Instant Artistry

The deceptively simple act of responding to a student's just stated contribution completes our triad of core skills. Its links with the ability to ask questions and listen to students' replies are as organic as the connection among the leaves of a shamrock. This instructor has found response to be the most demanding of the trio. Why? Because responding to a student requires a number of complex, interrelated, on-the-spot decisions. Together, responses have a powerful cumulative impact upon the quality of the day's discussion—and they are all but impossible to prepare for.

The scarcest resource in this context is time. Response is the art of the immediate. Some of the most important information needed to formulate a response is the stuff of a moment. What happened in the previous few seconds? How did the last speaker conclude her presentation? How do I read the interest and confidence levels of the speaker as well as the present mood of the class? One has but seconds to process these data plus relevant argumentation from prior classes, assess the current academic position of individual students and the entire group with respect to the material, predict what next steps might be appropriate, and decide how to proceed.

Many varieties of response are possible. For example, one might ask a further question, restate the speaker's points, request additional information, or offer a personal analysis. All of this requires instant consideration. Twenty or thirty seconds of awkward silence can seem like eternity to waiting students and their perplexed instructor. Time pressures tend to produce a reliance on the intuitive: "right instincts" and "inspired guesswork" are familiar allies in such situations. But perhaps one can move a bit beyond the intuitive to give some theoretical and operational support to inspiration and guesswork. David Sudnow offers a helpful suggestion. The artist's challenge, he reminds us, is "the organization of improvised conduct."[9] My own modest efforts to bring some order, some disciplined artistry, into the domain of improvisation are based on one key assumption: simplicity (of approach) enables an instructor to manage complexity. In that spirit I work with a three-step regimen.

First, I listen to each student's comment with two interrelated points of reference in mind. I try to understand and evaluate its academic worth and simultaneously I prepare for what to say and do when the commentary has been completed. In dealing with the latter dimension, where matters of process are extremely important, I apply a mental model developed by systems researchers—the "decision tree." Decision trees articulate possible alternatives by leading one through a series of yes or no choices. By thinking in terms of a simple decision tree, an instructor can narrow the "next-step" alternatives to manageable choices and anticipate the consequences of exploring one branch at the cost of ignoring the other. The tree I use has but two major branches, each with a few extending limbs—a useful simplification. In discussion teaching, it is not only what you know, but what you can remember—in time—that counts.

When a participant finishes her statement, I have two choices: either continue the teacher-to-student discourse or shift to a student-to-student mode. If I choose the teacher-to-student option, I can either go on with the first speaker or shift to another. If I continue with the first speaker, I have three basic action alternatives to consider. We can *explore* her ideas jointly—clarifying assumptions, checking the quality of the analysis, testing the reasonableness of her conclusion. Or I can *extend* the breadth and depth of her comments by asking her to comment on related ideas presented by her associates at other times during the discussion. Can she link those thoughts to her argument? Or I can *challenge* the points she has just made, citing contrary evidence and perhaps presenting a different interpretation of the problem. Can she defend her conclusions? If I decide to shift immediately to another student, I must decide whether to repeat the same question just asked of the preceding speaker, modify that question, or suggest a different question. Then, I again work along my "tree" by repeating a cycle of exploring, *extending*, or challenging.

If I want to follow the other major branch of the decision tree and highlight student-to-student (not teacher-to-student) interaction, I work with three basic alternatives. I can simply step back and turn the discussion over to the class with minimal guidance. Alternatively, I can reask the previous question, or raise a related question and suggest that the group focus its collective attention on those issues. Or I can provide some structure and direction to the dialogue by asking two students to present their (contrasting, I hope!) points of view on the primary issues of the case and then let the class proceed from there.

The use of a decision tree that matches academic objectives and personal teaching style can relieve some of the time pressures inherent in making a response. One arrives in class with a framework that lays out general, "first-order" options as well as secondary steps that might follow from each potential choice. These early steps, of course, need to be considered in light of situational specifics—your immediate reading of the class. But, having part of the action equation in mind enables one to get off to a fast start and to make appropriate decisions in a matter of seconds. And there is comfort in knowing that these early response options have been experience-tested, if only schematically. In practice, moreover, as one's log of teaching hours lengthens, one's comfort level improves as recollections of what actually worked—or bombed—in similar situations grounds one's general assumptions and sharpens one's ability to predict.

Second, having worked through the extended ramifications of my response with the help of a decision tree, I need to bring other considerations into play. When Inge finishes her argument in support of airline deregulation, academic training, plus the pressure of time, tend to direct my attention to the appropriateness of her economic analysis and the logic of her recommendations. An effective response, however, must consider additional factors. What will be the possible impact of the up-coming dialogue on her personally? Is this the first time Inge has spoken in class—volunteered? Has her previous behavior suggested unease at presenting ideas to the class? Will anything in the tone of her comments endanger her relationship with her peers?

An instructor's response at such a point must anticipate and deal with certain inevitable contradictions: What is the best course of action for individual student, class, and the instructor? In trying to balance these often conflicting needs, I try to keep a number of benchmarks in mind:

• Will my response put the speaker at high risk in terms of self-esteem or peer relationships? Scoring a teaching point, even a very important one, is never worth the sacrifice of a student.

• Will my response balance the needs of the individual student and the wider group? Will it focus attention on matters of interest to many members of the class and not simply the speaker of the moment?

• Will my response balance the immediate interests of the class with the need to cover the instruction program of the day? Ignoring students' interests minimizes their involvement; failure to cover material essential for understanding upcoming assignments threatens future progress.

• Will my response stretch the group's knowledge of subject material and its discussion expertise and yet permit honorable retreat if my expec-tations are unrealistic?

• Will my response fit the norms and values of the learning com-munity—cohere with terms of the teacher-student learning contract?

• Will my response balance the amount of available class time with that needed to explore the topic in appropriate depth?

Third, the wisdom of William Blake—"He who would do well must do it in minute particulars"[10]—has encouraged me to work up a number of very practical rules of thumb, guidelines for responding to students' comments.

• I correct, or call into public question, only major errors of fact or judgment, not minor misstatements of content or inconsequential flaws in the logic of an argument. It is an ineffective use of class time to seek perfection in every contribution. Worse, one runs the risk that students will perceive the instructor as a scold or nitpicker, not a supportive partner.

• When I do try to clarify a questionable conclusion, I offer the stu-dent an immediate opportunity to restate or reformulate his position or conclusion as well as an opportunity to question me. Teachers are fallible too.

• If a student presents an "off the wall, out of left field" comment—fascinating, internally consistent, admirably presented, but far wide of the mark—I immediately acknowledge the originality of the observation and note that, while an exploration of the argument at this time is inappropriate, I will try to return to it later, or would look forward to discussing it after class. I give similar treatment to contributions that relate to the topic of the day but not the specific point of discussion that we have reached. Maintaining the integrity of the class's path of inquiry is essential; tangents tangle thinking.

• When the group does not seem fully to appreciate the value of a peer's observation—one with exceptional insight and potential for advancing the group's analysis of the problem at hand in major ways—I call for repetition: "Would you please share those observations with us again? I'm not certain everyone thought through the full implications of what you just said!" A response of this sort communicates a need for further disciplined reflection upon a peer's suggestions.

• In preparing to respond to a superior contribution, I try to remember that praise, like blame, has its perils. It motivates, but also may encourage students to "play to the front of the room." In responding, I try to minimize public praise of a student's contribution, however excellent, in favor of having her peers recognize that accomplishment through their attentiveness, succeeding questions, and statements of approval. When the instructor's recognition of a student's contribution seems appropriate, I often send a personal note explaining why the comments were particularly helpful or speak to the student after class. In other instances, I refer to the comment in a summary or in succeeding discussions. When the accomplishments of the overall class need to be recognized, particularly early in the semester, my response focuses on the process by which the group worked through analyses. I try to avoid "blessing" a particular set of conclusions. To do so may well reinforce the student's stereotypical notion that there is but one "right" answer, and the instructor rewards no other.

• Confronted with an extremely emotional comment, based on incomplete evidence—a black-or-white judgment where logic might suggest a gray solution—I respond to the affective component first. Every era has its hot issues—abortion, the greenhouse effect, toxic waste, and nuclear power spring to mind at this writing—and their tendency to arouse irrational classroom polemics can best be defused by an acknowledgment of the range and depth of feelings involved. The speaker and the whole group will then have a better chance of finding constructive ways to analyze the substantive issues at stake.

• If a quiet participant should enter the discussion—uncertain of his or her ability to apply course concepts and perhaps uneasy about public speaking—I almost inevitably offer a supportive response. Even when the speaker's comments are of marginal quality, one can virtually always find something worthy of next-step inquiry. In such situations, I try to increase the probability of continued support by selecting, as the next contributor, a participant with a record of being supportive to his or her peers.

Response is probably the most challenging discussion-leading skill. Over time, it is possible to work up a typology of questions and enter the classroom prepared with a range of choices and alternatives for a particular discussion. And the laws of listening are universal; daily classroom practice is but a continuous refresher course. But our profession knows less about response. How can one prepare for an action that will, in practice, be almost instantaneous? One certainty is that due appreciation of the importance of response raises any instructor's chances of thinking with, not for, students.

Anticipated Outcomes

Serious thought about questioning, listening, and response can increase a discussion teacher's expertise and sensitivity and suggest teaching practices whose effectiveness will be obvious to any observer. As classes improve and individual students form strong, cooperative learning communities, instructors who teach in the active learning modes feel gratified, inspired, wiser. Yet we are never present when our true product—learning—is delivered.

The poet Amy Lowell compared an "idea dropped into the subconscious" to "a letter [dropped] into a mailbox." Applying her image to our profession, I would say:

> Teaching is like dropping ideas into the letterbox of the human unconscious. You know when they are posted, but you never know when they will be received or in what form.

When we instructors learn to pose skillful questions, practice true listening, and respond to the process of a class as well as its content, we increase the likelihood that our students will not only receive the ideas we posit, but reflect and act upon them in the years ahead.

NOTES

1. John Ciardi, *Manner of Speaking* (New Brunswick, NJ: Rutgers University Press, 1972).
2. Neil Postman and Charles Weingartner, *Teaching as a Subversive Activity* (New York: Delacorte, 1969), p. 23.
3. Quoted in Edward Hallett Carr, *What Is History?* (New York: Alfred A. Knopf, 1969), p. 9.
4. Paolo Freire, in a presentation given at the John F. Kennedy Library, Boston, MA, February 15, 1986.
5. Postman and Weingartner, p. 23.
6. Rainer Maria Rilke, *Letters to a Young Poet*, tr. M. D. Herter, rev. ed. (New York: Norton, 1954), pp. 34–35.
7. Charles Gragg, "Teachers Also Must Learn," *Harvard Educational Review*, vol. 10 (1940), pp. 30–47.
8. Douglas Hofstadter and Daniel E. Dennett, eds., *The Mind's I* (New York: Basic Books, 1981), p. 156.
9. David Sudnow, *Ways of the Hand: The Organization of Improvised Conduct* (Cambridge, MA: Harvard University Press, 1978).
10. William Blake, "Jerusalem," in *The Complete Poetry and Prose of William Blake*, ed. by David Erdman (Berkeley: University of California Press, 1982), p. 205.

PART IV
Critical Challenges

10

Patterns of Participation

JULIE H. HERTENSTEIN

IN A DISCUSSION CLASSROOM, students learn in two ways: through their own active participation and through the contributions of others. By attending to patterns of participation, the teacher can enhance both forms of learning, improving the overall value of a discussion while helping individual students develop their skills in speaking and listening. The latter is especially important, because discussion skills have broad, almost universal, relevance outside the classroom. In fact, when professional education relies on discussion methods, it is often with the conscious goal of helping students learn to communicate more effectively.

Students' contributions can themselves be viewed as having two dimensions: what the student says (content) and how he or she presents it (process). The content of a comment demonstrates the student's knowledge of the substantive material; in evaluating content, the teacher would consider the reasonableness of the approach the student has taken to solve the problem and the quality of the analysis supporting the solution. Attention to content ensures that the discussion focuses on critical topics and that issues are thoroughly analyzed. Virtually all instructors recognize the importance of content.

Process variables often receive less attention. Process includes such factors as the relationship of a student's contribution to earlier comments, the organization of the presentation, and the timing of the contribution. Tone is important too: an angry voice can be convincing, a well-placed joke effective. Attention to process can enhance the order, rhythm, and logical development of the discussion. The instructor can help students improve the discussion by asking thoughtful questions, providing necessary clarifications, and summarizing the comments of others.

Process skills learned in the classroom can help students in other settings. Colleagues may ignore a good idea if it is brought up at the wrong moment in a meeting; a proposal may be turned down if its sponsor does not carefully listen to other people's concerns and respond appropriately. Students will face a lifetime of such discussions: managers give performance reviews and attend meetings by the dozen; scientists debate the merits of research projects and evaluate the outcomes; government administrators must interact with elected officials. Practice in the classroom can help students prepare for these challenges.

Good teachers intuitively understand the importance of process. The following hypothetical interchanges illustrate its importance.

Powdered Dessert Mix Case Discussion

Teacher: Today we are going to discuss the proposal presented to the board of directors to approve the full-scale production of a new powdered dessert mix. Are the funds spent for test marketing the dessert mix relevant for the board to consider when approving full-scale production?

Bob: The board has to consider *all* costs related to the powdered dessert mix in making their decision to approve or reject full-scale production. If costs are incurred in test marketing, then they must be considered as part of the costs associated with this product.

Lisa: But when the board makes the decision to implement full-scale production, the money which was already spent on test marketing isn't relevant. It's a sunk cost.

Bob: What do you mean it's not relevant? It's over a quarter of a million dollars!

Diana: It seems to me that we need to clarify our assumptions about the timing of the test marketing expenditure. I'd like to ask each of you, are you assuming the board is making their decision before the money has been spent on the test marketing, or are you assuming that the test marketing has already been completed and paid for before the board's deliberations on full-scale production?

Whereas Bob and Lisa both address the question posed by the teacher, the main value of Diana's comment is to expose an unstated difference in the two prior speakers' assumptions. Most likely, Bob is assuming that test marketing is part of the program to be authorized; he has not really taken in Lisa's point about sunk costs. Diana eases the discussion process by pointing the way out of this impasse.

Discussion of the Use of the Narrator

Teacher: In the novel *The Good Terrorist*, by Doris Lessing, our information about most of the events and personalities is presented from the main character's (Alice's) point of view. How does Lessing's use of Alice as narrator limit or enhance our understanding of the novel's themes? In other words, how does Lessing use form to reinforce the novel's content?

Jan: Alice feels like an outsider in the group of activists and therefore her perspective is the most critical, the most objective, and the most useful to us, as readers, because she isn't taken in by everyone.

Chris: I don't agree. Her sense of difference is obvious to you precisely because she is the main character. Every one of those characters would see him- or herself as "different" and misunderstood if Lessing put us inside their heads. I think Alice's seeming objectivity is really misleading. This could be, in fact, the point: Lessing *wants* to mislead us temporarily. Do you think that's true?

Terry: Lessing is trying to make a political statement in this novel about the motivation for activism, and I'm afraid that her statement could easily be seen as a reactionary position. I think that you are letting a discussion of Lessing's style distract you from the real subject. Where does Lessing stand in relation to the leftist politics of the characters?

Jo: I think that Chris's point about Lessing's use of an "unreliable narrator" is another way of addressing just the issue you raise, Terry. It's just that Chris is talking about Lessing's use of form to illuminate her theme, and you are talking about the theme directly.

Jan and Chris are listening and responding to each other. Each builds on the other's contributions, adding to the substantive content about the use of a narrator. Terry's comment breaks the flow of the discussion by abruptly abandoning the unresolved issue of Lessing's goal in using Alice as narrator; Chris's question is left unanswered. The timing of his contribution, which is valuable in itself, suggests that Terry has not been listening to the other students. The disruptive comment leaves the class (and the teacher) in a dilemma whether to resume the discussion of the use of the narrator or carry on with political activism. Fortunately, Jo gets the group back on track with comments primarily oriented to the discussion process.

Discussion of Performance Measures

Teacher: Today we're going to evaluate a proposed change in the measure used to evaluate the performance of division managers in a decentralized firm. Previously this firm based the incentive compensation of division managers on the amount of profit they had earned. Now it proposes to base incentive compensation on the division's ROI (return on invest-ment).* Is this a good idea?

Pam: ROI will encourage the division managers to take actions in the com-pany's best interests because it will hold them responsible for the assets entrusted to their care, as well as for the amount of profit they earned. After all, you can always increase the amount of profit you earn by investing in more assets. The issue is whether division managers are investing wisely: that is, whether their assets earn a satisfactory profit relative to the amount they cost.

Sarah: I'm George Daniels, division manager for the Building Products Divi-sion. I can see that my bonus is going to be based on the ROI I make. Since those smart staff guys at headquarters have figured this thing out, they must want me to make decisions which will make ROI go up.

Therefore, I won't let my customers buy on credit anymore. It's cash, or no sale. That will get my accounts receivable down to zero, which will reduce my investment, and improve my ROI.

Rick: But you can't eliminate credit. You will lose customers to your com-petitors, who all offer credit; credit's essential in this business. It's just like Sears; if they eliminated credit purchases, their sales would go down. The reduction in sales and earnings will more than offset the reduction in receivables; as a result, ROI will go down.

Pam responded to the teacher's question with a well-reasoned argu-ment. But Sarah sees the potential for abuse or misinterpretation of the ROI system. To illustrate her point, she assumes the role of a key man-ager and presents an exaggerated argument. Her facts and reasoning are wrong when her position is carried to this extreme, as Rick correctly points out (and as Sarah herself realizes). By playing a role, she raises the important issue of risks associated with the ROI proposal. Sarah clearly contributes to the substantive learning, as fellow students are forced to articulate their opposition to her position. They make explicit the point that Sarah acted out dramatically.

To some extent, students learn the process skills illustrated above by observing one another and profiting from both good and bad examples of discussion behavior. But the teacher can greatly facilitate their learning

---

*Return on investment is a fraction. The numerator is the profit earned; the denomi-nator is the investment in the business unit being measured.

by developing individual profiles of participation and sharing those observations with students.

Observing Content, Process, and Frequency

To help students develop participative skills, the instructor should try to discern the pattern of contributions made by a student over time. Content and process should both be systematically observed, as should the frequency with which comments are made.

The substantive *content* of students' remarks reveals whether they are learning basic course material. To interpret a student's progress, however, the instructor needs to consider not only the content of contributions but also the background and expertise of the individual. Early in the course, for example, a profile indicating that a student has grasped basic concepts but has not yet applied them in a sophisticated way might reflect acceptable progress for a novice without prior expertise in the subject. In a more expert student, however, the same pattern would be unacceptable, suggesting that he or she was loafing rather than trying to apply known concepts to new, more complex situations. In fact, educational objectives may not be the same for all students. Perhaps the goal for novice students is to acquire basic skills and understanding, whereas students who have a background in the area should develop an understanding of the relationship between their area of expertise and other relevant areas, and learn to communicate effectively about the subject to a less-informed audience. By understanding the different levels of prior expertise and appreciating students' different goals, the teacher can interpret their participation individually.

Reviewing the content of a series of comments also reveals whether students are developing a broad range of skills. For example, can a business student perform both the quantitative analysis to determine whether an acquired company will be profitable, and the more subjective analysis to assess its fit with the acquiring firm's culture and strategic direction? Can a medical intern both pose the proper questions and diagnose the disease? Patterns of class participation can show that students are mastering skills appropriately or highlight recurrent types of errors that reveal misunderstandings to be corrected. The teacher who understands content patterns can structure better participation opportunities for individual students in the future. Is he ready for difficult questions? Does she need practice with more straightforward questions? Should he be probed with follow-up questions? Observations of the *process* dimension will shed light on a student's progress toward acquiring discussion skills and becoming an effective member of the discussion group. Attentive listening is a crucial skill. A good listener builds on the contributions of others, relating comments to, but not repeating, previous statements. When a question is asked, the careful listener answers it instead of moving in a different direction. He or she can support good arguments, challenge assumptions, point out inconsistencies, and probe weaknesses in the analysis. The careful listener knows when and how to synthesize and summarize the comments of previous speakers, and when to shift the discussion to new ground.

In addition to listening carefully, students must present information effectively. They should identify important points, organize them logically, and state them succinctly while noting important assumptions. Students must provide supporting evidence and persuade others to accept their positions. They must be willing to answer questions, respond to criticism, and consider new evidence, modifying an earlier position when warranted.

Recognizing process patterns allows the teacher to give students opportunities to participate in new ways, or to coach them to change bad habits. Helping individual students in this way also improves the quality of the overall discussion. When the discussion is coherent and purposive, rather than a series of random, unrelated comments, everyone benefits.

Frequency is the final element to consider in profiling class participation. Frequent participation is not necessarily good, particularly if the student's contributions are mediocre. Infrequent participation is not necessarily bad; in fact, the most effective contributors are often students who carefully choose their opportunities. They avoid wasting "air time" on mundane comments; when they do speak, consequently, fellow students recognize that an important insight is likely and listen attentively.

However, a student who rarely or never speaks misses the opportunity to develop discussion skills, and the instructor may wish to intervene. Some teachers use background information available before the course begins to identify students likely to be infrequent contributors. With such early identification, the teacher can make a special effort to involve these students in the discussion, to look for their hands, call on them, and remember their contributions.

A change in frequency merits attention. An increase in frequency may indicate growing confidence with the new subject. A sudden drop in frequency may indicate that a student has tuned out because of boredom, or has given up on his or her ability to learn the material. (Alternatively, of course, it may indicate personal problems.)

Remember that "it takes two to participate": the student who volunteers, and the teacher who chooses one raised hand rather than another. Sometimes changes in the frequency of a student's participation reflect the teacher's behavior. For example, encouraging occasional speakers to talk more may mean calling on regular contributors less often; the result will be an "artificial" decline in their participation.

Providing Guidance and Direction

Analyzing content, process, and frequency enables the teacher to give guidance that both shapes the contributions of individual students and ultimately adds to the quality of the discussion. Teachers can influence class participation through their interaction with the class as a whole and with individual students.

Expected standards of performance in participation should be explained in early class meetings. It is more productive to identify desired behaviors explicitly than to keep the rules of the game a secret, hoping that students will guess them correctly. Tell students, for example, that they should consider how their contributions fit into the discussion. If it is less important to speak often than to make valuable contributions, that too must be emphasized. Let them know that brevity and organization are favored over long-winded expositions.

Explicitly communicating standards is particularly important if students have had little experience in discussion courses or if the standards applied in their earlier courses were different. Failure to explain the ground rules deprives students of the opportunity to learn and develop skills, and it may impede the development of good class discussion processes.

As class follows class, the teacher can give feedback to the students to illustrate and reinforce the expectations explained at the outset. For example:

> I thought yesterday's discussion was excellent. What impressed me was your ability to identify the source of the conflict between the two groups, and to develop specific recommendations to manage this conflict in the plan of action you developed.

> I'm having difficulty following this discussion. The comments seem to me

to be random and unrelated. I don't think you are listening carefully and responding well to each other.

I'm not hearing any in-depth analysis to support your assertions. Where are the facts to back up your positions?

At times, in-class guidance to *individuals* may clarify what is expected for other students. For example:

A student interjects an unrelated comment into the discussion, and the teacher responds: "That's a good comment. I'd like to deal with it later when we've finished with the issue we're currently discussing."

A student asks a question. A second student raises his hand, is recognized, and proceeds with a different point. The teacher says: "I don't understand how your response relates to the question just raised."

Use this kind of feedback with caution, however. A confident student whose abilities are respected by peers could probably tolerate the implicit criticism; a shy student, speaking for the first time, might be devastated.

Throughout the course, the teacher will find it useful to provide guidance during discussions. Explicitly telling the class what is being done well, and why, reinforces good performance and motivates students to try even harder. As they develop basic skills, feedback encourages them to more sophisticated levels of performance.

Guidance should be offered to individual students as well—in student-initiated conferences or office visits, periodic formal evaluations of participation, or informal meetings after class. A good approach is to present an overall impression of the student's participation, liberally laced with specific examples, and then make suggestions helpful to his or her development.

Some students do only one or two things well and need to be encouraged to develop other discussion skills. For example, they may consistently provide excellent summaries, but never advocate their own point of view; they may *always* ask questions (or never ask questions); or they may respond only to questions that can be answered "yes" or "no."

Such patterns alert the teacher to pursue a broadening of students' activities and talents. It is important to seek clues that suggest how the student can best be helped. Is the monosyllabic student using English as a foreign language? If so, the instructor might allow him additional preparation time by asking him a day ahead to begin the following day's discussion. In other students, however, this behavior may be due to shyness or lack of confidence. Investigation may reveal the source of the student's discomfort and suggest alternative strategies.

Some students undermine the effectiveness of their contributions by calling attention to their uncertainty ("This may not be important, but . . .") or by failing to respond to questions or criticisms, thus appearing to back down. A tip from the teacher may enable them to eliminate such self-defeating behavior.

Students should be given guidance on the key elements of content and process that influence the quality of their contributions. Identifying what they do well builds confidence and encourages them to seek opportunities for using these skills. Contrasts between strengths and weaknesses can also be useful. Consider the following examples:

> Your numbers are good, but your explanation of what they meant was poorly organized. In preparing the numbers, you need to think about how to present them and, specifically, how to organize that presentation.

> Your summary demonstrates that you have a firm grasp of feminist psychoanalytic thinking on the concept of subjectivity. Now can you make an attempt to integrate or critique these theories from your own viewpoint?

> Your analysis of Chantal Akerman's camera technique in the film "Je, Tu, Il, Elle" is particularly enlightening because you contrast her cinematic choices with those you might typically expect in a more conventional film.

> You are able to take technical concepts and make them accessible to nontechnical people, as when you explained the Newtonian principles and their relationship to the theory of relativity.

> In the class on ABAC Manufacturing your analysis was very good, but in the class on Lowden Corporation your analysis was weak because you failed to distinguish between the fixed costs and variable costs.

> You have clearly identified and presented the three strands of repeated imagery patterns in John Ford's film, but you have not yet explained how these patterns relate to the film's theme. You're learning how to listen, and I now find that you're responding to your classmates and building on their comments. Your response to Sam's plan last Thursday was right on target.

Sometimes the instructor should respond selectively. Many problems may be apparent in a student's participation, but no one could solve them all at once. Selecting one or two allows the student to concentrate energy and attention on a manageable task. Since the primary goal is to develop the student's skills, the teacher should emphasize skills that the student can capitalize on, or problem areas where the student can improve. The selection will depend on students' backgrounds, skills, and abilities. For example, suggesting that a shy student "jump right into the discussion" is not particularly useful. It would be more helpful to spend time identifying topics of particular interest or situations in which the student might feel relatively comfortable contributing (for example, summarizing what fellow students have said).

It is important to have a sense of priorities, as some problems must be solved before others can be addressed. A natural progression of skills may be implicit in the course content. For example, perhaps students must first be able to make accurate factual observations before they can analyze and evaluate these data, then formulate creative solutions to the problems identified in the analysis. If a student is unable to observe basic facts, this skill should be emphasized first; otherwise no progress to problem-solving is possible.

Remember that students are learning. Their discussion skills are developing, not developed. Their knowledge of course content is beginning to evolve, and many consider themselves woefully inadequate when compared with their peers or the teacher. They can be embarrassed or humiliated by a thoughtless comment from the teacher. While constructive criticism is necessary for students' development, teachers should distinguish between those with sufficient self-confidence to hear criticism in the classroom and those who need a private conference.

Patterns and Profiles

To help themselves track their students' progress in acquiring discussion skills, teachers will find it helpful to keep records of individual students' class participation. In developing such profiles, the instructor should consider the complex interaction among content, process, frequency, and individual background. Eight brief examples will suggest the nature of such profiles, as well as the kinds of feedback that might be offered, and questions and participation opportunities structured to develop the student's personal skills.

> *Example 1.* Fred had not taken any related courses in this subject area. Initially, he said very little in class, although he actively listened to the discussion. In his infrequent contributions, he made elementary points, and he appeared somewhat intimidated by students who were seemingly more expert. Over time, however, Fred participated more actively and

substantively; he volunteered for increasingly difficult (though still not the most challenging) questions, and provided competent answers.

Fred's profile indicates that he is a strengthening participant. A novice in the subject of the course, he is becoming familiar with the material and carefully selects questions he feels capable of answering. The teacher should provide positive reinforcement, identifying the good comments made and underscoring his progress, and encourage continued acquisition of substantive knowledge and development of discussion skills.

> *Example 2.* Diana had her hand in the air all the time; she spoke several times every day if called on. However, she made very little contribution to the discussion. Often she simply repeated what others had already said; at other times she made assertions or offered opinions that she did not support.

Diana's profile seems to be that of a frequent, low-quality participant. It would be useful to speak frankly with her, indicating that her ease at participating in discussion is good, but that she needs to think more about furthering the progress of the discussion. She should attempt to be more selective in her contributions, waiting until she has a significant point before raising her hand. The teacher will probably want to call on her less often and, when she does speak, press for the relevance of the comment, encourage depth of analysis, and ask her to explain how her comment relates to the previous discussion.

> *Example 3.* Robert has seldom spoken in class. The difficulty of characterizing his participation is compounded by its variable quality: he made two brief, insignificant comments and provided one excellent, well-organized class opening.

Robert's profile is that of an infrequent participant. Such students present a considerable challenge since there are so many possible reasons for infrequent participation. Keeping in mind that infrequent participation may be due to such deep-seated causes as shyness, language problems, or culture, the teacher should talk to Robert to try to uncover other possible explanations. If, for example, his unfamiliarity with the material makes him uncomfortable when the discussion becomes sophisticated, he can be encouraged to participate early in the session, as the groundwork is being laid. Identify topics in the course that particularly interest him and encourage participation on these topics; make a particular effort to call on him when these topics are discussed. For some students the problem is volunteering, not participating; that is, they have great difficulty raising their hands, but contribute comfortably and effectively once called upon. The teacher may ask such students if they would like to be called on when their hands are not raised; after several such opportunities, they may find it easier to volunteer. Be careful, however: unexpected calls may terrify some infrequent participants and make it even more difficult for them to join in the discussion.

> *Example 4.* Scott participated regularly, although virtually all of his contributions were made in the last third of the discussion. The one discussion skill he showed was summarizing information previously presented by his classmates.

Scott's profile indicates that he may be a strategic participant. Such students create strategies for participation, often designed to get them out of work; the teacher needs first to recognize that there is a pattern, then decide how best to deal with it. Scott may not have read the material assigned for the class, but instead based his comments on the early discussion. Or he may simply feel more comfortable summarizing than presenting new information. In any case, a useful response is to describe to the student the pattern you have observed and indicate a desire for a broader range of participation. Call on him earlier in the class, perhaps even when his hand is not raised, and in situations that call for discussion skills other than summarizing.

> *Example 5.* Susan contributed to many discussions. Her comments often shifted the discussion to an analysis of whether the plan being considered was ethical; she consistently raised some very important points for the class to consider. Other students began to anticipate this pattern; when topics were discussed that clearly raised ethical issues, they turned toward Susan, waiting for her to raise her hand.

Susan's profile indicates that she tends to be a single-subject participant. In her case, the theme was ethics; in other students this pattern might take the form of always recommending the hiring of a consultant to cure corporate ills, or instituting government programs to solve social problems. Each comment in itself may be useful, but there are two problems with a consistently repeated theme. First, the single-subject participant is not broadening her knowledge and learning new approaches to the subject. Second, other members of the class may become dependent on her and fail to develop their own positions about this class of issues. It would be helpful to discuss both of these concerns with Susan. Seek out opportunities to include her in the discussion of other topics;

when "ethics" arises in the class discussion, make it a point to call on other students.

> *Example 6.* Although Ginger was quite articulate, she participated in the discussions with only moderate frequency. She preferred to wait for an interesting controversy or an issue on which she had something unique to contribute. Ginger appeared to be consistently well prepared; she listened carefully and followed the flow of the discussion; if called on when her hand was not raised, she responded thoughtfully and knowledgeably.

Ginger is a well-prepared participant. Because she chooses her opportunities carefully, fellow students recognize that her contributions will be important, and look forward to hearing her comments. To reinforce her behavior, tell Ginger that her approach is effective; she may be concerned that she is not speaking frequently enough. Be grateful for students such as Ginger, for they are real assets to the class discussion.

> *Example 7.* Jim enrolled in the course with some prior knowledge of the subject. He leaped into the discussions early to display his expertise, often using jargon, which he did not bother to define. He treated students with less expertise somewhat disdainfully.

Jim's profile reveals that he is often a dysfunctional expert. Talk with him about the positive role that someone with expertise can play in the discussion. If he shares his knowledge appropriately, the class will begin to seek his expertise actively and he will become an effective participant. But Jim must learn to listen carefully, to communicate concepts without jargon, and to treat his fellow students with respect. When elementary questions are asked, the teacher may want to ignore Jim's hand, and call instead on a novice. When Jim speaks, he should be asked to explain concepts until other students agree that they understand his explanation.

> *Example 8.* Liz was keenly aware of the process of class discussion. She noted, for example, when the discussion was getting off track or when the important points on a topic had been covered and it was time to move on. To further the progress of the discussion, Liz often took the initiative to summarize or suggest a new topic.

Liz tends to be a process-oriented participant. Let her know that you welcome her careful listening and her help in guiding the discussion process. Encourage other kinds of participation as well. For example, if she merely names an appropriate next topic, ask her to present her position on that topic.

Table 10-1
Profiles of Student Participation

Student	Content	Process	Frequency
Fred, a strengthening participant	naive initially, increasing in substance	response well organized, carefully selects questions	low, increasing
Diana, a frequent low-quality participant	adds little substance, fails to support assertions	listens, but repeats others, makes no useful contribution	very high
Robert, an infrequent participant	quality varies from insignificant comment to excellent opening	no evident problem, but little data	very low
Scott, a strategic participant	good content, but always derived from earlier in the discussion	offers excellent summaries; however, only summarizes and always late to class	adequate
Susan, a single subject	consistently a single topic	comment carefully placed in discussion, articulately presented	adequate
Ginger, a well-prepared participant	excellent—challenging topics or issues, knowledgeable, thoughtful	excellent—careful listener, follows flow of discussion, articulate, well-organized contributions	moderate, but adequate
Jim, a dysfunctional expert	accurate, but hidden in jargon	poor—answers questions inappropriate for his expertise, fails to explain clearly, treats others disdainfully	high
Liz, a process-organized participant	sometimes weak: may add little to comments of others	provides summaries, changes topics or returns to earlier points in a way that facilitates the progress of the discussion	moderate

Table 10-1 summarizes the participation profiles for these eight students. Recognizing such patterns helps the teacher understand individual students and identify the appropriate next step in their development.

An awareness of participation patterns will also help the teacher lead a more effective discussion. Suppose, for example, that a discussion has bogged down. Students are discussing a complex issue; the material is new and confusing to them; different interpretations abound. The discussion teacher could allow the class to simmer in its confusion, trusting it will eventually sort things out; she could directly intervene, explaining the correct interpretation and eliminating the confusion; or she could help the students clarify the issue themselves. In the last case, she must carefully select a student to speak. Fred, a strengthening participant, may not have sufficient expertise to handle this complex issue; Diana, a low-quality participant, is unlikely to provide the required interpretation with clarity. The teacher might turn to a student with prior knowledge of the subject matter, although a "dysfunctional expert" like Jim would require careful handling (controlled questioning) to avoid exacerbating the class's confusion. Ginger, well prepared and articulate, might also be a good choice.

Tracking Class Participation

It may be useful to adopt a routine, systematic approach to the collection of class participation data rather than rely on impressionistic memories. A structured method of note-taking is likely to result in more detailed recording of relevant information. Besides noting that Mary did not speak, for example, the teacher might also observe the sling on her arm; perhaps her silence is due to pain, not lack of interest or preparation.

Profiles change as students learn and develop new skills. By continually recording raw data from discussions, the teacher uncovers changes in patterns as they evolve. Teachers should guard against becoming captives of their original perceptions or a single memorable incident. Systematic data-gathering enables teachers to recognize the changing character of students, and to listen and understand with open minds.

Methods of recording participation data will depend on class size, subject matter, and other factors, including the teacher's personal preferences. Consider two alternatives, a small seminar, and a large class:

> *Small seminar.* The seminar, which meets once weekly, consists of six graduate students; most students were well known to the teacher before the start of the semester. This is the teacher's only discussion seminar.

> *Large class.* An instructor teaches three discussion sections in two undergraduate courses. One course has two sections of forty students, meeting twice a week; the other course meets once a week, and has thirty students. The teacher has had little, if any, prior contact with the students.

The first step is to have some place to record the data. A useful form will provide room for the student's name and background information, and comments on each class meeting, identified by date and topic.

In the small seminar, background data may include information previously known to the teacher such as the student's proposed thesis topic. In the large class, similar background information (major field, expertise in the subject, relevant work experience, goals for taking this course, prior experience with discussion courses) might be obtained from student records or supplied by students on the first day of class.

It is best to record information while the contributions are fresh and clear in your mind. In the small seminar, the teacher may make notes only after every two or three meetings. In the large class, it may be important to record data sooner, lest comments be forgotten or impressions of different classes blur (particularly if more than one section discusses the same topic).

While relatively detailed notes may be kept for the small seminar, a comprehensive record is neither practical nor necessary for the large class. You need only sufficient information to develop a profile of the student's performance; it is particularly valuable to make a note when the student plays a significant role in the discussion, such as opening the class or dominating the analysis.

Some examples may help. In the interchange quoted earlier in which students discuss use of the narrator, the teacher might make the following notes on Terry:

> Recognized issue of motivation for activism, an important theme. However, timing disruptive, in middle of unrelated discussion, caused point to be lost—they didn't pick up on it. Not listening carefully.

For Pam, in the discussion of performance measures:

> Responded to teacher's question: favored ROI. Organized. Good support for position.

Some teachers have little trouble recalling details of the discussion; others find it more difficult. Experience suggests several techniques that can help you identify who spoke and what they contributed:

> Page through the information sheets you have developed for each student. Reviewing these records, and concentrating on students one at a time, will help in recalling what each said.

> If you use assigned seating, or if students routinely sit in the same seats, a seating chart can be developed and reviewed. This technique, like the

first suggestion, helps focus on individual students but with the added dimension of spatial relationships. It is particularly helpful if you remember that a comment came from one part of the classroom, but have forgotten who said it. Focusing on the students who sat in the area may stimulate the memory.

If, before class, you prepared a list of students to be called on, review it to check whether they were called on, what was asked, and what they responded.

Blackboards are often used to record important points during a discussion. Noting what is written there will help you remember who contributed that point to the discussion.

If you prepared an outline of points to be covered or afterward made summary notes of the content covered, reviewing those notes may help you recall the stages through which the discussion progressed and remember who participated at each point.

Finally, if observers or course assistants are present, they can be asked to record who says what, or to help recall this information after class.

Participation in discussion classes provides an important opportunity for students to learn speaking and listening skills they will need in the real world. Teachers can help by explaining the importance of process and by providing opportunities for students to practice emerging discussion skills. Continuous profiling of the patterns of student participation allows the teacher to adjust teaching tactics and tailor opportunities for participation appropriate for the individual student. These profiles also provide the basis for individual coaching.

For some instructors, profiling will raise the further issue of evaluation. If patterns of participation are so important, shouldn't students be graded on their comments? And if they are to be graded, shouldn't process receive as much weight as content and frequency? All three, after all, contribute to students' skill at carrying on discussions.

However grading is handled, as participants develop skill the quality of the discussion will improve. That is rewarding and satisfying in itself. The greatest joy, however, comes when a student says that, because of your dedication to profiling, feedback, and coaching, "You made a difference."

11

Teaching Technical Material

BRUCE GREENWALD

AT LEAST ONCE EVERY TERM, an extremely anxious student arrives at my office clutching a textbook that has not been assigned in the course and is too technically detailed to be of use to anyone not intending to teach the subject at an advanced level. Reading this text has left the student fixated on a single, very precise question. If I will answer only that one question, I am promised, everything will become clear. As it turns out, the question cannot be answered usefully without addressing at least three other less precise, but unasked questions; moreover, the student's question is generally irrelevant to any practical understanding of the course material. But I have found that immediate, direct attempts to set the student straight are seldom successful. It is better to answer the single very precise question as posed and let the student decide what to do next.

Some students leave my office apparently satisfied. Most stay and talk about their determination to master the course material despite an inherited inability to deal with "this kind" of course—especially in comparison with more technically gifted classmates. (I have taught finance, statistics, linear programming, and decision analysis to MBA students and economics to undergraduates.) Invariably, these students do well in the courses in question (usually much better than they think they have done), and just as invariably, the answer to that single very precise question has nothing to do with their success. By the end of the term, they have typically forgotten both the interview and that once-crucial question. By then, if the course is successful, its insignificance to a useful understanding of the material has become apparent (if only unconsciously).

This archetypal experience illustrates many of the characteristic problems of teaching technical material. First, the student's action, however misguided in a broad sense, fairly captures at least one aspect of the situation. Many of the questions that arise in a technical course really do have clear-cut "right" and "wrong" answers, if only within the context of the technical discipline itself. There is a body of knowledge that must be conveyed. An introductory economics course is not successful if half the class understands the implications of downward-sloping demand curves and half the class does not. Such a model of market behavior has an internal logic that every student should grasp and be able to apply, whether or not it precisely and accurately describes a real-world economy. Also, it is usually not enough that students leave a science course with a general idea of the laws of motion (or of physical chemistry); they must also know something about how to apply them precisely in particular situations. Consequently, in a "technical" course, the instructor (as opposed to students) must directly provide proportionately more of the material to be learned than in a nontechnical course. Hence, the student's recourse to a textbook and his or her tendency to focus on a precise question, to which the instructor should have an answer, accurately reflect an important aspect of technical teaching. Instructors of technical material do have to provide right answers, even if they are not answers to each student's particular questions.

Second, technical courses often demand modes of reasoning that are unnatural and/or nonintuitive. That is why students often find textbooks beyond their competence. A technical discipline almost invariably pursues a highly developed theoretical and empirical approach that is not part of the intellectual equipment of even a well-educated layman. Multidimensional quantum field theories in particle physics are simply not interpretable in terms of everyday modes of thought. Thus, control of the context and sequence in which material is presented is especially critical in a technical course. Answering single, very precise questions out of context is of little value, and students who go to the library on their own initiative often do themselves more harm than good.

Third, students bring to a technical course an extraordinary capacity for anxiety. Many of them initially know nothing about the material involved, and their native intellectual instincts may lead them further astray. Despite hard work, these students may get nowhere in preparing for class, and will therefore be worried and frustrated at the beginning of the session. Whereas classmates can often provide valuable assistance in nontechnical courses, that source of help is not available in technical courses, unless the more advanced students are especially patient and unusually gifted at explaining the material. Moreover, many students approach a technical topic with serious misgivings about their ability to cope (for example, "math anxiety," although mathematics is not explicitly involved). These misgivings are likely to be intensified by the wide range of student abilities typical of most technical classes and the individual comparisons these generate. If the consequent anxiety becomes serious, students are likely to tune out of a classroom discussion that seems confusing, to seek enlightenment elsewhere (often by long, ritualistic reading of unassigned texts), to absorb very little, and to have a thoroughly unprofitable and painful educational experience. In the encounter described above, for example, the student's single, very precise question has more emotional than cognitive significance. The reassurance offered by a satisfying response is far more important than the enlightenment provided by a correct one. As a result, failure to give an appropriate answer is an invitation to trouble.

Fourth, the student's fixation on a single, very precise question illustrates a common response to technical material and the anxiety it arouses. Students expect that by proceeding step-by-step through a technical argument and by being able to reproduce that argument (if only by rote), they can achieve at least a passing (in the grade sense) mastery of the material. From elementary school on, they have learned to expect unambiguous answers to technical questions; hence they seek solace in precision, whether meaningful or not. They expect also that technical enlightenment both requires and follows from mastery of detail, that there is a logical progression to the subject matter, and that technical content comes in neat, complete packages. They expect to learn finance, econometrics, or decision analysis in a way that they do not expect to learn business policy or human resource management. And although a truly effective technical course may moderate such expectations, they must nevertheless be largely accommodated; otherwise, student dissatisfaction and anxiety may defeat the educational purpose of the course. The expectations that students bring to a technical course may be more important than the reality itself, and must, therefore, be both accommodated and overcome if a technical course is to be truly successful.

One natural response to these difficulties is to present technical material clearly and carefully in a tightly controlled classroom environment. That approach might seem to indicate a lecture format as the most appropriate way to present technical material. But my experience suggests that a discussion approach is more effective, particularly when students must ultimately apply their technical knowledge to practical problems.

Successful discussion teaching forces students to go beyond learning abstract principles and to apply them to the messy world of everyday reality. (My experience has been primarily with the case method, in which students learn through analysis and discussion of specific real-world situations, typically involving a decision that must be made. But any discussion approach that focuses on solving problems would also be applicable.) These exercises help students appreciate both the value and the limitations of the technical skills they acquire. They learn not to be discouraged by the complexity, lack of information, and the time constraints of actual decision situations, and also to distinguish between the useful central kernel of the theoretical approach and the peripheral details whose significance is swamped by the uncertainties and ambiguities of real life.

A discussion approach also helps students learn to communicate the conclusions of a technical analysis clearly and effectively. In most undergraduate and professional school courses, this means being able to communicate with and persuade a nontechnical audience, a skill of no small value. Technically able people who lack this crucial talent are ineffective in many real-world situations. At best, they waste everyone's time; at worst, they are labeled "geniuses," than which there is no more deadly compliment.

Finally, discussion teaching provides invaluable opportunities for exploring and, with luck, expunging "wrong" modes of reasoning. Technical disciplines often run counter to common ways of thinking that are deeply ingrained. If these common modes of thought are not exposed and corrected, they usually return to create confusion when students try to apply their hard-earned technical knowledge. A lecture course that lays out material in an irresistibly orderly way often masks these pitfalls. For example, a major problem in learning decision analysis (a set of techniques for making systematic decisions in the face of irreducible uncertainties) is the students' instinctive tendency to suppress uncertainty. They are natural Calvinists. Left to themselves, most students first try to "decide" which particular sequence of events represents the divinely ordained "future." Then they plan against this single contingency rather than against the whole range of possibilities (weighted by probability) from which the inherently uncertain future will unfold. In a lecture environment, students never come to terms with this tendency. Even if specifically warned against it every day, they never really understand how much of a problem it is. But, in a case discussion context, students will suppress uncertainty in actual decision situations and see the undesirable consequences of this approach (for example, it ignores the risks associated with a particular course of action when the "certain" outcome does not materialize).

These benefits must, of course, be realized while dealing with the special difficulties of teaching technical material. Right answers must be conveyed and reinforced by the instructor. Unfamiliar modes of reasoning must be taught to students. Perhaps most important, student expectations and anxieties must be accommodated. Imposing a careful structure on the course material is the most important means to those ends. Carefully thought-out and tightly organized course structure will allow right answers to be conveyed whatever the initial direction of a particular student discussion. At the same time, this structure will build into a systematic intellectual process individual lessons and points to be made. Finally, a tightly organized structure will reassure students that the course is heading in a coherent direction and that the necessary material can be mastered according to traditional standards. A loosely structured course, no matter how adventurous and potentially stimulating, will achieve none of these goals.

This structure must be imposed at all levels of a technical discussion course: on the sequence of classes, on individual class sessions, and on exchanges with particular students. Overall, course structure is probably most critical. It is very difficult to overcome poor organization of the sequence of cases with sparklingly well-orchestrated case discussions; similarly, even the most valuable individual exchanges will not compensate for a poorly organized class session. Therefore, in developing a technical case discussion course, the primary need is to give an efficient and reassuring structure to the material: first, on the course as a whole; second, on planning each case discussion; and third, on individual exchanges with students.

This emphasis on structure stands in marked contrast to one view of the discussion approach, which holds that it should be a largely unguided investigation in which students and teachers collaborate to break new ground. In this view, the instructor functions primarily as a referee in allocating the available discussion time, at most nudging the discussion back on track when it runs too far afield. If such a model is ever appropriate, it is certainly not suited to the teaching of technical material. Students' expectations alone dictate that a discussion course in a technical area be highly structured. The challenge is to impose this structure in a way that does not stifle the free flow of ideas. However, where a compromise must be struck between free discussion and structure, the wisest (and safest) course with technical material is to err on the side of structure.

Establishing and Announcing a Course Structure

It should be possible to describe the structure of a technical course in a narrative that takes no more than five minutes to deliver. At its simplest, the narrative may be simply a definition of a class of problems and a taxonomy of techniques for dealing with them. If some topics logically precede others, the rationale for this sequence should be stated. At a minimum, the narrative should list the major blocks of material to be covered and show how they form a unified whole. Such narratives are essential because they represent a core view of a course and are a means of keeping both teacher and student efforts on track.

The first step in developing this kind of narrative is to identify the basic blocks of material to be covered. For a new course, a fundamental review of the potential subject matter may be required; in other situations it may be helpful to look at related courses and textbooks. Each block of material should then be considered in relation to the overriding goal of the course (for example, to solve certain kinds of differential equations, to understand the workings of financial markets), refining or expanding topics as necessary. Then the sequence of blocks of material should be planned; some topics may have to be covered early in order to provide a basis for understanding others. If the narrative that emerges from this process is too complicated, then the entire process should be repeated with an emphasis on simplification. If the narrative is too spare, then some blocks of material might usefully be expanded.

The goal is to create a coherent framework for the course, not to discover a preexisting "correct" structure. Alternative narratives may work equally well. For example, in a finance course whose eight sections were taught by different faculty members, the most successful teachers had quite different narrative views of how the material fit together. One related the various topics covered to the decisions faced by financial managers (estimating cash needs, selling securities, setting dividends, making capital investment decisions, and so on). Another spoke in terms of managing the liability and asset sides of a firm's balance sheet and of coordinating those decisions. The third focused on interactions among a firm's financing decisions, its external environment, and its financial performance. What distinguished the less successful teachers from these three was the lack of a simple organizing narrative; some of the less successful teachers had very complicated visions of how topics fit together, while others had no framework at all. The important thing was not having the *right* simple narrative but having a simple narrative of some kind.

It is extremely important to share the narrative with students. They must be repeatedly reminded of how individual case discussions fit together. At a minimum, the basic narrative should be reiterated as each major block of material is taken up, showing how that particular topic fits into the overall structure.

Setting Limits on Material

In organizing a technical course, it is essential to limit the amount of material—both the level of detail and the number of topics—to be covered. Students who feel they face an enormous amount of impenetrable material are likely to be greatly reassured (and correspondingly better motivated and more successful) if they are told that there are only a few things they really need to know. An experienced instructor taught me this lesson in relation to teaching a ten-class module in econometrics (normally a subject covered in two to three term-long courses). He advised me to announce to the class the five "things" they needed to know about econometrics. Subsequent case discussions could then focus on the application and elucidation of these five things. Moreover, he assured me, it did not matter what five things I chose, as long as they covered most of what I thought was important about econometrics. The important point was that the students could not effectively absorb more than five things in the time available; trying to do more would inevitably mean achieving less.

Setting the Level of the Course

In deciding on the complexity, detail, and amount of material to include in a technical course, the instructor must strike a balance between challenging students at the top of the class and preventing disaster among those at the bottom. When students have a wide range of backgrounds and technical aptitudes, it can be difficult to strike this balance. As a rule, losing students at the low end of the class constitutes the greater danger. Among perhaps forty colleagues I have observed at work, the ones who had trouble with their classes typically aimed their material either consciously or unconsciously at the upper half of the class. In contrast, even teachers who I thought were simplifying the material to a painful extent were well received by, and clearly beneficial to, ambitious, hardworking, and highly intelligent students. The lesson is clear: when in doubt, select a lower level for the material.

If a course is taught at a "difficult" level, so that some of the material is beyond the reach of some of the students, the weaker students must be reassured that they will not be abandoned. It is helpful in this connection to hold regular review sessions (perhaps three a term) summarizing the material for a particular course segment. (The instructor will be more than amply compensated by the reduced demand for office appointments.) To keep review sessions as small as possible, they should not be open to students for whom they are unnecessary (but who choose to use them as either a timesaving device or a security blanket). If possible, they should be conducted by the teacher. One major aim of review sessions is to lay out the simple things that are at the heart of the course, and the credibility of an appropriate authority figure is crucial for this purpose. Finally, review sessions should not exceed the limit of a student's ability to concentrate: about two hours.

Establishing the Party Line

Because technical material involves nonintuitive and unfamiliar kinds of reasoning, students cannot be expected initially to distinguish "right" from "wrong" arguments. Ideally, the value and nature of a proper analysis should emerge organically from a carefully orchestrated case discussion, while the flaws in mistaken approaches are pitilessly revealed. In practice, however, students may easily miss these lessons. Too often, after a class in which the arguments of one student were—in my view— irredeemably destroyed by those of another student, I have been asked by other participants who was "right." With technical material many students have a capacity for belief in false gods equal to that of the most primitive cargo cultists. Accordingly, the instructor must be prepared to establish a party line by announcing, usually in a closing summary, which arguments are right and which are wrong. For these occasions it helps to have a mental list of major true and false points for each segment of the course (for example, finance students must not think they can outguess the market as a whole in predicting future interest rates).

It is also important to indicate what is important and what is trivial or peripheral. It is not realistic to expect students, especially those with relatively weak technical backgrounds, to make such judgments for themselves. Perplexed by collateral reading, a textbook, or comments made by "expert" members of the class, students often ask questions about difficult points that are not central to the basic thrust of the course. In this situation, a party line on relevance should be laid down publicly and unambiguously.

Using Texts and Handouts

Particularly in discussion teaching, there are dangers in assigning too much background reading. If students rely heavily on written sources, they may put less time into analyzing case material assigned for specific classes, and the quality of case discussions may deteriorate. At worst, students will be learning largely from the prepared theoretical materials rather than realizing the benefits of the case discussion approach. Even in a lecture context, providing too much background material may be dysfunctional. Once when teaching economics, for example, I acted on the democratic principle that no one should have to come to a nine A.M. class and handed out detailed lecture notes during part of the term. In reading examination papers, I was surprised to find that the students almost uniformly performed less well on the topics for which notes were available. Class attendance had not fallen off when I began to provide notes, but I suspect that attention had.

It is not a good idea to organize a case discussion entirely around an assigned textbook. If the text includes material you have decided to ignore (and it almost always will), it will generate endless unwelcome questions and significant confusion and anxiety as students begin to suspect there are gaps in the education you are offering in class.

Success in structuring a discussion course depends as much on experience as anything else. A course outline that looks good on paper may prove ineffective in an actual classroom; changing perspectives may establish the importance of material once deemed irrelevant. Instructors should expect to make mistakes in this area—and then to learn from their experience.

Structuring Individual Case Discussions

As with the course itself, each case discussion should be planned around a simple organizing structure. It is not necessary to construct a detailed script (with student stooges filling in the appropriate blanks) or even to decide on the order in which issues will be discussed. Planning may involve no more than assigning groups of students different advocacy positions and preparing questions to bring out the main points at issue.

Unfocused discussions are particularly harmful in technical courses, when students feel, quite rightly, that there is a hard core of material that must be learned. When case discussions go nowhere, students become uneasy and anxious, since they fear that this material is escaping them. Anxiety impairs their ability to learn and contribute to the discussion, reduces the quality of discussion further, and, in a vicious cycle, generates still more anxiety.

The Importance of Closure and Final Summaries

When technical material is being taught in a discussion framework, it is important to reach some kind of closure in each class. At the end of the session, the instructor should briefly summarize the central points raised in the discussion. If students have discussed a case designed to illustrate a particular method of analysis or technique, this should be pointed out and explained. The summary, which should take no more than five minutes, can be prepared in advance. Other discussion sessions are intentionally more open-ended. In such situations, an extemporaneous summary should emphasize the points that emerged as particularly significant. To raise issues that were missed in the discussion serves little purpose and heightens student anxiety. The summary should clearly distinguish (a) "right" from "wrong" arguments, and (b) central issues from peripheral ones. When a discussion has been poorly focused, possibly leaving students confused, it may be worthwhile to reiterate the central points at the beginning of the next class.

Timing

In planning a particular case discussion, it is essential to give thought to the *pace* at which the discussion should be carried on. Only so many minutes are available, and some cases are inherently "longer" than others, involving more complicated material and more intricate analysis. If a case is a long one, a fast pace must be set. An instructor should be prepared to cut off tangential discussions rapidly and to drive relatively quickly to a conclusion. Rapid and precise questioning will communicate a sense of urgency to students; in the extreme, an instructor may even need to treat as tangents some potentially relevant points in order to reach closure in the time available. With a short case, on the other hand, the instructor may allow discussion to be more wide-ranging and give students substantially more latitude in developing their own thoughts. The overall design of a course should balance "long" and "short" days, since an extended sequence of either type will test the patience of students.

To keep the discussion on track, it is useful to set approximate *benchmarks* for the development of individual segments of the analysis. Technical discussions are particularly susceptible to this kind of control, since the appropriate technical analysis of a case can often be outlined in advance. By attending to these benchmarks, the instructor can recognize when the pace of the discussion should be adjusted. In preparing to discuss a decision theory problem, for example, you might estimate that the first third of the class time should be spent developing an appropriate decision tree; then, if the tree is not complete when the class is halfway through, you had better start moving faster.

With experience, instructors will learn how much material they can expect to cover in the time available. Almost certainly, it will be less than they initially anticipate. (In my first case discussion class, I spent three-quarters of the period covering roughly one-third of the planned material and had to force-march the students through the remainder.) It is usually easy for lecturers to defer to the next class any material they have not covered by the end of the hour. But when each class session addresses a new case, the instructor cannot readily revive the previous day's discussion. Consequently, it is better to include too little material in a discussion than too much.

Blackboard Space

The use of the blackboard space can be critical when extended numerical calculations are an essential part of a case analysis. Nothing is so disconcerting (to both teacher and students) as trying to refer to a previous calculation only to find that it has disappeared in a frenzy of erasure. To ensure that the important numbers stay visible as long as needed (not erased, not hidden behind sliding boards), the instructor needs to think explicitly in advance about where critical calculations will go.

Since many technical case discussions involve exemplary formats for presenting numerical data (for example, pro forma balance sheets, an income statement in finance, decision trees in decision analysis), the board plan may also involve establishing a template into which students' numbers will fit. Then, as the discussion evolves, a neat, readable, and familiarly organized presentation of a case's numerical data will gradually emerge from the uneven flow of student comments. Seeing this happen reassures students and provides a valuable focus for further discussion.

Developing a Numerical Analysis

When a particular numerical analysis is central to a case, that analysis must be reproduced and completed with reasonable accuracy during the case discussion. As a rule, a consensus set of numbers should appear on a classroom board.

Unfortunately, consensus can be hard to reach. Where case "facts" are ambiguous, students make different assumptions. They make more or less trivial arithmetic errors. And even when the basic numbers are the same, students present them in very different formats. Nevertheless, there is usually a degree of common ground (that is, standard formats from previous cases and "natural" assumptions) toward which the discussion should aim. The more familiar a set of numbers, the more easily they will be understood by students.

One way to proceed is to ask one student to demonstrate his calculations. If the numbers are broadly correct, he can be asked to amend them in response to objections or corrections by other students. If the numbers are clearly idiosyncratic, in either nature or presentation, then another student must be chosen, and—given the usual tight limits on the time available—quickly.

Alternatively, the instructor may ask individual students to go through exemplary calculations and then reveal to them a set of "official" numbers. This approach saves time and is therefore unavoidable for long complicated calculations. Beside reducing the need for real-time mental arithmetic, it keeps the teacher from being confused by the numbers later in the discussion. And the "correct" numbers are reassuring to students. Yet, overreliance on "official" numbers has serious disadvantages. Students do not get to see how easily alternative assumptions can be factored in, once the basic thrust of the analysis has been understood. Querulous students may find fault with and nitpick at official definitions, whereas they would be more likely to accept variations that had been voted or decided on in a democratic way. If the majority of students made deviant assumptions, they may find it difficult to follow the official numbers. Most important, the use of official numbers encourages students to rely on the teacher rather than themselves, diminishing the value of a case discussion approach. In practice, therefore, a balance should be struck between using official and student-generated numbers. Time constraints and the need for closure should be the determinants.

Whatever course is chosen, a teacher has to be familiar with the basic numbers involved. There is no faster way to lose a class than to be confused and incoherent in deriving the numbers in a case. (If a teacher is weak in this area, it is probably safer to rely on the students.) Conversely, having the necessary numbers at one's immediate command provides reassurance to students quite out of proportion to the pedagogical value of the numbers themselves.

How can one master the numbers? It is probably unnecessary (and impossible) to precalculate and memorize all the necessary numbers (both right and wrong). Better to establish a clear template into which individual calculations can fit. (In case of disaster, an instructor can always cut off a discussion in which the numbers seem to be heading God-knows-where.) In addition, it is valuable to remember certain bottom-line numbers (as a corrective to student errors, an anchor in a storm of confusion, and a basis for further calculation and discussion) and orders of magnitude (for example, profits should be in millions, shipments in thousands). Indeed, these relatively few critical numbers should be recorded in discussion notes lest memory fail.

It is also helpful to remember important wrong numbers—those that arise when common mistakes are made. For example, in projecting cash flow, depreciation must be subtracted from "accounting costs" to arrive at "cash flow costs." Suppose that a failure to subtract depreciation leads a student to calculate cash flow costs as $3.9 million (when they are really lower). Remembering that number will immediately alert a teacher to what is going on when a student announces that cash flow costs are $3.9 million. Responding quickly with a question about the treatment of depreciation saves a good deal of time and builds credibility with the class. How can an instructor identify important wrong numbers? Experience and the advice of colleagues will be useful guides—as will the mistakes you make yourself in going over the material.

Beyond the considerations outlined above, the structure appropriate for a particular case discussion will depend largely on the nature of the students and the material. Once again, experience will provide valuable guidance. In some situations, the subject itself provides a structure. For example, a discussion in decision analysis might be organized around the decision tree, which identifies the appropriate sequence of decisions and uncertain events. In finance, balance sheet and income statement projections often serve the same function.

Especially when new material is being introduced to relatively inexperienced students, the underlying framework of a discussion may be a detailed script that allows only brief (but frequent) student responses. At the other extreme, the structure may consist of first letting one side of a question be argued (usually whichever side is favored by most students), then trying to elicit a strong counterargument, and finally attempting to reach a synthesis. In general, the more latitude allowed students (consistent with obtaining closure and maintaining a clear direction in the discussion), the more fully the benefits of a case discussion approach will be realized. With technical material, however, it is better to have too much structure than too little.

One of my colleagues unwittingly but vividly illustrated the difference in this respect between technical and nontechnical material when he switched from teaching managerial economics (a highly technical subject) to business policy. His own style changed not at all: he ran a highly controlled and structured class in both courses. His business policy students rebelled, complaining that he stifled discussion and expected them to act like trained seals, producing prescribed responses on command. His managerial economics students regarded him as the very model of what a case discussion teacher should be.

Managing a Technical Case Discussion

A variety of techniques are useful in managing a technical case discussion that allows students as much freedom as possible without losing sight of the basic structure of the class or failing to obtain closure. In no particular order, I offer these suggestions.

1. *Try to limit students to relatively short contributions, each of which makes a single major point.*

In technical courses, students usually have difficulty following a classmate's long, complicated contribution unless it is unusually cogent and well organized. Such statements often contain a number of points, which may be individually interesting and worthwhile but, taken as a lump, are difficult to follow and invite diffusion of the subsequent discussion. As the discussion loses focus, its value as a vehicle for conveying and understanding technical material deteriorates.

2. *If a student makes a comment that contains multiple points leading in different directions, rephrase the contribution to emphasize one of those points (or, more broadly, one direction) before asking the class for responses.*

A student may be allowed to open the discussion with a relatively long and free-form statement of what he or she regards as the main points in the case. The instructor can then set an appropriate direction by summarizing one particular set of points made and asking for responses to that issue.

3. *Short internal summaries are a useful device for focusing a discussion and redirecting it toward a selected issue.*

The more a teacher talks, the more passive students become, so interim summaries should be brief: not more than two minutes long. Also, since such a summary tends to stop the existing discussion in its tracks, it should be followed by a question designed to restart the class in an appropriate direction. When an active discussion is following a useful direction, there is no need to interject summaries. They should be used to redirect a discussion that is going no place or to refocus the class following a series of apparently unrelated comments. Fortunately for the latter purpose, the summary need not be very closely related to what has gone before (particularly if the immediately prior comments are especially unintelligible).

Suppose, for example, that Student A has made a completely impenetrable remark. Not knowing what was meant and dreading to ask for clarification (since Student A, while sometimes a valuable contributor, can, on his day, cast a dense fog over the entire class), you simply call on Student B. Student B responds in a similarly opaque way. In quiet desperation, you call on Student C. Student C answers in a language that you strongly suspect is neither her nor your native tongue. This is the time to say, "Let me summarize this discussion . . . ," followed by a summary of your own and a preformulated question to the class.

Finally, internal summaries are useful as a means of conveying the party line and/or identifying the official significance of a controversy that arises during discussion.

4. *Tangential points should be treated carefully and, for the most part, suppressed.*

Tangents come in several varieties. The worst is the *highly technical point* or *question* raised by one of the class "experts." At best, these contributions raise peripheral issues that waste valuable time. At worst (and most commonly), they create confusion and anxiety. If the point is followed up, it becomes difficult to convince other students that such points are truly unnecessary. The polite way to deal with these tangents is to offer to discuss them outside a class. But, if ever manhandling students is permissible, it is here. Squelching out-of-place "expert" comments not only bolsters less able students, but benefits the "experts" themselves. It is far better that they learn the cost of their behavior (which is usually a highly dysfunctional form of showing off, since they could always have raised the same points privately) in the classroom than in the harsher world outside.

A second kind of tangent that should be rapidly suppressed is the *solipsistic interjection*. Typically emerging after a full discussion of common errors in developing a set of numbers, this comment begins, "But my numbers are different. . . ." Such points should be referred to an outside-class meeting.

A third common tangent is the *point out of order*, which comes in two varieties. The first is an important point that is irrelevant to matters currently under consideration. Such contributions should be acknowledged (perhaps recorded on a side blackboard) and deferred, with the observation that they are irrelevant. At an appropriate later time, these points can be recalled, preferably by returning to the students who originally raised them. The second kind of point out of order is one that is not likely to figure significantly in the case discussion. It should be acknowledged (and perhaps recorded), but then ignored.

A variant of the insignificant point out of order is the *stupidity bomb*: a student statement, often made with considerable flourish, that makes no sense at all. The best response is to mutter something unintelligible in a friendly tone of voice and move on rapidly.

Two final types of tangents can serve useful functions in discussion if they are properly controlled. The first is a *repetition* of a point already fully discussed. In most cases these repetitions should be acknowledged and passed by. However, repetition plays an important role in technical teaching. Students do not pay attention 100 percent of the time. Even when they do, they often initially miss the import of an argument. Repetition helps to ensure that important material does not disappear into either of these gaps. Thus, if time is available, allowing students to elaborate on a point already made may be a useful way of reinforcing material. For example, shortly after I began discussion teaching, I watched in surprise as a colleague allowed three students within twenty minutes to bring up the same point and develop it in some detail. A highly effective teacher, my colleague was adept at passing over unwanted remarks, so it was clear that none of the repetition was inadvertent.

Also potentially worthy of pursuit is the tangent that embodies a *common mode of "wrong thinking."* Indeed, the opportunity to pursue such mistakes is a significant advantage of the case discussion approach. The key to success is to be prepared for the opportunity, to understand how to lead the student into an obviously indefensible position, and to have a simple example (or range of examples) to reinforce the wrongness of the point being made. Under these conditions, the discussion that results will be carefully controlled, efficient in its use of time, and educationally profitable.

Highly trained teachers with a natural affinity for their subject may not find it easy to identify common modes of wrong reasoning. Students' mistakes may simply seem idiotic and unnatural. It helps to remember your own and your fellow students' wrong turnings in first learning the material in question. Alternatively, seek the advice of experienced colleagues. Effective teachers almost invariably have identified common ways students go wrong and may have developed effective methods of dealing with the problem. Your own experience will provide further clues. Once you have encountered a particular kind of "wrong reasoning" twice, it is well to be ready for it at least once more.

5. *Close questioning of a single student is an effective way to elucidate a method of approach or calculation.*

This procedure has several advantages. First, the instructor can select students who have roughly the right numbers or the right approach, so that their explanations are unlikely to lead down a blind alley. Second, close questioning slows down the class and allows the instructor to bring out the technical reasoning involved in as much detail as seems appropriate (for example, by asking a student *why* he multiplied certain quantities to produce a result). Third, close questioning of a single student focuses the discussion tightly so that rapid progress is made—an important consideration when time is at a premium. Fourth, concentrating attention on an individual student heightens the interest of the class, if only because there is a hint of potential blood in the water. Therefore, students subjected to this treatment should not be ones who tend to freeze or become inarticulate under pressure.

6. *Questions from students should almost always be referred first to other students.*

Requiring students to talk to one another provides technically well-trained students with an opportunity for developing their expository skills. Moreover, once the instructor begins to answer questions, he or she will be rapidly inundated with other questions, and discussion will come to a slow, wheezing stop. Students will then begin to rely on the teacher rather than themselves, and preparation and future discussion will suffer. Forcing students to answer each other's questions reinforces the lesson that they are responsible for their education—a useful lesson to learn, since in life-after-school the instructor will not be available to answer their questions. However, this rule ought not to be inflexible. In technical subjects, there is usually an enormous communications gulf between more and less able students. Technically gifted students are often not very good at explaining material or answering questions posed by their less well-prepared peers. Thus, if no clear answer to a question has emerged from the class itself, after two attempts (aided if necessary by intervention to elicit fuller explanation), you may answer it yourself, being careful to preface your explanation appropriately: "So what you [referring to the student experts] are saying is . . ." This takes time. A question that is not of wide interest may be better answered after class.

7. *Try to pose tightly focused, unambiguous questions in directing the discussion.*

Open-ended questions, a valuable tool in nontechnical subjects, also have a place in technical discussions, but that place ought to be carefully planned. Ambiguous or open-ended questions often generate tangential responses, which may then have to be suppressed, wasting time and possibly disconcerting the students involved. Such questions should be reserved for occasions when enough time is available for a relatively open, free-form discussion.

Suppose the instructor asks, "Is Company A's policy of preemptive plant building wise?" That is not a question susceptible to quick resolution, nor can the answer of a particular student be easily predicted. A more focused discussion can be produced by asking whether Company A's estimates of the likely future profits from this strategy are realistic.

The instructor may narrow the discussion further by requiring that any responding student examine the particular assumption concerning profitability that he or she believes is most important to Company A's projection (or to Student B's criticism of those projections).

8. *The weight of critical response and pressure should be directly related to a student's confidence and command of the material.*

This universal principle of case discussion management should be observed with particular care when dealing with technical material, since student anxiety and lack of confidence are especially serious problems. A student exposed to severe criticism in a discussion of a nontechnical subject like organizational behavior is protected to some extent by the notions that (a) many issues in organizational behavior are subject to honest differences of opinion (even among experts), and (b) everyone knows *something* (and often far more than just something) about organizational management. In a subject like decision analysis, students have no such reassurances. Indeed, many are conditioned early to feel that they have little aptitude for technical material; a critical response from their teacher may confirm them in this view. A lack of confidence will in turn impair a student's ability to master the material and, more important, will minimize any chance of its being used by that student outside the classroom. Moreover, attacking weak students will rapidly silence most of the class, leading to a quick deterioration in the quality of discussion.

For these reasons, the basic rule in dealing with students who are neither self-confident nor in command of the material should be that *no comment is a bad comment.* Irrelevant or repetitive comments can be accommodated with a nod and a scribble on a side board. Comments that are ambiguous and probably incorrect should be interpreted and rephrased in the best possible light before responses are invited (the ambiguity of case facts provides valuable running room here, since almost any comment is right in certain circumstances). Even comments that are flat-out wrong should be either ignored (with an appropriately grateful but unintelligible utterance) or followed up as gently as possible to maximize the overall educational value of the exchange. It is important not to appear patronizing in doing this—a possibility to which students are usually extremely sensitive.

Students at the upper end of the scale can and should be treated less gently. Such treatment challenges them, helps them to learn to respond on their feet before large groups, and may teach those students who are prone to parade their abilities aggressively some of the dangers of becoming self-proclaimed experts. It is also useful for the rest of the class to see that these experts can be closely questioned and are not always right.

These rules apply as well to grading policies. Students are apt to interpret poor grades in technical courses as overly authoritative measures of their attainments. Thus, although manifest incompetence should always be properly rewarded, I believe generosity at the lower end of the grade scale is appropriate. At the upper end of the scale, high standards seem equally appropriate. Therefore, a rigid quota system that treats the upper and lower ends of a grading scale in the same way is out of place in a technical course.

One final point should be made about managing a technical case discussion. As a teacher becomes more experienced both with the material and with a particular class, increasingly less rigid control is typically needed to lead a well-directed discussion to a satisfactory conclusion. Therefore, particular devices in this list can be used less frequently and the maintenance of tight control can be abandoned more often. The result will generally be a freer and more valuable discussion. However, in the first days of class, or for an inexperienced teacher, this is usually not a wise course of action.

Conclusion

Student expectations are an important constraint on the way technical material is taught and presented—as important as the nature of the material itself. For example, as noted at the outset, when students bring very precise but misguided questions to office hours, an instructor should probably not waste energy pointing out their fundamental irrelevance. Unless time and context allow for a full explanation of the point at issue, in a form that the now-disoriented student can understand, any response other than answering the question on its own terms intensifies the student's anxiety and causes endless trouble. Given students' diversity, inexperience, and discomfort in dealing with technical material, a refusal to accommodate their strongly held expectations involves swimming up a very rapid stream indeed.

To accommodate these expectations within a discussion teaching approach, structure and careful class control are essential. When the necessary groundwork has been laid in a well-planned sequence of classes, a student's single, very precise question can be answered within a structure that firmly and correctly establishes its implications, meaning, and importance. This point will never be reached, however, unless the instructor has carefully structured the sequence of cases, the discussions in individual class sessions, and individual exchanges with students.

12

"To See Ourselves as Others See Us": The Rewards of Classroom Observation

JAMES AUSTIN WITH ANN SWEET AND CATHERINE OVERHOLT

> Oh wad some Pow'r the giftie gie us
> To see oursels as others see us!
> —Robert Burns, "To a Louse"

A DEEP PARADOX of discussion teaching is the isolation of instructors, even in the most populous classrooms. We cannot physically perceive the class from the students' point of view, and the disparity between their grasp of the material and ours creates a metaphorical gap between us. In addition, the intense concentration of simultaneously managing the discussion flow, monitoring the students' progress through the material, and planning the remainder of the session creates a sort of tunnel vision.

Prolonged isolation can produce lethargy and the risk of professional stagnation, as I can attest from personal experience. In fact, a sense of lethargy led to my odyssey in observation. After fifteen years of apparently successful discussion teaching, I was disturbingly complacent. Then a colleague, Chris, whose teaching I greatly admired, invited me to co-teach a faculty seminar on discussion leadership. I accepted, with some trepidation, and chose to experience the seminar as a student first. The course included twelve case discussions, each focused on an incident that posed a challenge to a teacher. In class, my mind operated continually on three levels: I analyzed the problem facing the protagonist in the case, engaged in the discussion, and—spurred by the stark knowledge that I would sit in his chair the next year—carefully observed Chris leading the discussion.

His teaching techniques, different from my own in many respects, opened invigorating new possibilities for me. Observation began to seem a wellspring of vitality, and I wondered what further insights might emerge from *being* observed. The hunch that observing and being observed could produce wonderful opportunities for new learning was an important impetus to my odyssey. My co-teaching experience the following year confirmed this hunch: directly after the first class, I met with Chris, who led the first discussion, and another colleague, Ann, whom he had asked to observe the session. Ann's observation notes—a transcript interspersed with insightful remarks and process queries—helped Chris "see" student demeanor he hadn't had time to notice during class, "hear" tones that had slipped by in the intensity of his concentration, and "feel" the hesitation in some comments and the acerbity in others. Her notes catalyzed a series of self-critical comments from the discussion leader. I had found the class's discussion stimulating, with high involvement and wide participation. Chris's eagerness to learn reminded me that teachers, however good, can always improve, so long as we never stop being students.

We continued these "class after class" meetings throughout the seminar—each of us profiting from two other people's perceptions and analyses of what had happened in the discussion. After the seminar, we agreed that these sessions had nourished us with a commodity rare in teaching: feedback. How, we wondered, might one harness the power of classroom observation to help other teachers develop?

Answering this question became the goal of a research project in which Ann and another seminar participant, Catherine, joined me. We interviewed colleagues, held classroom observations and discussions, and ran workshops to elaborate on observation methods and techniques. The project persuaded us that it is possible to practice straightforward, useful techniques of observation and to describe them cogently for other teachers. What follows is an experiential collage of insights from our work.

Benefits of Observation

Observation can be a mutual gift between the observer and the observed. Both stand to gain self-awareness, perspective, an introduction to new teaching techniques, and fresh enthusiasm for their craft. The instructors with whom we worked noted many practical rewards. When one experienced case method instructor encountered difficulties in teaching an executive education program for the first time, he invited a colleague to observe a few sessions. The colleague identified five teaching practices that didn't suit that group of older students. With this feedback, the teacher made adjustments and became the teaching star of the program.

A teacher in his first year, who acknowledged a tendency to "zing" individuals with sharp remarks when their logical analyses were weak, initially felt that his rapport with the class made sarcasm a useful tool to challenge students and enliven discussion. Being observed opened his eyes. He reported, "My department head observed some classes and pointed out that some students appeared hurt by my remarks, and my insensitivity to the hurt might be undermining my credibility with the rest of the class." Together, the teacher and his department head identified ways to push for rigor without risking personal offense.

Another case method teacher, pleased with his open-ended discussions, prided himself on being nondirective. A colleague who observed his class, however, pointed out that he consistently went on "fishing expeditions" (asked questions in a very controlling way) to make transitions from one topic to another. The case method teacher reported, "I have now learned that I can stop the discussion when important issues have been aired and say that it's time to turn our attention to another topic. In the end, that's much less directive."

Still another discussion leader wished for a "fog button" on every student's desk. She knew that, while some students were on top of the complicated material, others were tuning out in confusion masked by expressions of keen interest when she looked at them. She asked a fellow teacher to sit in and "watch the action away from the ball" to tell her which students were fading out, and to what extent, when she focused her attention on the speaker. Her observer provided a fuller reading of the situation than she could possibly have made unassisted, and suggested some ways to gauge the fog level.

These instructors sought help with problems, but observation is more than a diagnostic tool for probing dysfunctional classroom practices. Observers can also help good teachers become even better and can reap enormous benefits from watching experts ply their craft. One much-admired teacher noted, "When I was a new teacher, observing other classes was the most important thing I did to improve my own teaching." Thoughtfully watching another teacher's behavior and its effects can prompt reflection on one's own behavior and reveal new options and possibilities. One instructor mentioned seeing a teacher accomplish things he wouldn't have believed possible. Another commented, "I had taught that material three times and it had never really worked, but the way Professor X used the blackboard made all the difference in sparking the discussion."

Given all these benefits, one wonders why observation is so seldom attempted. To some, the practice suggests evaluation, which carries the threat of exposure to painful criticism. This threat is particularly intense with discussion teaching because of the teacher's comprehensive involvement in the interactive learning process. Decoupling the process from evaluation can alleviate this threat, but even when the goal is only to provide feedback for self-improvement, the teacher under observation needs a positive attitude toward professional development.

It must be acknowledged that many people who have experimented with observation have been disappointed. One new instructor commented, "I received generalities and didn't know what to do differently to address them." Another added, "Observation is only as good as the observer's ability to record data and discuss it afterward." In short, our profession has lacked an effective set of observational techniques, tools, and perhaps even clear terminology to describe the process. Useful observation requires careful thought about objectives and methodology. And no one will deny that it takes time, although its benefits can be powerful. The process we will summarize maximizes efficiency and effectiveness by emphasizing sharp focus, the use of straightforward recording techniques, and tight coordination and cooperation between the teacher and observer.

The Three-Part Observation Process

A successful observation process involves three stages: before, during, and after class. Each has its unique set of choices and considerations.

Before Class

The first critical decision facing the teacher to be observed is: Who shall do it? Should the observer be someone of similar, greater, or less experience than the instructor? Some teachers opt for a buddy system, in which two teachers of comparable experience and rank visit each other's classes and share notes afterward. Working with an equal may be less intimidating than working with a senior faculty person, and peers can readily identify with one another's concerns. One teacher mentioned, "I find that if I just invite a junior colleague to sit and watch me and give me some feedback, it is not threatening. But if I have senior faculty members sitting there watching, evaluating as well as giving feedback, I am very worried about it."

More experienced teachers can, however, provide a valuable resource: experience. They can spot aspects of teaching that younger colleagues might miss. When selecting a senior colleague as an observer, it may be useful to cast the process as a mentoring experience. Decoupling observation from evaluation can make the experience less threatening, and accomplished, experienced teachers can reassure as well as threaten. The teacher might also consider selecting a respected senior colleague from a different academic field. Such a colleague can concentrate more on the teaching process than on the content of the discussion.

A teacher in his third year commented, "Everyone has an idiosyncratic approach to teaching. Some shy and retiring people do fabulously well, and so do some aggressive people who run from one end of the classroom to the other. And all in between. You have to get the right person who is able to extract some common element to success, whether it is trust or the kinds of questions you ask. But the observer should never say, 'I teach well, so therefore you have to teach like me.' " This instructor added, "The most useful observers have been those who comment on the way the class responds to the things I do."

With training in targeted observation, otherwise inexperienced observers can become valuable resources. In our group, one experiment that succeeded (not all of them did!) involved inviting an undergraduate working as a course assistant in a graduate school of business administration to observe a section of the course. Before observing, the assistant received extensive training in diagnostic skills from the professor who headed the course. Then, by observing him lead several discussions in his section, she became familiar enough with the teaching process to make helpful observations to other instructors in this large, multisection course. To make her observation less threatening, she provided feedback only to the instructor she had observed, reporting to the course head only if she had observed one of his classes. In effect, the course assistant developed into a very useful extra set of eyes and ears for the instructors.

Some teachers ask their students to observe occasionally. One new teacher solicited written observation comments from his students halfway through the course. "They pointed out aspects of my teaching behavior that I was totally unaware of," he noted. His new awareness let him adjust his behavior and have a very successful first teaching experience. Another colleague met with a small volunteer group of his students every few weeks to discuss their perceptions of how the class was going. This practice prevented unpleasant surprises at the end of a course.

Whoever is chosen to observe should next meet with the teacher to hold a "class before class" to define a clear focus for observation. Without this step, the observation may lose a great deal of power.

The particular aspects on which the observer might concentrate are almost limitless. The instructor may wish to learn how his or her gestures or facial expressions affect the class. Or the issue might be calling patterns: Does the instructor favor one part of the room (or type of student) and overlook others? Or the focus might be upon intellectual rigor: Are there moments when students seem to wriggle off the hook too easily? Does discussion tend to become diffuse? If so, what is the instructor doing when this happens? In our project, one teacher felt difficulty in making transitions from one topic to another. Another had trouble starting discussions and achieving closure. A third wanted to improve his use of the blackboard. But the teacher need not point to areas of discomfort; the observation could focus on polishing techniques rather than troubleshooting. Without exception, the instructors and observers who participated in our project considered their brief before-class agenda setting to have been time well spent.

During Class

A complex process, in-class observation rests on simple questions—when, how, and what to observe. One way to answer the "when" question is: frequently. A well-focused, single-visit "snapshot" can provide salutary perspective, but two or three observations are even better: then patterns can emerge and adjustment efforts can be made. In general, observers should avoid both the initial classes of a course, when the student-teacher "learning contract" is forming (unless that process is on the observation agenda), and the very latest sessions, when little time remains for corrective action.

On the day of observation, the "when" question can best be answered: early. The observer who arrives before class can get the feel of the environment, watch the students' interactions as they arrive and take their seats, and observe the instructor's setup process. If possible, the observer should find an unobtrusive position in which to sit. One instructor cautioned, "The more visible the observer, the greater the temptation to teach to his or her expectations."

Selecting a method—the "how" of observation—offers a rich field of choices, but four basic techniques stand out: semitranscription, taping (audio or video), "discussion-mapping" and checklists, and what one experienced teacher called "observation by exception." These techniques may be used singly or in combinations, to meet the needs of a given observation.

Semitranscription provides rich data for observer and instructor to analyze. In this method, the observer makes rapid notes that capture various aspects of the process at key moments—how things look, sound, and even feel at specific points in the discussion. The observer watches for moments when the particular issues upon which he or she is focusing come to the fore, and then makes comprehensive, even verbatim, notes of what the instructor says and does, and how the students seem to be responding. Semitranscription notes can also address the pace and emotional atmosphere, and add the observer's running comments. Did the class lose energy here? Did the class recoup? Was this a turning point? Did a new topic emerge? Is the observer wondering about a road not taken? Semitranscription is useful when the objective is to provide an information base for general reflection on the session, and it can prompt recall of events whose importance emerges only after the fact.

Audiotape recordings can catch moments of interchange for the teacher's private self-analysis, and videotapes can augment such records by capturing body language. One instructor has a collection of about a hundred cassette tapes of his discussions, accumulated in just two years of case method teaching. He considers these tapes invaluable, because "you need to tape yourself and listen to what you say, what clues the [students] are giving you that you have missed, whether you talk too much, whether you are really doing what you are trying to do." This instructor has probed his observation data, playing the roles of both performer and observer. Ideally, however, he would like to have others listen with him and raise questions or make comments from their own viewpoints.

Audiotape is helpful to capture tone and inflection. For a teacher concerned about a particularly complex or new teaching plan, the tape would provide a necessary level of detail. Videotape can provide an objective record of the instructor's physical actions—an obviously important tool for working on nonverbal communication skills, but its use is technically more difficult than audiotape.

Both taping formats or in-class observation can provide raw material for "discussion-mapping," in which one keeps track of the type, frequency, and timing of key aspects of the discussion such as the instructor's questions and responses. These can be elaborated into quantitatively based discussion profiles. In some cases, observers draw actual maps or seating plans to note instructors' calling patterns and other aspects of classroom dynamics such as student-to-instructor versus student-to-student interchanges. In other cases, observers note specific kinds of occurrences—awkward transitions, for example, or instructor interruptions of students' comments. Whether based on tapes or primary experience in the classroom, discussion maps and profiles can document classroom patterns with great precision. They are very helpful in revealing unconscious patterns in the use of teaching techniques. One new instructor commented, "Discussion teaching now doesn't seem like such a mystery. I think I can actually learn how to do it because my colleagues and I can watch each other and provide feedback."

In "observation by exception" the observer waits for teaching challenges (exceptional moments) to arise, and notes how the instructor handles them, for better or worse. Perhaps someone throws a smoothly progressing discussion off track with a comment. What exactly is the comment? How do students react? How does the instructor respond? What happens next? In observation by exception, one experienced teacher noted, the observer attempts to "put himself in the teacher's shoes and look for options that might have been chosen." The rationale is that we can learn more from our most difficult moments than from run-of-the-mill experiences. Observation by exception is appropriate for general troubleshooting, where no specific area is designated for observation.

The most successful observation techniques we tested in our project do not try to cover everything that goes on in the classroom. Targeted observations, designed by mutual agreement between the observer and teacher, ensure relevancy of feedback, increase the motivation and receptiveness of the teacher being observed, and create an agenda for the observer and teacher during feedback sessions. As one teacher put it, "It is essential that instructors and observers have the same scorecard." The agenda for each observation should guide the observer's choice of techniques.

What to Observe. Two elements—instructor and students—constitute the classroom dynamic, just as physical elements constitute matter. The observer's task is to employ a sort of check-and-balance system in assessing each element's part in the whole. To ensure against missing the forest for the trees, the observer might first "take the temperature" of the class by looking at its gestalt, or general context. Do things in general seem to be going well? Do the students appear interested? Do they relate well to the instructor? Are they clearly learning things that matter to them? Are they paying attention to each other as well as to the instructor? If these elements are in place, fumbles and awkward moments are less significant.

One way to get a feel for the gestalt is to observe how the class starts and ends. Are the students early or late? Do they enter with energy or reluctance? Do they engage one another in lively dialogue? Do they continue the discussion after class, gather around the teacher, or merely disperse? The observer may also focus on the apparent level of preparation and interest. No one can actually see feelings, but observable cues can indicate the level of rapport in the classroom. Many instructors have found it useful to receive an outsider's assessment of intangibles such as respect, warmth, sensitivity, formality, tension, antagonism, and cooperation, as well as their causes and consequences for the learning process.

Observing Instructional Techniques: Questioning. Productive discussions depend on asking the right people the right questions at the right times. Because they are such powerful instructional tools, questions are often the central focus of good feedback. The observer should note the kinds of questions being asked and their apparent effects on the discussion process.

In the typology of questions with which we and our colleagues worked, information-seeking questions—the "who, what, when, where" variety—establish a common information base for subsequent analysis, indicate the level of students' preparation of the assigned reading material, highlight the importance of certain categories of information, and lower the barriers to student participation. Useful as they are, such questions can become dysfunctional at times. One teacher was frustrated by a discussion that seemed to drag and students who appeared bored. An observer noted that for the first forty minutes of class the instructor had asked mostly information-seeking questions. Together, the teacher and observer concluded that the students had disengaged their attention because these questions had elicited contributions that added little value or intellectual discovery to what the students had already gotten from preparing the material. The observer's notes supported this insight by showing that the students' attentiveness had picked up during the last part of the class, when the instructor's questions became more analytical.

Analytical questions, of the "why" and "how" type, can challenge students to think deeply and look for causes. Another type—action questions—can quicken the pace of discussion. For example, questions such as "What would you do with that worker who was drinking on the job?" will generally focus attention and accelerate the pace as the student states a course of action and others react to that statement. In contrast, an abstract question that asks for generalizations—such as "What lessons about managing the effects of job-induced pressures can we take from this situation?"—often slows the pace of discussion because students need thinking time to address these higher-order issues. By relating the type of question to a resultant lull (or spurt) in the discussion, the observer can help the instructor see what types of questions he or she tends to ask and how these affect the pace of discussion.

An observer might look for clarifying ("Could you elaborate?") questions, which elicit specificity or extend an analysis; evaluative questions, which call for judgments; hypothetical ("What if?") questions, which stretch students' thinking to consider new situations; and predictive ("What will happen?") questions, which force students to extrapolate and assemble reasons for their forecasts. Exclusive reliance on a particular type of question is generally a red flag. Observers who record questioning patterns will increase awareness and understanding of this key tool and strengthen both the teacher's and their own capacities to plan questions for future sessions.

Observing Instructional Techniques: Response. Instructors often greet students' comments with a further question, but other responses are also available to shape the discussion. Although one instructor's class began well, students stopped answering questions and started quizzing the instructor in the middle of the discussion. This puzzled him until his observer's record revealed that he had put a graph on the board and explained it. By assuming the role of information-giver, he had become the class "expert." In response, the students began posing questions and the instructor provided more answers, thereby turning the ostensible discussion process into a lecture for nearly ten minutes. By focusing on how the instructor responded to students' contributions, the observer was able to help explain an otherwise mysterious episode.

Echoing the essence of a student's comment or repeating in abbreviated form can give recognition and encouragement or highlight a point. Some echoing may be desirable for keeping a class on track. Too much is likely to become disruptive and detract from a smooth flow of student-to-student interchanges. One experienced case teacher was surprised when a colleague's observation notes showed that he was echoing or interpreting most students' comments. "I think it was a carryover from teaching in company executive programs where I needed to be more directive," he said, "but I was using up time and disrupting the flow unnecessarily." Interpretation goes further by distilling or rephrasing the student's remark—useful if the comment is long, complex, or confusing. When the observer notes that a class is going awry, a tally of the instructor's particular kinds of intervention may indicate the source of the problem. In instances like this, discussion maps, profiles, and even simple checklists can prove valuable.

Observers can also look for responses that give explicit instructions to the class or a student—directives such as "Let's now discuss . . ." or "Please hold off on that topic until later." Or one might focus on the instructor's summaries, which bring closure or highlight issues or conclusions; or the use of transitions, which tie parts of the discussion together. The tone and volume of the instructor's responses can also affect students' reactions. Do they come across as cold, intimidating, friendly, encouraging, sarcastic, attention-getting, monotonous, perfunctory, or enthusiastic? A new teacher, observing an experienced colleague, was pleasantly surprised to see that "So what?" could be used to elicit deeper analysis from the students. "I had shied away from asking that, because I thought it would be too aggressive and intimidating, but the tone and body posture he used signaled strong encouragement to the students."

Nonverbal responses, which can greatly affect the tone, pace, and mood of discussions, are also readily observable. In one session, the observer recorded just the discussion leader's body language—facial expressions, hand movements, body posture, eye contact. The observer interpreted the message of each nonverbal signal—encouragement, interest, excitement, puzzlement, pleasure, request to stop, request to continue—and was struck by the richness these cues added to the discussion process. In the "class after class," the instructor was intrigued to have this silent, almost instinctive side of the process verbalized and interpreted. Another instructor was surprised to learn that his serious expression tensed his class and that students relaxed visibly when he smiled.

Among the other nonverbal signals that an observer can monitor, movement within the classroom—sitting, standing, walking, leaning— can greatly affect the mood of a class. One instructor was unaware that his pacing back and forth distracted students' attention from the content of his closing remarks. One observer was impressed to watch a teacher increase student-to-student interaction during a discussion by walking to the side of the classroom and sitting in one of the empty student seats for a while.

In general, monitoring frequency and type of responses can often point to why classes are not going well. Does the instructor talk a great deal? The best classes often include a great deal of dialogue among students and relatively little prompting from the instructor. The instructor's use of the blackboard and other visual aids can also influence the pace and quality of the discussion. Observers can note the frequency and intensity of their use, legibility of handwriting, and effect on the class.

Observing Students in the Discussion Process. So far we have focused on observing the instructor, but it is the reactions and behavior of the students that reveal the learning process. In the instructor-class interplay that creates the special dynamic of discussion learning, discussion leaders constantly "read" the verbal and nonverbal actions of their classes. But the instant demands of leading a discussion prevent teachers from capturing and remembering all the student signals. Observers can help them take more accurate readings.

Observers can gather useful information by tracking students' participation patterns. One teacher was surprised to learn that she called on students on the left side of the room three times as frequently as those on the right. This explained the apathy she had noted among those on the right. Another teacher learned that all his students directed their responses to him, not to other students. In his next class he explicitly redirected students' comments to other students. An observer's record of the percentage of students who participate indicates the breadth of student involvement and may pinpoint over- or underparticipators. Classroom observations have revealed, for example, that women students tend to speak less often and more briefly than men, and with different presentational styles. One instructor learned from his observer that he consistently interrupted women students more than men. In his case, observation provided the instructor with an opportunity to develop better techniques to manage student diversity.

An observer can take further readings on the students' learning process by recording their level of attentiveness, interest, excitement, preparedness, listening acuity, depth of analysis, cumulativeness of comments, frequency of discovery, and insights. It is important to remember that dysfunctional behavior of students may result from some past event: for example, the tone set by the instructor on the first day of class, or a blow-up in a previous session. Some poor discussions have no immediately observable antecedents. In such cases, when the instructor appears to be doing all the right things, the observer might simply note the evident disparity between technique and result.

In general, however, if the students appear bored, restless, or confused at some point in the discussion, the observer will probably find links to some behavior that the instructor can control, such as questioning, requesting certain types of analysis, suggesting particular topics, or managing his or her demeanor. Even if the observer cannot establish the causal linkage immediately, it is useful to note the instructor's actions and the discussion topic at that point. Later, the observer and teacher can reflect on that specific portion of the discussion, a process that often sparks very productive introspection by the teacher.

Finally, the observer can focus on the students' grasp of the material, noting the depth of analysis and the technical correctness of the discussion. Some teachers, who desire feedback specifically on these matters, ask observers to concentrate exclusively on substance: the data, concepts, techniques, and analyses covered in a given discussion. In such sessions, the observer may wish to note what questions spur the most thorough comments or probing interchanges.

After Class

If observation during class is the heart of the enterprise, the after-class debriefing is its head. During this part of the process, instructor and observer share information, compare perspectives, and educate one another. The observer should act with sensitivity and respect, and approach the instructor at a level appropriate to his or her teaching experience. Delivering complex, sophisticated suggestions to a new instructor incapable of acting upon them would be as counterproductive as oversimplifying for a thirty-year veteran.

Whatever the instructor's level of experience, information overload is a great danger in the after-class process. Two young discussion teachers learned their lesson when they made a pact to sit in on three or four of one another's classes and then meet for feedback sessions. At their first "class after class," the teacher who had led that day's discussion found her head whirling. Her observer-colleague was telling her more than she could take in. They agreed to focus future observations and feedback on specific areas.

The debriefing should be selective. If a tape has been made, only those portions should be reviewed that are relevant to the specific focus of observation. The review of any quantitative records also should be limited. The observer who has taken notes on what might have happened—but didn't happen—should focus on a few graspable exceptions. One third-year teacher commented, "The after-class session should be a discussion built around the observation data, not a lecture." One experienced observer usually begins by asking the instructor, "What do you think went well?" and then asking the converse, "What didn't go well?" Her perception is that teachers have a reasonable sense of what they do well and not so well, and that the role of the observer is to help the teacher look objectively at those strengths and weaknesses and develop the capacity for self-assessment. Rather than quickly rendering judgments, which can make an instructor defensive and stifle discussion, the observer should, as one professor put it, "let the notes talk." The value of this approach is captured by one observer's comment: "The observer holds up a mirror. It can tell you what you shouldn't tamper with, and what is working well, as well as the most glaring problems that will give you the greatest opportunity for impact if changed."

Instructors were unanimous in requesting specific operational comments. They wanted observers to help them identify particular behaviors, their effects, the reasons for their occurrence, and ways to improve. But the observer's role is more than just technical. An instructor who had come to discussion teaching from a traditional school, where she had been considered a brilliant lecturer, fell into such a depression about the leaden exchanges in her discussion class that she seriously considered leaving teaching. Her department head visited her class several times during her devastating first semester and encouraged her. His optimism gave her hope. When students complained about irrelevance in the course, she started clipping current articles and introducing them into the discussions to stimulate livelier interchanges. And it worked! Her observer had done nothing but counsel hope, but that support sustained the instructor until she found her own way to grow. Emotional and intellectual help are interwoven in the observation process.

Both instructors and observers agree that the postclass session should be held while the discussion is fresh in their minds. As one senior instructor mentioned, "I must debrief with the teacher quickly because the half-life of these impressions is short." At the same time, however, the observer needs a chance to review, organize, and interpret his or her observation notes and to plan for an effective class after class. One professor's goal for this session is to leave "with the instructor feeling that change is both necessary and possible, and that there is a plan." Planning for change and actually changing are the final steps that convert the observation process into professional growth.

The Odyssey Continues

My odyssey in observation began with a discussion after a faculty teaching seminar and flowered into a stimulating research project. Like my colleagues in the project, I feel that I have become a better teacher as well as a better observer—and helped others to do the same. All this because observation lets us "see ourselves as others see us," hear ourselves as others hear us, and even feel something of our effect on others. With observation, every class has the potential to push our knowledge of teaching further. This invigorating voyage of discovery has a destination but no end.

13

Discovering the Semester

LAURA L. NASH

IN THE FORMAL ACADEMY that we call a college or university, the whole art and business of education has long been dominated by one fact: teaching is subjected to a chronological limitation. Course content, classroom location, and student populations regularly change, but the opportunity for formal teaching nearly always remains fixed to a defined unit of time, usually called the semester.

So universal, artificial, and unyielding is this chronological construction of academic reality that we as teachers regularly take the concept of a semester for granted. To some, the semester is nothing more than a time slot: an unremarkable bowl to be filled with lectures and topped by grading duties. To others (perhaps on the receiving end of teaching), it is the time between returns to "the real world."

But the semester is more than a bureaucratic unit of measurement. For us, as for the ancient Greeks, time is a concept closely related to accomplishment, and the semester is one important place-marker for a student's learning experience. For the teacher, it offers a larger forum for fulfilling communication and learning goals than any individual class.

In this essay I would like to explore the learning possibilities that are inherently tied to a semester-long perspective. My comments can be applied in a limited way to lecture courses, but the main focus is on how the fact of the semester can be used as a resource to enhance discussion leadership.

The Architecture of a Semester

Every course has its own architecture, and the shape of the semester provides its basic framework. Some courses resemble a Mayan temple: each class is a separate but identical step up the steep slope of learning, and the semester's end is simply the last step. Both teaching role and learning process are affected by this architecture. Learning is achieved in a serial, uniform fashion while teacher and student stand worlds apart. Like supplicants, the students are supposed to climb steadily in fixed degrees of ascent only to arrive at the truth, which is enshrined in the temple at the top. The instructor is the high priest outside the temple door, supervising the supplicants' journey up the steps and mediating their exposure to the mysteries of the temple. When the student finally reaches the last step, he or she undergoes the initiation rites of final exam and term paper. Students lay their parcels of knowledge at the instructor's feet and depart, only to be replaced by a new set of students the following year, who will make the same ascent via the same kind of classes.

Such a teaching architecture makes the path to knowledge predictable, replicable, and largely under the teacher's control in terms both of content and classroom dynamics. It also implies that when the last step is reached, the knowledge to be gained runs out. Such an approach seems best suited for the acquisition of highly factual content by extremely self-motivated students, but it severely limits the knowledge process of most academic subjects.

In the architecture of a good discussion class, the learning framework is more like the process of raising a New England barn.[1] Everybody participates and contributes to the knowledge process, whatever his or her level of skill. People have to work together to get the job done. They learn from each other. They socialize partly for the fun of it but also to ease cooperation on the job. In such a learning architecture, progress is not readily confined to serial steps of equal proportion such as are represented by lecture classes. Learning can be irregular and is often unpredictable—a function of social interaction as much as of intellectual design.

Such a process undercuts many of the familiar distinctions between student and teacher (such as imparter and receiver of knowledge) and wipes out the premise of uniformity that typically governs the lecture format. *And yet design there is.* Just as barn raisings required an experienced barn master and a fairly standard product design to ensure a workable end product, so too, the discussion course must have a guiding expert and a fine design to fulfill overall academic learning goals. This design, however, must take into account the special dynamics of the building process while conforming with the standard intellectual skills that a given course seeks to represent.

One of the greatest pitfalls of discussion teaching is a failure to channel the fluidity and irregularity of the process within an overall design.

Though the building process has inherent learning value, extensive class participation in itself is not enough. Like the master builder at a barn raising, the instructor has an experienced acquaintance with the craft of his or her particular field, and bears the responsibility for making sure that the group's efforts produce the desired result. A barn must be built. To put it in familiar terms, the discussion leader is responsible for both the process and product of the learning experience. Both aspects should be productive from the individual participants' perspective. Both aspects should be planned for by the instructor.

The fact of the semester gives teachers the opportunity to create a learning design that recognizes the vagaries of this educational process and product. In a discussion format, some classes will inevitably seem to make more progress on the barn than others. If the instructor views learning as a product received in class-long increments, he or she can easily fall prey to severe emotional highs and lows, depending on the discussion of a particular day. This volatility will greatly increase the risk of overcorrecting and overcontrolling either the content or discussion activity of the next class.

Valuable in itself, the social learning process must be given time to develop. A semester-long perspective not only lessens the anxieties associated with the ups and downs of specific classes, it opens up many opportunities for planning a richer and more appropriate course design. A successful building process then paves the way for future barn raisings in other parts of the academic community.

By recognizing the dynamic and varied architecture of the semester, the instructor gains access to a much larger pool of teaching resources than are available to one who views the semester merely as a set of replicable, modular units called classes. Four planning and discussion tools are particularly important for the discussion leader. These are the possibilities for achieving:

1. Variety and stability
2. First-hand expertise at multiple skills
3. Risk and reparation
4. Creation of a learning and learned society

Time, which the great Roman philosopher and poet Seneca once suggested was the revealer of truth (*Veritatem dies aperit*), can also be the teacher's resource for stimulating social interaction, intellectual risk-taking, student independence, the acquisition of multiple skills, and the opportunity for recovery when things go awry.

Resource #1. Variety and Stability

The Mayan temple metaphor contains a profound truth about the nature of learning: progress by replication and repetition, no matter how exquisite the material, eventually trivializes the progressor. All those identical steps up to the temple made the priest and the shrine, not the supplicant, the focal point of the process. Passive submission to the prescribed paths to truth, rather than active self-discovery of it, becomes a limiting mode of learning in both an intellectual and a psychological sense.

The serial lecture course, even when perfectly prepared and delivered, runs the risk of trivializing the student's role in the learning process. Future academic growth may be stunted; indeed, even learning within that class may be subverted. Often, for the first few weeks of class, students read books and articles with zeal; but as the classroom environment becomes totally predictable, they become totally passive about their own engagement in the topic of the day. Readings are strategically abandoned until exam time's panic; meanwhile the professor is left to do all the thinking.

The discussion class is vulnerable to the same effects of monotony if each class design duplicates the last. The lively debate and interplay between participants during a single successful class can be transformed into a mechanical and ultimately aimless technique if repeated in some twenty discrete units over a semester's time. If, however, a discussion class is conceived as a dynamic process over time (like the barn raising), then the instructor can plan for the variety of material and environmental agitations that characterize real life. Such variations may seem risky: they eat up time and potentially overwhelm a scheduled syllabus. But if one plans for variation, social eccentricities, and shared control of the class, a course can be transformed into a unique and dynamic experience. It is a view to the semester that allows one the luxury of making such plans.

Most obvious, perhaps, is the opportunity over a semester's time to introduce a *variety of resource materials*. During class time the use of visually stimulating media, outside speakers with personal expertise in the field, oral reports, or contemporary articles from newspapers and journals invites the student to break through the rigid packages of learning that are so frequently proffered in the standard textbook-lecture approach. But change for its own sake will accomplish little. If variety is allowed to become a gimmicky and manipulative teaching technique, it will be as predictable as any other teaching approach. The point of using the semester for variety is to allow for a more dynamic and self-motivated learning experience. The newspaper article or outside speaker needs to be channeled in such a way as to challenge the students to make a considered response, to think in a new way, to discover for themselves the significance of new facts, and ultimately to be able to share this discovery so as to help others build on what is being learned.

The semester also allows scope for variety in students' preparation for class, through library work, team reports, survey material, and experimentation. When learning materials are presented in precooked pouches, they strengthen the assumption that knowledge will always come in packages off the shelf. If formal education suggests a metaphor for life, it should not be the shopping mall.

Every class presents an enormous choice of resource materials and modes of presentation. Selection is a matter of multiple purposes, which include at the very least finding a match between curiosity, academic rigor, environmental disturbances, and the probable social mood of the class. Say, for example, you want to teach the technical acrobatics of cost accounting. A lecture on the mechanics of determining the cost of producing five different widgets will certainly present the techniques efficiently in terms of teacher time, but will be less likely to engage the students' active participation or help them understand the underlying reasons for cost accounting. There are ways to turn the drudgery of such exercises into active and pleasurable experiences—say, a zany problem about ice cream flavors with a discussion of why one should or should not produce the costliest flavor, followed by a sampling of the same product at the end of class. Which learning process seems more likely to stimulate mastery of the technique and successful application in real life?

Variety of presentation materials is also enhanced by attention to the *variety of moods* that groups adopt as they move through a semester's material. Some classes may deliberately deal with subjects that provoke extremely sensitive and personal feelings, such as Willy Loman's dismissal in *Death of a Salesman* or Martin Luther King's death discussed in a contemporary history class.

And there should always be at least one class that provides the opportunity for psychological victory, that moment when students realize they have mastered the materials and no longer need the teacher's assistance. In a lecture course, such moments are typically reserved for assignments outside the classroom. But if teaching is meant to empower students from an intellectual standpoint, then the victory class provides group reinforcement in this effort, even if little new material is presented that day.

There are other ways in which the discussion leader can encourage group contribution throughout the semester. In taking a first pass at a new concept, I often try to draw on every student's experience. Polling students about their first associations with, say, the concept of trust, not only engages the entire class in active inquiry, but also establishes the variety and richness of such concepts. From this basis the wisdom of a particular philosopher or author can be discussed with greater immediacy and group understanding.

Some of the moods of a discussion class cannot be predicted. A semester allows time to react to the unexpected environmental agitation and take corrective measures. No one can predict what a student who believes his or her religious beliefs or ethnic background has come under attack will say. But one can help set up a productive response to such difficulties by using the semester's time to build group respect and the foundation of trust that will be needed in such crises. One can also be ready for the sudden onset of illness. Every teacher should have an emergency lesson plan, prepared at the semester's outset, that can run on autopilot. The material could be a film, or a special reading, or an interactive problem on paper—anything that has a special command on students' attention and does not require 200 percent of the instructor's energy and participation.

The larger and varied social life of the university beyond the classroom presents its own challenges to course content and discussion mode. There is an *automatic variety provided by the social environment* of an unfolding semester at school.

This environmental fact can work for or against you, depending on your own sensitivity and feel for balance. To teach a class that requires heavy outside preparation the Monday after homecoming weekend is to invite disaster. A predictable decline in attendance on the Friday after Thanksgiving does not necessarily dictate a wasted lecture. If you leave some slack in your syllabus, that can be the day to hold a more intimate, smaller group discussion of some of the important and continually knotty themes that have been introduced so far.

My favorite parable concerning the classroom impact of the college's social environment comes from Brandeis University. A visiting art history professor was lecturing on Jan Steen's famous seventeenth-century painting of Esther, Ahasuerus, and Haman. It happened to be the day of the Jewish holiday of Purim, which celebrates Esther's defeat of Haman's plot to massacre the Jews. That evening most of the Brandeis students, Jewish and non-Jewish, would be gathering at the university chapel to hear the reading of the story of Esther. By tradition, it would be a rowdy campuswide event. They would boo the wicked Haman and cheer the brave Esther each time their names appeared in the text.

None of this was known to the visiting professor. As soon as he put the slide on the screen, the students began to cheer and boo. When they quieted down he began to relate the story of Esther as depicted in the painting. But he didn't get very far before his students were booing and cheering again. Mystified, he pretended to ignore the interruptions, but each time he spoke the cheering and booing began again. Finally he threw down his pointer in exasperation and stormed out of the lecture hall, furious and confused. Eventually some students found him and explained what had occurred.

Many instructors fail to recognize the environmental hazards of the semester because they are not really integrated into the social life of the institution. From junior faculty bent on mastering the material and achieving tenure to established chaired professors whose schedules are dominated by national academic affiliations, teachers find it is easy to confuse their own social environment with that of the students—or to see no environment at all! Many a course has been planned and presented as if it existed in an antiseptically sealed chamber wherein a student's whole existence was confined, periodically brightened by fifty-five minutes' exposure to the professor's wisdom. Presumably the rest of a student's time would be spent in a kind of half-life behind a massive volume on the basics of organic chemistry.

How different is this concept from the academy's original setting. Inquiry took place outdoors in the agora (the marketplace) or at the dinner table among friends and citizen professionals. Bringing the learning and discussion process into a realistic environment is a wonderful teaching resource, whether the instructor invites students to a mid-course gathering at his or her home (when class size permits) or simply introduces food and drink into the classroom. Such acts help establish a participative learning environment and dispel the image of the enshrined and distant professor/priest on the podium. I am reminded of Samuel Johnson's marvelous parody of pompous traditional depictions of mentor and student:

> Hermit hoar, in solemn cell,
>   Wearing out life's evening grey:
> Smite thy bosom, sage, and tell,
>   What is bliss? and which the way?
> Thus I spoke; and speaking sigh'd;
>   —Scarce repress'd the starting tear;—
> When the smiling sage reply'd—
>   —Come, my lad, and drink some beer.[2]

Once the instructor recognizes the common humanity of student and self, the real-life examples come more easily, and course material can be harmoniously paced with outside activities without provoking jealousy or resentment.

Part of the secret to achieving such a balance is to place oneself in the life of the semester. Participation in an extracurricular student activity—from helping organize a lecture series for a student club to coaching an intramural team—may do more to improve an instructor's sensitivity to a college's social environment than an inspection of the academic calendar.

Participation in university life can be emotionally instructive as well as tactically informative. Engaging in the larger life of the university sensitizes the discussion leader to social dynamics that will surely assert themselves in the classroom itself. If you know that students X and Y are hotly contending for the position of editor-in-chief of the school newspaper, it will be easier to anticipate and defuse their explosive and disruptive exchanges in economics class over the issue of deficit spending. So too the instructor can *plan* for times of generalized personal stress— when medical boards are administered or senior honors papers are due—and schedule less participative sessions.

In short, the discussion leader can take advantage of the environmental and intellectual rhythms that mark a student's learning experience in any course. These natural variations in mode of learning or social calendar provide the jumping-off points for creating your own variations in presentation and thus a more diverse classroom experience for students. Such variation provides more than entertainment or intellectual stimulation. When classroom learning meshes harmoniously with the rhythms of the students' larger environment, they are more likely to retain it in the real world.

Resource #2. First-Hand Expertise at Multiple Skills

The semester also provides the discussion leader with the time, resources, and intellectual perspective for helping students develop a fuller range of learning skills. In comparison with lectures, the discussion process over an entire semester allows students and teacher to engage in first-hand learning experiences that invite a larger variety of substantive understanding.

The physicist Richard Feynman (who served on the Rogers Commission investigating the *Challenger* disaster) summed up his philosophy of learning in a simple story from his childhood. He and his father used to take long walks together, observing the structure and form of nature and inquiring into the meaning of these observations. After one such walk, during which they discussed the ecosystem of parasites on a bird's feathers, another little boy challenged Feynman to tell him the name of a bird. Much to his friend's scorn, Feynman hadn't a clue. Unperturbed, he observed: "After you've been told the name of a bird, all you know is the human name for that bird. You don't really know the bird."[3]

As other essays in this book suggest, discussion teaching at its best helps students both to gain a personal knowledge of the bird and to master traditional human modes of knowing that bird, whether they be techniques in art, zoological classifications, or the words of Edgar Allan Poe's famous poem. This is an organic view of learning that creatively combines external environment (that is, other people's thinking in the past and present, or old and new facts) and internal mental systems. The student not only receives knowledge, but *creates* it, with the rest of the class. As in a barn raising, all participants in the process should come away with new skills and heightened social experience.

The acquisition of such expertise takes time and cumulative wisdom. Most courses are organized around a logical, sequential arrangement of the material. But if the instructor thinks of each class as a little pellet of wisdom, so will the students. The relevance and transferability of material they learn will be severely limited.

An awareness of the semester time frame opens the door to planning for a greater variety of materials, analytical skills, and social dynamics in the classroom. Given that a semester marks a cumulative experience punctuated by significant discrete insights and exchanges, the complexity of classroom dynamics requires a correspondingly complex set of perspectives on learning. To facilitate a student's acquisition of the many kinds of knowledge to be gained from participation in a course, it is helpful to measure a classroom discussion against a backdrop of multiple time frames and multiple learning points.

The discussion model of learning requires a new perspective on the individual class. It is not an isolated moment in time during which one presents a neat parcel of knowledge; rather, it comprises a combination of learning points viewed in relation to both the long and the short term. Besides the immediate content being mastered, one must also consider its relation to previous and future lessons. Inherited social dynamics from previous discussions will inevitably color the current discussion and the roles people play, and new twists will alter future directions of the learning process. To cope with this complexity and channel it productively, an instructor must maintain a multiple focus on present, past, and future, both in analyzing course content and in judging a single class. Ideally, a mode of analysis learned in the third class will still be relevant at the sixteenth class (and for the rest of life). Course planning should reflect these interconnections. One of the most effective ways of provoking an aha! is to present a new puzzle whose solution rests on material learned more than a month earlier. (You mean that stuff is still relevant?)

I like to think of the multiple time frames and multiple perspectives of a course as a story to be told. The techniques of the novel can be adapted to incorporate the longer-term accomplishments of the semester into the immediate goals of the discussion experience. Foreshadowing, flashback, repeated themes and variations, climax and anticlimax—all the elements of technique and perspective that make for a good extended story—contribute to the success of a semester as well.

Take an intermediate foreign language class. Often the first half of the semester concentrates on building translation skills, and secondary critical material is withheld until later. Such an approach mechanically parcels out various kinds of wisdom in hierarchical order. What you do in the last half of the course—the outside reading assignment or term paper—is "better" and "smarter" than in the first.

But treating each class as a step up the ladder of expertise risks demeaning the learning that has already occurred. By implying a sequential hierarchy toward the attainment of an intellectual product, you may undermine the learning process itself.

When each new product (the next class) implies the obsolescence of the last, the value of learning, like that of the buggy whip, is totally dependent on the temporal environment in which it appears.

By changing the time frame in which you plan the course content, you can transform the character of the learning experience from factory manufacture of knowledge to an organic integration of academia and real life. For example, you might foreshadow the themes of the secondary literature that will be assigned in six weeks by asking students to consider the same issues in general terms during the first week of the course. They might be asked to contemplate these issues with reference to their own experience, to analyze the concepts first-hand. Then again, as you begin to plow through the translation, the slower, methodical pace of translating can be punctuated with a return to the same theme from the standpoint of the text itself. By the time the secondary material is introduced, its role has been *experienced* as necessary to the building process and the

skills required to make use of secondary material are more eagerly acquired and retained.

One professor uses the dramatic device of suspense and contrast to
heighten the immediacy of the learning experience. She assigns a particularly thorny problem concerning the explication of a passage in the
New Testament to be completed outside class. On the surface the problem appears to defy interpretation; no one of subgenius intelligence gets
very far with it, despite a recent exposure to techniques for digging into
secondary sources. The class discussion that day begins with individual
feelings of dark defeat and moves to intense group debate, which is
frustratingly inconclusive. But as the professor introduces additional historical material and relevant Old Testament prophecies, the problem is
gloriously unraveled. The shared insight leaves students with a first-hand
enthusiasm for the use of history in solving important textual and theo-
logical problems.

Another kind of victory class applies lessons learned earlier in the
semester to new purposes. Jaded instructors may see "contrast and compare" as a time-worn assignment, but as a learning technique within the
context of the semester it is invaluable.

Again, anticipation and planning are keys to success. If you set up the
recurring insights early in the semester, they can be recalled later on.
For example, I used to begin a course on adolescent heroes in ancient
literature by inviting the class to free-associate on what adolescence
meant to them. This topic required no book learning. Even the most
reluctant literary critic had something to say and could participate.

Throughout the semester we referred back to this initial statement
about the meaning of adolescence. We explored points of similarity between youths today and those of ancient Greece. There were startling
differences and remarkable similarities between contemporary experience
and ancient adolescence. Students had the opportunity to assimilate new
historical facts or literary types into their concept of adolescence. In
short, the learning process invited the possibility of relevance, and self-
discovery. These insights might not have been as immediate had we not
anticipated the repetitions and tapped the class's stereotypes and impressions before they were exposed to the course material. The semester
allowed historical perspective *to develop* among the group rather than be
passed on by a third party through neat lectures.

Just as there are multiple time frames to consider in planning for a
class and assessing its progress, the successful discussion class should
stimulate *multiple learning points*. At each session, the individual stu-

dent will be accumulating multiple skills (for example, exploration of academic concepts, analytical expertise, communication skills). Moreover, *the entire class* will be similarly engaged in the discovery process, but in different ways and at different rates of discovery. Students also will be learning how to learn together, an important skill for any field requiring teamwork and complex analysis. Thus the group's learning process should also be planned for, and the fact of the semester provides the necessary time for such nourishment to take place.

To exploit the cumulative expertise that the entire class is intended to develop, it is helpful to keep these process goals in mind as you plan the arrangement of substantive material. The first few classes can be used to set the stage for future discussions, even if some content must be sacrificed. In those early sessions, keeping the length of the semester in mind can help a new instructor slow down on substantive material or build in enough time to pursue intellectual sideroads that may lead to better learning. At Harvard Business School, for example, Chris Christensen plans his course around three phases of the learning process: (1) romancing the participants to gain their commitment to a group process, (2) group-building to increase the efficiency of the discussions and help ensure success, and (3) victory. For him the semester allows the opportunity to take risks with the classroom time, for establishing through practice the ground rules for the discussion. Obviously a one-day seminar could not be approached in this manner, but would require more straight teaching of content. But the reality of the semester allows an instructor the luxury of delaying some of the content while firming up the learning process itself.

Christensen's three-stage organization of the course is but one way of exploiting the semester's opportunity for establishing multiple educational goals in the classroom. Another way to remain mindful of process issues is to record in a personal journal the progress of the class in both academic *and* discussion skills. This is a particularly useful antidote to those desperate days at the end of the semester when one's impulse is to cram in every bit of substantive material that has not yet been covered.

Planning for a balance between process and substance helps to avoid the danger of *overpacking*. In the search for variety and multiple learning points, many instructors tend to add extra frills without dropping anything. This is especially true when planning is carried out by a teaching group, rather than an individual instructor. Overpacking is like the "rich and damp cake" that Captain Hook gave to the lost boys in *Peter Pan*; it will poison the entire group's ability to engage in an effective discussion process. Christensen has suggested a handy rule of thumb to forestall overpacking: decide what you want to do for the whole semester, then drop 50 percent!

Resource #3. Risk and Reparation

The discussion class is potentially much messier than a lecture course. The instructor cannot control the specific path the class will take, however masterfully he or she keeps the overall goals in mind. In this sense, there is a risk of failure.

The stakes are also high for the students, whose participation is being graded. In a discussion class, an off-the-mark comment brings public exposure, not private intellectual failure. Meanwhile, the instructor faces the hard trade-offs of salvaging a student's ego versus maintaining rigorous academic standards for the group learning process.

The semester justifies and to some degree mollifies the certain risk of discussion teaching. Both teacher and student have the time to make reparation for past mistakes. Failure then becomes less significant than when every class is seen as a discrete unit. A semester allows both instructor and student to take greater risks. If a student "bombs out" in a class, it's not the end of his or her grade. Nor is the learning opportunity of the whole group fatally jeopardized by the potential failure of a slower participant.

Both students and teachers often have difficulty remembering that student participation can mature and evolve over a semester. It is easy to fall into static relationships in a class, to type students into a few categories: the summer-up, the shy one who never talks but always buttonholes you after class with perceptive comments, the one who usually makes a comment from left field, the disrupter, and so on. In a good discussion class, student and teacher roles should evolve continually over the semester. By taking the long view, an instructor is more likely to facilitate this growth.

At the beginning of the very first class I ever taught, an elderly woman approached me with a list of detailed medical instructions to be followed should she have a heart attack! I was derailed before I ever started and never called on her for fear she'd die. In retrospect it is clear that every class was for her a major hurdle of nerves. Had I been more mature at encouraging discussion skills, I might have recognized that the semester was her extended opportunity for cultivating self-confidence in class participation. I could have begun with a small and concrete question in one class, and at another time challenged her further. But such long-term perspectives rarely assert themselves in the instructor's panic to get every class perfectly crafted.

Students will venture more readily into new intellectual territory knowing they may stumble, if they also know that you will provide many opportunities to recover during the semester. To build trust in the group, the instructor has a responsibility not only to encourage risk-taking during group discussions but also to demonstrate reparation early.

The ancient Greeks had a proverb that was often invoked to summarize the point of tragedy: *Pathemata mathemata* ("learn by suffering"). Much wisdom can come from openly making a mistake *and* seeing it through to completion. I often meet Harvard Business School alumni who recall with relish how they were shot down in one class only to triumph in the next. They are usually delighted with the memory of their own experience. Interestingly, they can always recall the specific academic point that was being made on these occasions.

Constructive failure depends on an instructor's ability to help repair the damage. It is the semester structure that provides the time and opportunity to reconstruct a student's ego or analytic approach. I recall one occasion when a particularly argumentative executive—call him Bob—from a defense industry company made a number of illogical analyses in class and was soundly defeated by the group. Ten sessions later the case was about Boeing, and the instructor deliberately asked Bob to open the discussion. He presented a brilliant analysis that drew heavily on his own experience. Both the class and the instructor acknowledged his excellent participation. The instructor was able to deal with Bob's earlier defeat by keeping the semester's agenda firmly in mind. He knew that there would be a chance for recovery down the road, and in the meantime he established the possibility of recovery by repairing the damage for other students who had similarly failed.

Several practical techniques are useful in this process. Keeping an index card on each student is invaluable. A card's worth of personal information volunteered by each student (past work experience, sports, high school) will allow the instructor to draw on his or her potential strengths in class. This approach is particularly helpful for drawing out the relevant participator. These same cards can be used to keep track of participation, and to remind yourself who needs a chance for reassurance or recovery in the next class.

Eye contact is another repair tool. Often a student who made a poor comment one day will not raise his or her hand the next. But if you

continually make eye contact and direct some of the summary and positive remarks to that student (implying that you knew that he or she knew
the same thing), you increase the chance that he or she will jump into
the fray again.

Of course some risks, such as burnout, are best avoided entirely. The
longer perspective of the semester should help the instructor reduce, if
not eliminate, such risks. One can, for example, help students pace
themselves by spelling out what is to come later. If you are going to give
a particularly time-consuming assignment in three weeks and it is a
crucial benchmark in the grading process, you can suggest students
schedule themselves accordingly.

Anticipation also gives students spiritual encouragement as the long
semester nears its close and the course content becomes more difficult.
Say you plan to teach an extremely problematic and not immediately
entertaining piece of literature near the end of the semester (or a very
difficult math formula, or a tedious testing technique). In anticipation
of student burnout and discouragement around the beginning of December or April—just when this concept will be introduced in the course—
you begin to joke about it early in the semester. You make cryptic remarks such as "You think this is bad; just wait till we do X." Or
"Remember this when we get to my favorite equation, X—it will help."
Pretty soon X begins to symbolize a new stage of accomplishment and
intellectual maturity. Your support of their effort to learn X is now well,
and humorously, established. By the time X arrives, it is a familiar and
tantalizing package whose contents must be examined. The semester has
allowed you to set the stage for victory rather than discouragement.

Resource #4. Creation of a Learning and Learned Society

It is important to use the semester as a means of *creating a community.*
The people who worked together voluntarily on early New England barn
raisings were already members of the same community. They knew each
other's quirks of character; they had already engaged in many mutually
beneficial experiences; they had experienced conflict and resolution between members of the group.

By contrast, a class group is a particularly artificial affiliation of people.
Its members are thrown together for four months not because they particularly like each other or have similar backgrounds, but because they
want to (or have to) learn the same subject. They do not usually know
each other's quirks, nor is there any previously shared constructive experi-

ence among them. The typical American primary school experience, with its emphasis on competition and individual achievement, has probably precluded *any* shared learning experience at all.

Thus a major goal of the discussion class instructor must be to create a learning and learned society out of the various people who attend his or her course. That sense of community is essential to the group effort to build a course of learning together.

Again, the semester provides the time for such a process. If the class is going well, an artificial affiliation of individuals will gradually become a dynamic community of knowledge builders. One can help this transition by adopting in class the rituals and customs that normally build community: personal introductions, conversation, shared meals, common goals. The instructor also has the responsibility for establishing early on the ground rules for the community's discussion sessions: how people will be acknowledged and allowed to participate, how they will be cut off for the sake of continuing or changing the topic, how their contributions will be recognized, and how they will treat each other. A teacher has the power to create a mutually respecting group, a Byzantine hierarchy, or a shark pool. One needs to think in advance about the kind of climate that will be created.

With careful planning and execution, *the discussion class has the potential to create its own learned society.* By the semester's end, this group will have passed through many of the variations of life: through trial, error, victory, and friendship. Plato once suggested that truth could be discovered only through the discourse of friends. As a small mirror of life, the semester allows the time for a class discussion to evolve from an orchestrated dialogue into such a discourse among friends. As a step in the attainment of knowledge, it is giant indeed.

At the same time, it is a fact of university life that the society that has been created will also be destroyed by the constraints of the semester. The group will dissolve when the door is opened at the end of the final exam. Ideally, however, the semester and the group will have provoked an intellectual and perhaps social transformation of individual students that they will carry on to the next stage of their intellectual journey.

How does the astute instructor bring the semester to a close? There is a sense of portion and fixity about an academic course that is reinforced by the fixity of time allotted to the class for learning. Some professors treat the last class as simply the last step up the pyramid—no different from any other that has preceded. Others try to include the entire universe of knowledge in dramatic imitation of the grand finale.

Both approaches seem inappropriate. The former marks a final failure to see the semester as a unit of pedagogy and its last class as a special occasion. The latter reminds us of Stephen Leacock's oft-paraphrased description of the fictitious Lord Ronald:

> He flung himself from the room, flung himself upon his horse
> and rode madly off in all directions.[4]

More sensibly, the teacher might keep in mind the paradoxical responsibilities presented by the multiple goals of the semester: the classroom learning process must be brought to some kind of closure, the discussion community must take its farewells, the intellectual victories must be acknowledged.

The larger intellectual issues, however, demand immortality, and it is entirely appropriate to give them a new start as the semester draws to an end. I have in mind something akin to the conclusion of Robert Joffrey's 1967 multimedia ballet *Astarte* (named, I believe, for the Phoenician goddess of rebirth). At its close the leading male dancer turned his back to the audience, stage center, and began walking to the back of the set, shedding clothes on the way. Each backdrop was lifted as he progressed until finally only the brick wall of the building was exposed. The dancer, now nearly or totally nude, ceremoniously opened the small door at the back and walked outdoors. Curtain down. Audiences were startled and delighted. The boundaries between dance and life had been broken. The dancer had been reborn at the end of the dance.

So too the boundaries between the semester's course and the student's intellectual life must be broken in the final class. This is the time to focus on the open-ended philosophical question, the sticky textual problem that plagued later critics, the historical demise of the movement being studied, the observable or logical phenomenon that led to subsequent scientific or mathematical discoveries—whatever keeps the questioning alive and analytical skill relevant. In this way the last class can prompt the rebirth of intellectual spirit that one hopes to encourage in students.

Conclusion

The concept of the semester—an organic unit of considerable lifespan—can free the instructor to use a greater variety of resources to enrich classroom discussion. The semester will have its own variety of rhythms, times of intimate contemplation, Mach 2 leaps of effort and learning, and letdown that need not be regarded as wasted simply because they weren't perfect packages of wisdom perfectly transmitted and received.

Planning for this process, taking an organic view of time's progression, and maintaining a long-term perspective during class will require a very different approach from the traditional methods of course planning. Writing twenty-five discrete lectures that convey a fixed body of material is radically different from the dynamics of discussion group teaching. In the first case the teacher deposits a cluster of perfectly formed frog's eggs in a warm puddle and hopes that they will hatch. In the second, the teacher accompanies the tadpoles through the hazards of growing up together in the pond. Survival in this primordial soup of discussion can be stressful, but the evolutionary leaps in intellectual growth are worth getting your feet wet.

The tone of the last class? To my mind the only way to bring this dynamic, semester-long journey to closure and rebirth is through celebration.

NOTES

1. For the analogy, see Don McCormick and Michael Kahn, "Barn Raising: Collaborative Group Process in Seminars," *EXCHANGE: The Organizational Behavior Teaching Journal*, vol. 7, no. 4 (1982), pp. 16–20.
2. Boswell, James, *Life of Johnson*, vol. III (1777), p. 159.
3. Richard P. Feynman, *"What Do You Care What Other People Think?" Further Adventures of a Curious Character* (New York: W.W. Norton, 1988), pp. 13ff.
4. Stephen Leacock, "Gertrude the Governess, or, Simple Seventeen," *Nonsense Novels* (New York: John Lane, 1914).

14

Encouraging Independent Thinking

JAMES WILKINSON AND HEATHER DUBROW

"I DON'T KNOW if this is the answer you want, but . . ."

The student's eyes are fixed on the instructor, watching for a sign that it's safe to proceed. If the teacher's expression seems disapproving or puzzled, the student prudently shifted ground. Classmates watch and listen, so that when their turns come they will at least know what *not* to say. If the instructor smiles or nods, they relax. Such exchanges educate, but what do they really teach? A pernicious lesson that many students have already learned all too well: how to kowtow to authority.

To help our students develop the more valuable capacity to think on their own, we must counteract, not reinforce, this lesson. Discussion teaching provides one of the most promising opportunities to transform students' disabling deference into thoughtful independence. Indeed, we believe this should be one of the main goals of any discussion class. Yet even in discussion courses, most students will not risk originality without a great deal more guidance, encourgement, and support than most instructors offer. It is rarely enough to announce that class participation is required or that part of the course grade will be based on verbal contributions. As the familiarity of our opening scenario suggests, powerful forces inhibit the spontaneous display and development of independent thought.

Only when students stop deferring to others' opinions can they learn to identify and assess problems, form reasoned, defensible interpretations, and reach and test conclusions unaided. Of course, classes and individual students differ in the way in which they acquire these skills. For convenience, we shall present the phases as a tidy sequence—healthy questioning of authority, analysis, and the formation and testing of reasoned judgments. But in the classroom, these steps may occur in scrambled, or even reverse, order. Sometimes the phases even overlap; but it is useful to recognize them as components of a single process that leads to intellectual independence.

249

In group discussions, we teachers can help students drop their cautious conformity and examine received views by involving them in open-ended dialogue. We can pose questions and offer responses in ways that help them evolve their own ideas step-by-step. The purpose of our questions and assignments should be to encourage, stimulate, and—when necessary—challenge students to articulate and test their beliefs. We should use the classroom as a forum where students can learn to distinguish between convincing and unpersuasive evidence, sound and faulty logic, promising and poor solutions. As for sheer enjoyment—an element of education that we often underestimate—a class where students have mastered the basics of independent thought becomes a lot more fun for both them and their teachers.

In the pages that follow, we shall draw primarily on our experience as teachers in the social sciences and humanities to describe ways to encourage students to question authority, analyze facts and ideas, and develop defensible interpretations for themselves. In closing, we shall briefly note some of the changes in classroom behavior these new intellectual habits may cause, and their benefits.

I

If we are to coax students out of the shelter of received opinion, we must consider what made them seek such protection in the first place. Why do so many students defer to what they perceive as authority—be it a teacher, a textbook, a famous scholar, or another student who appears especially knowledgeable? One fundamental answer is uncertainty. Most students are painfully aware of how little they know, and how difficult it is to arrive at genuine knowledge. Deference to supposed experts of all kinds betrays their yearning for certitude in a world where, sure of very little, they must nonetheless perform well academically. How easy, under these circumstances, to assume that the source of an opinion guarantees its substance. Rather than debate the merits of a particular idea, they invoke an expert's name and think it proves their case.

Some students' need for security leads to a further, equally flawed assumption: every question has but one correct answer, and the teacher knows what it is. A study undertaken some years ago by William Perry at Harvard College suggests that most entering freshmen subscribed to this comforting belief, confirmed by the multiple-choice examinations most of them had encountered in high school and on their SATs.

This assumption is not always wrong, of course. If we ask who succeeded Queen Victoria on the British throne, or who painted the portrait of Whistler's mother, the answers are not matters of opinion. Nor is it intellectually or politically useful for an undergraduate to question a competent teacher's explanation of the Krebs cycle or the principal parts of the verb *être*. In elementary language courses, mathematics, and the natural sciences especially, even college students must memorize a good deal of standard material that is not in dispute.

But some questions—including the most interesting—can engender several valid interpretations. In subjects where independent thinking is appropriate, good teaching should help students overcome their habitual deference and begin to appreciate the rich complexity of multiple solutions. To teach students to think independently, we must recognize that—worried about admission to professional schools or future job prospects—they may wish to placate or flatter us. After all, we can withhold a high grade or write a lukewarm letter of recommendation. Whether or not we realize it, our students frequently believe that the way to do well in a course is to mimic our views.

Then again, students may be genuinely awed by an instructor's reputation or demonstrated expertise and feel that only the ignorant or foolish would presume to question such a luminary. One of us, who had attended a high school that encouraged independent thinking, nonetheless became so impressed with the Great Man teaching one of her college courses that she studied for his first examination by zealously memorizing the theories he had proposed and corroborating them with additional evidence from the readings. When her exam came back with a mediocre grade and the comment "Too much material canned from lectures," she was surprised and puzzled. What the grader considered a flaw in her examination, she had seen as one of its chief strengths.

Whether motivated by uncertainty, ambition, or respect for expertise, students customarily begin the semester by watching for clues to what the teacher expects and how they can meet those expectations. Paradoxically, their eagerness to succeed, wish to please, and need for approval can provide the key to an effective strategy for encouraging greater independence.

From the very outset, we should emphasize that most questions have more than one side. It is not necessary to go to the lengths of the instructor who told his colleagues they must "never utter a conclusive statement"—thus breaking his own rule in the act of enunciating it—but one should mention conflicting schools of interpretation or alternative explanations where they exist. When an authority teaches students that authorities often disagree, they will remember and act upon the lesson more readily than if we hush up disagreements like disgraceful family secrets to be kept from the children at all costs.

Some controversies polarize an entire field of studies. Was Hitler's rise to power fortuitous or actively desired by the German people? Do children acquire langue by a universal genetic pattern or the unique structure of their mother tongue? European historians and developmental psychologists have proposed differing answers to these questions. A class discussion or a whole course could be organized around the issues each debate raises. Other controversies are more private. An instructor who has long disagreed with a colleague about a poem by Andrew Marvell tells students of the disagreement and makes the case for each interpretation when teaching the poem. Or the teacher herself may change her mind about a topic over time. Perhaps an art historian now considers Monet's final studies of water lilies far more original and important than they appeared ten years ago; perhaps a once-admired theory now seems deeply flawed. It is useful to show classes how our evaluations have altered and explain why we have abandoned some of our earlier views.

Naturally the extent to which we use such tactics will vary from class to class. At the elementary level too much controversy may confuse students, for beginners often require the reassurance of clear, unequivocal statements. Yet even novices may profit from some exposure to disagreement or opinions in flux. To pose alternatives is to create an "open space" where students can begin to explore the possibility of offering opinions of their own. And when these opinions emerge in discussion, we should welcome them. One way to convey a sense of welcome is to credit students for their contributions to class discussion. Referring to "John's theory" or "Mary's important observation" later in a conversation shows that we remember and value their efforts. Once students feel that they are associated with us in a common search for answers, they are well into the first stage of independence.

The open space essential for independent thinking can be maintained and enlarged only if our classroom behavior encourages those brave enough to enter the space. Sometimes it is difficult to remember just how vulnerable students really are. They fear humiliation; no one wants to appear foolish before classmates. Yet the first steps toward independence entail that risk. An instructor who criticizes students' opinions with caution and forbearance will reap the rewards of a livelier class as the semester progresses. Stress on what is positive and tact in correcting faults—always essential—are especially so in the early days of the term.

Assigned work can also threaten independent thought. In students' eyes, assignments represent value judgments. ("If these weren't good books, why would the teacher require us to read them?") Students often suppress their negative responses to assignments because they feel they must learn to like what everyone else manifestly admires. A senior Italian scientist, now in his seventies, still recalls a particular day in high school when his literature teacher had assigned a sonnet by a famous Renaissance poet. During the class each student was asked to comment on the strengths and weaknesses of the poem. Each explained why it was a work of genius. Finally a student in the back row arose and said in a perplexed tone, "Maybe I shouldn't admit this, but I didn't like the poem much at all," and gave his reasons. A hush fell over the class. They waited for the teacher to object. Instead he smiled. "You're right," he replied; "it's one of the poet's worst sonnets. That's why I chose it for you to read. You must learn to trust your own judgment. Petrarch was a great literary artist, but he was only human. Even great poets produce inferior work, and we must learn to recognize it." Including works of varied quality on a syllabus—and saying so—is one way to provide contrasts that can help students begin to make their own evaluations.

Another way to temper the authority of assigned readings is to tell the class why they have been chosen and what possible alternatives might have been offered. We can all become historiographers on occasion, encouraging our students to analyze the bents and biases behind editorial decisions in textbooks and the selection of authors in syllabi. "What assumptions about the canon of English literature may one discern in *The Norton Anthology?*" At every level students are interested in how a field is evolving and where it is likely to go. "Twenty years ago, we would not have been studying this" is the sort of comment that piques their curiosity and informs them that course content undergoes continuous transformation. For many, this comes as a surprise.

It is also important to monitor the volume of assigned works. Students can neither absorb the material nor consider the issues it raises if they are swamped. Teachers are often tempted to require more reading than their students can handle. Extensive assignments seem to signal rigor and seriousness. Some of us, in our enthusiasm, cannot bear to omit material of even marginal interest from classroom consideration. Some have simply forgotten how time-consuming certain assignments can be for beginners. Whatever the reason, we should try to confine assignments to a limit that allows true mastery. That limit will depend on both subject matter and students' skills. A beginning Russian class might spend a week on a few lines of poetry that more advanced classes could complete in minutes. But in general it is advisable to be conservative about the time an assignment will require. The quality of class discussion will provide a barometer for adjusting assignments as the course goes along. Many teachers discover that they assign less, not more, when they give a course a second time.

Monitoring the quantity of reading material, explaining assignments, and prompting discussion at the start of the semester represent deliberate ways to endorse independence. Yet teachers also communicate attitudes and expectations on other levels, sometimes unaware of the messages they send. Students both listen to what we say and watch what we do. If our behavior communicates that we do not really mean to reward independence—no matter what we've said—the proposed open space will disappear. To gain students' trust and ensure their willingness to take risks in the classroom, we must not take away with one hand what we offer with the other. Yet such consistency is not always easy to achieve. Like students, teachers need security. In fact, some of the most formidable barriers to developing independent thinking in the classroom lie not with them, but with us.

Troubling though it may be to admit, we often encourage dependency because we derive emotional benefits from our students' praise or compliance. The narrower the gap between their knowledge (or ages) and our own, the more pronounced this need may be. Uncertainty about our expertise can easily lead us to reward students, perhaps inadvertently, for following our private party line. We feel flattered if they adopt our opinions, threatened if they do not.

Even teachers who have outgrown such insecurity may discourage independent thinking in other, more subtle ways. The best way to teach independent thinking is to demonstrate it; yet sometimes our own views may owe more to authority than we realize. In all fields some critiques are considered more legitimate than others. These critiques may effectively delimit the boundaries of acceptable dissent. Many disciplines stigmatize what lies beyond these conventional limits as irrelevant or even inimical to the aims of the field. Thus, in most American departments of philosophy, metaphysics was long considered disreputable. For many economists, historical questions are "soft" and trivial. Until recently, management scientists dismissed the sociologists' long-accepted concept of "corporate culture" as hopelessly vague and impossible to quantify.

What do such judgments imply—high professional standards or narrow prejudice? At the very least, they demand scrutiny.

As we guide students toward independent thought, we may find ourselves forced to question or suspend a number of cherished assumptions. One of us remembers that, long after she had abandoned some of the tenets of New Criticism—the principal school of literary interpretation in which she had been trained—she continued to react sharply against the term "message" in student papers. Only after several years of filling margins with diatribes against the concept did she acknowledge that her distaste was grounded in New Critical principles she had never examined objectively. This recognition persuaded her that the word "message" and its implications, though liable to misuse, were not intrinsically unacceptable.

Maintaining the open space essential for independent thought often involves us in a version of balance-of-power politics in the classroom. Without our constant vigilance, debate may gravitate toward one of two extremes: automatic acceptance or unthinking attack. Sometimes students forge a tacit "nonaggression pact," endorsing their neighbors' comments and ideas in return for similar forbearance toward their own. On the other extreme, they may confuse intellectual acuity with belligerence and find fault with all the works or opinions they have been assigned to study. One of us discovered this problem, toward the middle of the semester, in a discussion group that had seemed to be going well. The level of class participation was high, and debate was spirited. But students had become so accustomed to attacking whatever author had been assigned that few dared to defend writers or views they genuinely respected. Here the solution was for the instructor to argue more strongly on behalf of his reading list than he might have done in a less combative class. Conversely, a pact of mutual support among students can be defeated if the teacher is willing to play devil's advocate for a time. Assuming that our objections to students' points are not capricious, but fair and clearly explained, we can show that criticism need not be confused with attack. In cases of this sort it is also especially useful to welcome, encourage, and support the first appearance of helpful criticism from a student in the class. The students will eventually follow our lead.

II

Teachers who keep sight of the ultimate goal—helping students learn to evaluate material on their own—can, with care and self-management, lead a class from conformity toward independence during the initial weeks of the semester. The first signs of such a transition may be unsettling. Rather than saying, "I don't know if this is the answer you want," students will ask questions that begin with "why." "Why are French historians currently so much respected in the United States?" "Why were we assigned a novel by James Fenimore Cooper when he writes so badly?" "Why should managers concern themselves with workers' morale?" When students begin to participate without self-censorship, the results frequently reflect their own perplexity. They do not know the answers—if they did, why take the course?—and the number of possible questions seems to multiply with frightening speed. At this point, we teachers may wonder whether this is really the direction we want for the course. Just how much should we encourage students to express confusion and disagreement with us? When does the questioning spirit become blind iconoclasm or dissent for dissent's sake? Fears—of losing valuable class time, of appearing foolish in front of the students, of a whole semester consumed by doubt or anarchy—may prompt us to rein in the class and reimpose order.

And we should. We cannot teach (nor should students be expected to learn) in chaos; it is the social structure of the classroom that distinguishes formal education from the inefficient pleasures of picking up a subject on one's own. But we must be careful to seek an order that leads not back to conformity, but forward, toward mature assessment.

When a book reviewer ponders a verdict on a novel, a business executive weighs the advantages of a new product line, or a scientist scrutinizes the results of a recent experiment, each performs certain distinct, though interrelated, operations. So do students. At the risk of oversimplification, we shall posit three steps—description, analysis, and evaluation—that may occur in class discussions. Description is the cornerstone of the process. To assess a book, product, or laboratory result, we must consider it in purely factual terms. Then we may analyze its parts and what produced them. Finally, we may venture an opinion about its significance and value.

Discussion teaching permits us to explore each of these steps and their interrelations through what we might call "linked questioning"—a series of related queries that focus on a subject from different, successive vantage points. We can ask first for factual detail ("What happened?"), then investigate causes ("Why did it happen?"), and, in some instances, conclude with a personal verdict ("Should it have happened differently?").

The description-analysis-judgment model is typical of classroom inquiry. Teachers often begin with factual questions because, being relatively easy, they are likelier to stimulate participation. Most discussion teachers have experienced the moment of unhappy silence that follows a question on which students can get no firm grip. In this situation, many of us retreat to questions of fact. "Well then, who are the main characters in *The Scarlet Letter?*" "Who can tell me by what amount the XYZ Corporation increased its earnings in 1980?" Such retreats do not signal defeat. Facts can lay the groundwork for subsequent inquiry into more fruitful, challenging topics, as teacher and students venture beyond "what" to probe "how" and "why."

Most students recognize facts; far fewer feel comfortable analyzing them. They can reproduce the informational content of assigned material with reasonable accuracy, but they tremble, or stumble, when asked to interpret that content. Why should analysis be so difficult? Perhaps because students are so seldom asked to do it. Or because the skills we need to discern a pattern within a mass of facts require us to regard reality as organized, and thus capable of being understood. Whatever the reason, mastering the skills of analysis is the greatest single barrier a student is likely to encounter along the path toward independent thought.

By asking students to analyze, we are really asking them to cut through inessentials to causes that customarily escape easy detection. We are asking them to find some order amid chaos. "What medical diagnosis best fits these symptoms?" "What is the chief difference between the American and French constitutions?" Identifying patterns is an ability that few acquire without coaching, and none without hard work. One frustrated householder with little mechanical aptitude finally learned to repair his ailing lawn mower when, after many fruitless attempts to fix the uncooperative machine, he realized that its ills must have a rational explanation. That such a self-evident truth should come as a surprise suggests the degree to which we tend to accept effects without searching for their causes. A poem moves us. Why? If we look closely, we find that certain key words and their placement trigger much of what we feel. A company outperforms its competitors. Why? Research reveals that its junior management has significantly greater responsibility than its rival's. The lesson we want students to grasp is clear: things happen for a reason, more often for several reasons, but rarely by chance.

How can teachers help students deduce causes once they have discerned effects? Often it helps to show them a concrete example of the type of analysis we seek. We can offer such a demonstration within the context of class discussion—"If we were going to analyze this problem, Joan, we might come to the following conclusions"—or distribute two- or three-paragraph essays to be studied at home. Another, more advanced, approach is to ask a question that invites students to challenge a particular interpretation. "Do you think we're really dealing with a problem of racial discrimintion here?" "Could we say that all of Stendhal's novels concern thwarted ambition?" The advantge of this gambit is that it furnishes students with a plausible generalization that is still open to query or change. From the very start, they can debate essentials.

Another approach to teaching analysis consists of drawing an analogy between classroom presentation and legal argument. The teacher can suggest that students pretend they are lawyers pleading a case before a judge and jury. To marshal an argument, they will have to select facts and suggest their causes. *Which* facts seem pertinent will depend on what they are trying to prove; moreover, analysis requires structure. Students come to realize that no lawyer would merely pepper the jury with details or statistics, or call witnesses at random. She would make an opening statement outlining what she intends to show, and then try to persuade the court through a careful sequence of exhibits and examinations of witnesses that explain the facts she thinks significant. The courtroom analogy can help students learn to focus and present their analyses. Once we have described the facts, we must analyze them if they are to yield a coherent, persuasive interpretation.

At this point, we are close to teaching students the principles of logical thought. How many students ensure that their presentations hang together? One aid to developing logical thought is to introduce students to elementary concepts in philosophy such as the syllogism or the distinction between necessary and sufficient conditions. Few students receive any training in such matters; a surprisingly large number find them useful, fun, or both.

The process of evaluation raises questions of proof as well as of logic. How does one support an opinion in class discussion? How much evidence makes a case? Some students confuse proof with intensity of belief. They preface statements with "I feel very strongly that . . ." and trust that their sincerity will carry the day. Like students who think that grades should be based on effort alone, the partisans of personal conviction must learn to test their ideas against a more stringent standard. One way to begin this process is to ask students to evaluate a point propounded by an authority outside the class. Criticizing a theory or verifying a hypothesis becomes easier when the verdict cannot hurt anyone present. The requisite proof will, of course, vary from field to field. But in general, the exercise will encourage students to confront interpretations with evidence. "Where can you find examples of what John termed Mark Twain's 'cynicism'?" "What data support the contention that 'cities breed crime'?" Whatever standard applies, students who understand how to organize facts into a pattern of evidence based on analysis will come to see that sound judgment is never arbitrary; it must be susceptible to demonstration.

Often discussions will become more penetrating—and more enjoyable—if they can be turned into informal debates. Unlike the legal analogy, the debate fosters teamwork. It is not necessary to assign affirmative and negative teams. Rather, the teacher should watch for patterns of agreement and disagreement in the class and suggest that people who seem to agree with each other's viewpoints unite to challenge those who disagree—and vice versa. When this happens, the class has divided into natural subgroups, and the members of each faction will have to bolster each other's reasoning even as they attempt to point out flaws in that of their opponents. The teacher's skillful questioning and alertness to students' styles of analysis and emerging points of view are crucial here.

By calling on speakers by name, distinguishing their points of view as they go along, and inviting other students to comment on their assertions, teachers can both subtly encourage opposition and maintain a stimulating pace as opinions evolve. When an issue is controversial, and opposing factions form of their own accord, students often muster an acuteness they would have lacked had they been assigned arbitrary positions at the outset. Once sides define themselves, our job as teachers is to help each faction focus on the important issues and to summarize conclusions periodically as the debate progresses. If there is too much superficial description, we may call for analysis; if opinions proliferate without support, we should ask for proof. Each side will have to sharpen its ideas as the opposition attacks its logic or proof.

The more proficient our students become at analysis, the easier it will be for them to master the final phase of evaluation: judgment. No longer content merely to reduce a problem to its essential features and speculate on their causes, they will now be prepared to evaluate conclusions, theories, theorems, and strategies on a scale running from poor to admirable. They will be able to answer questions like "Is this the best possible solution? What are its faults and virtues, and what trade-offs does it involve?" In learning sound judgment, students may do well to acquire the habit of viewing poems, experiments, or natural phenomena as answers to problems. This habit can become a powerful force to liberate them from simply accepting things at face value, and lead them to approach phenomena of all sorts as solutions to problems. This can foster judgments, for solutions may be evaluated. For example, how might we design a life form capable of living underwater? Streamlining the body and developing fins or a tail for locomotion seem essential until we remember seals or whales. The problem of underwater living, it turns out, permits multiple solutions, each with advantages and flaws. Enabling students to see marine biology—or any other field—in this way opens up a new dimension in their approach to learning and makes it active, not passive; liberating, not confining.

To judge an idea, we must consider its content as well as its intrinsic worth. The defensive strategy that helped the French win World War I, for example, helped defeat them in World War II. Similarly, a nuclear engineer who designs an atomic reactor without adequate earthquake safeguards has committed a serious enough mistake if the reactor is to be built in Boston, but a potentially catastrophic one if the intended site is San Francisco.

To raise the issue of context in the classroom, students might be asked to specify the frame of reference within which they are making judgments. "You say this is a fine painting, Peter. With what other art works are you comparing it?" Or we may plead for a neglected aspect of the problem under review, encouraging students to broaden a narrow outlook. "When you call this the best site for the new library, Sally, do you mean 'best' for the architect, the contractor, or the community?" Students often define issues as narrowly as possible, to make them easier to deal with. It is up to us to broaden their frame of reference.

Just as students' judgments often ignore significant contextual factors, so, too, they often undervalue the constraints that shape particular decisions—chastising politicians, for example, for making compromises without considering what the consequences of avoiding them might have been. Practical pressures like the state of the economy or population growth, cultural constraints like attitudes toward work or modernization, and technological limits like factory equipment or the transportation system all affect what people can accomplish. Difficult though it may be to keep such varied constraints in view, we should remind students of their presence. We should not make things seem simpler—and the freedom to choose greater—than they really are. At other times, students may need to notice that constraints they take for granted do *not* exist. During a recent class discussion, one participant argued that domestic public opinion would force Soviet leaders to adopt a certain position on arms control. Only after the teacher inquired how public opinion was expressed in the Soviet Union, and by what process its leaders could be voted out of office, did the student reflect, "I guess they're playing the game under different rules."

Then again, students and teachers alike may feel tempted to judge a work or piece of research too harshly because they would prefer it to be something else. Those who dislike the conventions of the early Victorian novel may think *Oliver Twist* "too romantic"; entomologists may believe that a series of field experiments devoted to plant adaptation should have focused more on insect behavior, and so on. It is neither productive nor fair for the class to concentrate its attention chiefly on what the author or naturalist has *not* done.

Discussion teaching, like the independent thinking it aims to stimulate, is often messy, open-ended, unpredictable. It places heavy demands on the teacher, who must respond to the unexpected while keeping the discussion on course. Yet this very unpredictability brings it closer to real life and helps participants develop skills with strong practical value. Perhaps more important, it allows students to discover strengths and explore opinions that might have gone unnoticed or underdeveloped in a more regimented learning environment. Prior conditioning may cause students to resist the first stages of independence, but once the teacher has truly opened a welcoming space in the classroom, discussions become more interesting, students more involved. Discussion teaching can accelerate the process through which students internalize skills and standards by making them responsible for *finding*, not just accepting answers. Students who can evaluate others' interpretations and theories can also evaluate their own. By a process of continuous inner dialogue, they become their own most acute and helpful critics.

Early in the semester, it is the discussion teacher's job to prod students tactfully but with enough persistence to move them beyond simply affirming others' ideas. By the term's end, if they have mastered the tools of independent thinking, they will have become difficult to teach in the conventional manner. They will reflect out loud on what their teacher has assigned or said in class, and challenge an interpretation or text with which they disagree. They will watch and listen to each other, rather than just the teacher, because they will care as much about other students' opinions and, by extension, their own. At times they will be eager to explore an aspect of the course that has little appeal for the teacher. They will make it clear if they consider assigned work tedious or dull. All these are signs of success as is the disappearance of the plaintive preamble, "I don't know if this is the answer you want, but. . . ."

PART V

Education for Judgment

15

Having It by Heart: Some Reflections on Knowing Too Much

JOHN HILDEBIDLE

THE CULTIVATION OF IGNORANCE may be a necessary step in the development of an effective teacher. As instructors we are continually expected to know a great deal, especially if we teach in a prestigious graduate or professional school. We are hired, in large part, for what we know; we must demonstrate what we know, publicly and repeatedly, in articles, presentations, guest lectures, and of course in the classroom, where our students quite justly expect us to know the answers to their questions and our own. Few things are so unsettling to a student as a teacher's admission of ignorance. Such moments are unsettling to the teacher as well, since our sense of authority and control in the classroom may depend on the conviction that we are the experts. There is no need to abandon that expertise altogether; but I do want to suggest that the role of a teacher is quite different from that of a scholar or consultant. As teachers, we may find honest and well-timed ignorance a decisive element in our work.

To resolve, or at least elaborate, this paradox, let me begin with Eudora Welty's novel *Losing Battles*, which tells the story of a family reunion in honor of the one-hundredth birthday of Elvira Vaughan. The family is sizable, and over two summer days in the 1930s a number of unexpected guests happen by as well. There is heroic eating and even more heroic talking; not surprisingly, the celebration is full of ghosts, most of them anything but dour. A ghost of particular interest is redoubtable Miss Julia Mortimer, who has been, for more years than anyone can number, the schoolteacher in the dusty, tin-roofed northeast Mississippi town of Banner.

Almost everyone who appears in the novel has felt Miss Julia's guiding hand and mind—not always comfortably or profitably; but not even the best of teachers can be universally successful. Welty's title suggests the various struggles going on in that particular time and place; Miss Julia provides a rather gloomy summary of her own battle, in a letter written just before her death.

> All my life I've fought a hard war with ignorance. Except in those cases you can count off on your fingers, I lost every battle. Year in, year out, my children at Banner School took up the cause of the other side and held the fort against me. We both fought faithfully and single-mindedly, bravely, maybe even fairly. Mostly I lost, they won. But as long as I was still young, I always thought if I could marshal strength enough of body and spirit and push with it, every ounce, I could change the future. [1]

Few of us must teach under the missionary circumstances that faced Miss Julia; few will encounter ignorance so fully on its own ground. But all of us will probably have moments in which we share her sense of defeat.

Of course, on our good days we reject her imagery of battle in favor of a belief in education as a communal and humane process; but there are days when only thoughts of warfare will do justice to the intensity of our effort and the stubbornness of the resistance it seems to face. And yet, if we are lucky—or rather, if we hold on to that rare combination of hard common sense and a starry optimism that is an essential part of a true teacher's nature—we will preserve the youthful sense of purpose that Miss Julia describes; we will continue to believe that we are, in even the tiniest of ways, changing the future. If we are honest, however, we will also acknowledge, as we look out over the classroom, that at any given moment, no matter how superbly the discussion is going, someone is missing the point.

Miss Julia's accounting grows darker and darker:

> The reason I never could win for good is that both sides were using the same tactics. Very likely true of all wars. A teacher teaches and a pupil learns or fights against learning with the same force behind him. It's the survival instinct. . . . But the side that gets licked gets to the truth first. When the battle's over, something may dawn there—with no help from the teacher, no help from the pupil, no help from the book. [2]

So far has Miss Julia come from the inspiration (it is her word for it) that drove her as a young teacher: instead of trying to change the world, she sees it as little more than a Darwinian conflict, with the "dawn" coming only rarely and by accident.

That far we need not, God willing, follow her, although we may pause to give thanks that we work in an atmosphere of academic gentility rather than Miss Julia's world of rural backwardness, single-minded clannish-ness, and comic exaggeration. And we don't have to take as gospel her own estimation of her work. The novel as a whole shows us how little she succeeded in making her pupils think clearly about a world even a mile wider than the peculiar corner of the South in which they were all born. But she has unquestionably left her mark. Her pupils—and we meet a fair sampling of them—cannot seem to escape the memory of her. "She was pretty smart, herself!" one of them remarks; "She rammed a good deal down me, spelling, arithmetic—well, history's where she fell down. . . . There's a heap of history I don't know, standing right here before you. . . . But she knew it all. She had it by heart." This particular fellow bears an even more distinguishing mark of Miss Julia's regime: he signs his name, always, with a question mark afterward. "Because she told you to?" someone asks. "Well, she told me not to."[3] Force of will does not always produce the result it intends.

Miss Julia has become a creature of legend, all-knowing, all-seeing, indomitable. That is both her heroism and her downfall as a teacher. Surely to live in the memory of our students is one of the prime ego rewards of the trade. Miss Julia, through ceaseless hard work, struggle, ability, and yes, sheer stubbornness, won that immortality, as did Socrates, Louis Agassiz, and the straight-backed woman, who, in the eighth grade, taught me to diagram a sentence, right down to the infinitives. But Miss Julia never seems to have overcome her own knowledge, which was rather monstrous (at least to the world she worked in). She remains a puzzling alien being in the minds of those who knew her, having left behind a rather grudging admiration and a perilous weight of memorized verse.[4] Perhaps, given the ingrown nature of Banner, Mississippi, she could not realistically have hoped for more; and by occupying a not inconsiderable part of the memory of so many people she, in a way, succeeded in changing the future. But not in a way we can altogether admire.

Miss Julia failed largely because she knew too much. That may be as much a condemnation of her environment as of her teaching technique, but the problem is not limited to those who work in cultural backwaters. Consider the following classroom exchange—hypothetical but still, I hope, representative:

> Student: I've finished reading *Walden* and I'm pretty confused. I mean, I see the point, but the book seems awfully *disorganized*, doesn't it?
>
> Teacher: Well, it will probably help if you keep in mind what stands behind the book—the kinds of things Thoreau had read. For instance, he

was Emerson's neighbor and, in a way, student. So a lot of what he's writing is an extension of things like "Self-Reliance" and "The American Scholar." And then there's the odd fact that stay-at-home Thoreau, who never seemed to go beyond walking distance of his home town, loved to read travel books, and those books leave their mark on *Walden*, too. So does all the natural history he read about and, of course, studied first hand. He says he took only one book with him to the pond, a book of Homer; that suggests that it helps to keep the classics (not to mention Eastern literature) in mind. And, of course, he had read a great deal of Romantic poetry, especially by Wordsworth. Maybe—even though he says he never read novels—he had a few books like *Robinson Crusoe* on his mind too, when he decided to write his own book about living a solitary and independent life. What I'm trying to say is that, a lot of the time, he's imitating or echoing books he expects his readers to recognize.

The teacher's remarks are not immediately offensive or utterly incomprehensible; they would serve well enough in a survey course of American literature, to open the subject of what is both old and new about Thoreau's book. Certainly, it is the kind of thing we all, in our various disciplines, do almost every day: lay out the groundwork. But this approach has some sinister implications. Consider the matter from the standpoint of the student who is reading *Walden* for the first time, who may even have enjoyed it, although some parts are no doubt either a bit tedious or downright annoying. He had thought that he was reasonably well equipped to understand the book. Suddenly he feels rather a fool; look at how much he missed, all those echoes and dependencies that *must* be grasped if the book is to be comprehended. The student, a little proud of himself for having done the assigned reading, now learns he needs to run out and read Homer, Emerson, Charles Darwin, DeFoe, and a number of other writers he couldn't even put a name to.

The discussion leader has done one kind of work very well, and may go on to provide a wealth of encapsulated knowledge, not to mention an invaluable list of books that the eager student will eventually want to read. But, at the same time, the teacher clearly put the student in his place and turned the eyes of the class away from the book itself. In effect, the student has been told that one can read nothing well until one has read everything. Of course, teachers should help students see books (or problems or cases) as part of a context, not just isolated units; we need to show students that learning is continuous and is necessarily pursued through multiple paths of inquiry. But what will be the rewarding task of a lifetime can be a demoralizing place to begin on a cloudy Tuesday morning.

Our hypothetical discussion leader has driven home to her hypothetical beginning students the enormous distance between her own mind and theirs. No doubt, she has spent the better part of a life working hard to accumulate the data now being offered. By showing how each newly acquired bit of knowledge has added to her literary joy and enlightenment, she stands as a vital example. It is true that the more you read, the more you understand what you read. But too often the distance, in knowledge and experience, between teacher and student, becomes a weight of moral condemnation: the beginner, the person with more questions than answers, with too many gaps in his prior reading, is encouraged to feel like an inferior life form. Too often students are battered with information, citations, terminology; and too often that battering bewilders rather than informs their reading and thinking. Too often they become convinced that, whatever the discipline, it is governed by a Mystic Code, and that only the rare and blessed (for which read "the teacher") have access to a decoder. The clever student will rather quickly grasp and borrow the teacher's version of the world; and, sadly, that student may then learn the least of all.

For the instructor, knowledge can be a way of asserting his or her essential value. But when the classroom becomes a showroom of egos, most other activities stop. And when the classroom becomes a place in which we demonstrate to students their own ignorance, as compared with our wisdom, everything is backward, since it is our job to help students enlarge and use their own wisdom, not just to admire or absorb ours.

It is always important to have someone in the room with answers, or at least with well-informed questions; and however much we may encourage (or command) our students to take on the role of discussion leader, we have to be there with the safety net. Refusing to show off our command of facts does not mean forgetting the *skills* we have. To put it another way, though we may forbear to dominate through information, we should not abandon the other techniques we use to direct, mold, and even control the class.

Nor should we play dumb simply to encourage a terribly insecure first-year student. That would resemble the "I'm just a simple country lawyer" routine that Senator Ervin employed (so unconvincingly) while searching the murky depths of Watergate. No student with any perception will buy that for a moment. No: to be truly effective and truly interesting to us, our ignorance, our willingness to reach and to pass the boundaries of our own certain knowledge has to be real.

Nor do I suggest that we become utter populists, willing to entertain any idea, no matter how ill-formed or ill-informed, without challenge. We do our students the greatest disservice if we do not expect intelligence from them. Instead I propose a reflexive version of the classic response to a very able student who comes up with an apparently perfect and complete answer, and who stands there smiling amidst charts, graphs, and self-satisfaction. With luck the teacher can find the factor that has been glossed over, can formulate the question that will force a new perspective on the problem. The point is not to topple the lovingly constructed castle with which we've just been presented. The question needed is the one that admires what has been done but keeps the minds of the class moving, intellectually, and reminds everyone (the teacher included) that few useful answers are complete and conclusive, since only the least interesting questions are, in the end, permanently answerable. As a grammarian might point out, the word *learning* is, properly, a verb masquerading as a noun: an activity, not a substance; something we do, not something we have. Poor Miss Julia seems never to have conveyed that understanding to her charges, perhaps because she had forgotten it herself, in her eagerness to ram learning down them.[5]

If students' best answers are merely way stations, what of our own? Our own information, particularly as we have assembled it into understanding and interpretation, is inevitably partial. If we are intellectually alive, we acknowledge that fact each time we read an article that casts new light on a subject we thought we knew well. But it is not enough to be honest with ourselves in private; we must also find a way to be honest publicly, in the classroom, and that is terribly risky. It is a gesture of limitation, an admission of how far short of godlike we are; and it is uncomfortable taking risks in front of a room full of relative strangers. But we ask students, every day, to take just such risks—to move into new subjects, to hazard partially formed ideas, to ask questions that reveal they haven't gotten the point. It doesn't hurt if teachers, too, take an occasional risk—but not, perhaps, on the first day of class or at a point when things seem altogether muddled, and not without establishing a context in which students can comfortably and productively admit that they don't know. The kind of public honesty I am suggesting must be grounded in real knowledge and in real trust; but those are the conditions we want to establish in any case.

How much information is "too much"? Over time teachers develop a pretty sound idea of the likely talents and needs of particular kinds of students; we can guess what will puzzle a group of sophomores who are not English majors or a class of second-year MBA students at a distinguished eastern professional school. But we must always retest our assumptions, and the simplest way to do that is to offer a diagnostic exercise: a case that requires insight rather than prepared information, an article or poem or story that allows even the beginning reader to show whether and in what ways she can analyze. It is probably better not to call such an exercise "testing," since that term suggests the possibility of failure, but we should define clearly that the purpose is to assess our supposed omniscience as much as the students' background and knowledge. If at all possible, the test should demand both speaking and writing (which will, by the way, enhance the teacher's reputation for rigor: "What? A paper assignment already?").

Then, with a better sense of what the class knows and its ability to apply that knowledge, we can formulate our questions and answers appropriately. Of course, the diagnostic process must continue and be constantly refined. And it will be if we keep our eyes and ears open and pick up the implicit and unintended information that the class provides each time it meets. A school principal once remarked that a good teacher conveys the impression that he or she knows everything that is going on in the classroom. He was discussing the problem of disciplining early adolescents, a subject that—blessedly!—need not concern us here. But his definition also works for the most advanced students. Though we may acknowledge gaps in our command of the numbers, of the texts, or the fine points of law, there is one kind of deficiency we cannot permit ourselves—an ignorance of the people in the room, as they are at a given moment: Who's confused? Who is half-asleep? Who needs a little stroking of the ego? Who needs to be left alone? Whose ego needs a little deflating? The personality of the class is endlessly changing, and learning about that personality is perhaps our greatest challenge in the classroom.

So there are certain kinds of knowledge we must have and use constantly. Know those students whom you're teaching at the moment: start from where they are, build on what they know (and of course convince them, happily, that they don't know everything). The trick is to show students how to get from where they are to a more advanced, more enlightened, more percipient place; and that will not be done solely or even primarily by pointing to that place—that is, by parading what we know already and what they "ought" to comprehend. It is better to provoke, cajole, beguile, seduce, hector, and incite (the array of techniques is almost endless) them to piece together a route of their own. It won't do for us to race ahead if they're rapidly losing sight of our backs.

Some small but significant steps can keep the race more equal. It is, for example, often productive to pause before answering a question. The silence may at first feel uncomfortable, but at the very least we will suggest that the question is worth thinking about for a while: if we are lucky, someone else may come up with a useful answer before we are forced to speak. We ought, repeatedly, to confirm that asking questions is a worthy act, that the ability to question clearly is a skill important not only to the leader but to the learner. It is not enough to assert this point; if we do not *act* as though it were true, we might as well save our words. To learn to cherish the students' questions as much as our own is a complex task. And unless students feel at ease in asking occasional questions that seem simpleminded, teachers have no way of knowing when they have left out the crucial first steps.

A teacher who has all the answers, always, does little to make the student (who at best has some of the answers, sometimes) feel at home engaging in intellectual dialogue. The class cannot effectively always meet on our ground; there ought to be a time, each day, when the issue under consideration either has no solution readily apparent to the teacher, or has so many resolutions that the teacher's is really no better than anyone else's. That ought to be an exciting time, when the class becomes a true community of inquiry. This is what we mean when we talk of open-ended discussions; this is what occurs when we teach material about which we have not altogether settled our own opinions, when we ask questions to which we authentically do not have answers, when we extend the ground of the discussion beyond what seems most familiar to us. But how many of our open-ended questions are really open-ended to us? And how comfortably do we deal with what ought to be both a delight (intellectually) and a compliment (pedagogically): the question from the class to which we must honestly respond, "I don't know. I never thought about that before."[6]

It is unlikely that Miss Julia Mortimer was fond of open-ended questions, or that she often let on that she didn't know the answers. Possibly her students seldom posed a question she hadn't thought of long before; she may well have been as universally accomplished as they believe. They can recall only one thing that she couldn't do better than anyone else: milk a cow. That suggests to me that her class should have met, now and then, in a barn. But the wonder with which Miss Julia is remembered is by no means all bad; perhaps it is mostly good. Her funeral cortege is long and distinguished, and she set even the least willing students an example of the astonishing capacity of the human mind. It would be presumptuous of me, after few years of teaching able, committed, well-prepared young intellectuals, to judge the work of the Miss Julias of the world, who daily face students with little skill, less confidence, and even less interest or time. She had aspirations for those whom she taught, and in that we should emulate her. If we find ourselves no longer interested in what will happen to the faces we see before us each Monday, we'd better consider a sabbatical or a career change. Miss Julia had an apparently endless store of energy, the kind of stubborn patience that allowed her to persist in an underappreciated and inadequately rewarded task; she had that patience that allows teachers zestfully to begin again, each fall, at the beginning.

I would really argue with Miss Julia only on one issue: the value of having it all by heart. A telling point is that she is remembered for what she knew, while her students recall only snatches of things she taught them. She—and therefore they—mistook the acquisition of data for the process of learning. I would rather be remembered for what others figured out, in my presence, how to do. As Miss Julia recognized (though with gloom, not elation), the most important and most memorable things often do not seem to have been caused, but simply to dawn. An effective teacher seemingly just happens to be nearby when the dawn comes. Of course, that appearance is usually misleading; one remains unaware of the accomplished teacher's long hours of preparation, the careful guiding of students toward their own discoveries. The credit, after all, should go to the person who has mastered something new. If we teachers always know it by heart, we deprive ourselves of much of the joy and wonder of learning. And that joy, in the end, is the ample repayment for the occasional discomfort of saying those short but significant words: "I don't know."

NOTES

1. Eudora Welty, *Losing Battles* (New York: Random House, 1970), p. 298.
2. Ibid.
3. Ibid.
4. Miss Julia's strangeness is summarized in a line I heard Miss Welty read

aloud, as a kind of welcoming rebuke, to a large audience of Harvard intellectuals: "She reads in the daytime."

5. The perils of knowledge-forcing are masterfully lampooned in the second chapter of Charles Dickens's *Hard Times*—a chapter all teachers ought to read, aloud if possible. My own small list of great pedagogical lessons in English literature includes the sad schooling of Paul Dombey in Dickens's *Dombey and Son* (and particularly the "report card" sent home for young Paul, which displays in all its absurd glory the evaluative double talk we still deal in); the long description of Ursula Brangwen's first months as a teacher in Chapter 13 of D. H. Lawrence's *The Rainbow*; and of course Muriel Spark's *The Prime of Miss Jean Brodie*.

6. It is worth mentioning the problem that arises when we are asked to provide information that we should long since have learned but somehow cannot come up with. (I once forgot, in the midst of what I believe was otherwise an informative class on the Supreme Court, how many justices serve on that body.) We can at least point out where the student might go to find the answer to her question (simply saying, "Look it up" will not always do justice to the fairness of the question, or to the complexity of finding information); or we can pay the student the compliment of looking up the information ourselves. In any case, my argument applies most fairly to those questions that demand judgment and interpretation, rather than raw data.

16

Undue Influence: Confessions from an Uneasy Discussion Leader

JOYCE GARVIN

SEVERAL YEARS AGO the local branch of a national social organization asked me to speak at its monthly meeting. Vaguely flattered because the program chairman had named me specifically instead of extending a generic invitation to the high school where I teach, I sampled the roast beef and virtuously declined dessert. My thoughts played around the literature/language curriculum we had recently refined to whet those critical, creative, and expressive skills that define the study of English. I felt relaxed, assured of a friendly reception. Indeed, my audience seemed very attentive. But I was cut down coolly as soon as I started to warm to my subject: how a teacher provokes critical thought during general discussion, developing in students the desire and capacity to make independent judgments. Hardly a bombshell, really just a preliminary platitude. With concerted timing, four rather grim gentlemen rose from the corners of the room and warned in unison: "Don't teach our children to think. We'll teach them to think. You just teach them grammar."

Well, I gawked, as though I had been slapped down for applauding universal peace. What kind of assault was this? The gentlemen were very clear as they discharged a broadside of complaints. They did not want their sons and daughters to question family decisions; sons and daughters were not supposed to dispute parental politics, morals, values. Literature was subversive stuff (stick to grammar) because it led young adults to consider ways and means different from those confirmed around the dogmatic dinner table. Advanced Placement (AP) English should substantiate home rule, not stimulate argument. (I wondered if they meant "discussion.")

Wrong, all wrong! But a little sprig of anxiety kept tapping away at the farthest reaches of my confidence. I tried to characterize those sessions that had left my classes high on words and ideas, when we had flowed out of the room on a swift current of dialogue. Most often we had been in passionate agreement. Despite careful inquiry—or maybe because of it—students had adopted my viewpoint, even though I had conscientiously urged alternatives; even though I had held my sentiment up to the light of reason and laid bare the seams, courting dissension.

Where were those "independent judgments" I had been touting? Was I somehow training disciples instead of critical thinkers? (By now I felt distinctly uneasy.) My students showed none of the familiar signs of intimidation. They felt free to deny, to insist, to counter. Still, they usually found me wrongheaded only on interesting but minor points. Whenever major ethical questions arose—literary discriminations often rest on the flawed behavior of characters—we seemed to agree. Over the following weeks I reexamined this happy concurrence because, obviously, I *did* want my students to think as individuals.

Just as obviously, thinking itself was not the real irritant agitating those formidable fathers: it was the nature of literature and other humanistic studies to stir moral reflection, even stern indictment, that had provoked their fusillade. Because my students were questioning principles rigidly maintained at home, I, their teacher and perceived leader, had become the enemy. Shades of Socrates, I was tampering. And I had to agree. Ironically alerted by four parochial horsemen, I conceded a disquieting truth: class discussion allowed me to exert "undue influence." To a degree that alarmed conscience, I was urging my own moral views on vulnerable young adults. I began to consider the complicated circumstances of teacher influence.

When students start to assimilate their discussion leader's values and opinions, a syndrome more compelling than simple imitation, then undue influence has taken root and, like crabgrass, it is hard to dislodge. Monitoring the endangered ground is tricky because the symptoms flourish under cover of free speech and the condition spreads rapidly and pleasantly. For better or for worse, teachers who frequently make converts—I do not think the word is too strong: followers brought from one set of ethical or social beliefs to another—have entered and altered their students' lives.

Don't teach our children to think. You just teach them grammar. In all fairness, my peppery critics were not really confining me to a grammar text. "Thinking" becomes forbidden fruit only when it causes students to criticize their parents. In most cases it is innocuous enough, a sometimes untidy, sometimes clear-cut, educational imperative.

So, when does thinking become a subversive activity? Students must, of course, learn how to make proper operational and theoretical decisions. Having absorbed basic information—facts, possibilities, procedures, priorities, data of all sorts—they must think out the most expedient way to solve problems. To the extent that she represents state-of-the-art scholarship, the discussion leader, like Father, generally *does* know best and should lead students to rummage around a problem pretty much as she would herself. This is not mindless yea-saying; most sound learning occurs through thoughtful imitation. Often there are routine equations to be supplied, right and wrong answers, wiser and poorer solutions. No competent teacher dispenses decisions like a drugstore. Insted, she enables students through dialogue and a hierarchy of questions and elaborations to develop *within themselves* appropriate patterns of thought. Each subject follows its own avenues of speculation intrinsic to the nature of that discipline. In demonstrating and transmitting these characteristic models of thought, the discussion leader is exercising *due influence*. Even my embattled Archie Bunkers would agree to this benign guidance.

Some liberal arts subjects, however, investigate and judge human behavior in ways that stir the moral sense without supplying definitive answers. In this no-man's-land of moral ambivalence lies the potential for *undue influence*.

From third-grade teachers nostalgically recalled in *Reader's Digest* to such memorable discussion leaders as Alfred North Whitehead, Hannah Arendt, John Crowe Ransom, and Ruth Benedict, made vivid in the book *Masters—Portraits of Great Teachers*,[1] many instructors evidently wield this additional influence. Their personal philosophy, not only their scholarship, makes a permanent imprint on their students' repertoire of ideas and feelings. When we teachers contemplate the thousands of young people captive to our voice over the decades, we ought to take stock of what they are inheriting from us.

By now, agonizing over reams of lesson plans, I have taken ample stock. . . .

Some popular and articulate discussion leaders command a following even when they do not seek one. Other teachers need not worry: they are unlikely to influence at all, certainly not unduly. They're just too cool to get involved, or they toot too strident a horn. The serious influencers are discussion leaders who listen and conjecture, who suggest answers as provisional, not chiseled in granite; who are passionate in their beliefs but not coercive. They do not consciously set out to plant a partisan flag. But passion is an even stronger catalyst than reason, and to such teachers adolescents willingly submit both mind and heart. These leaders must learn to mistrust the very gifts that mark their professional commitment. Guarding gesture and tone, they must censor themselves and throttle spontaneity. Sometimes. (Clear distinction here: lecturers are safe. Introducing a bristling controversy, a lecturer will not favor her own view unless she wants to. The self-contained presentation guarantees objectivity. But discussion is not so tame a creature. It leaps around; it's shifty. Snared by an unexpected but juicy comment, the discussion teacher speaks off the cuff. The deeper her belief, the greater the temptation to influence student thought.)

Words, words, words! Face it, teachers *like* to talk, and by prim definition alone we are hired to "influence," to produce an effect on the minds of others. This is the raw stuff of our jobs: leaving any course, students should be able to evaluate, with increased sophistication, whatever elements of physical, artistic, or ideational life that subject deals with. But the influence of math or science is so different from the influence of art. My subject, literature, dramatizes the dilemmas that underscore our private and public selves. This is very intoxicating material, intended to elicit moral judgment. That's the name of the game. My role should be mainly catalytic, guiding students into the light cast by a particular author and then helping them grapple with the social, ethical, psychological, political, or philosophical ideas reflected there. In sympathy or anger, even in bewilderment, they must face the human muddles and mysteries made concrete through character and action and setting. With all their might they must join the fray.

Sounding this call to high emotion, how could I "stick to grammar"? Did I want to remain objective when, like Flaubert, I pitied adulteress Emma Bovary; like Ralph Ellison, I rooted for the Invisible Man, even in a racist community (*especially* in a racist community); following Thomas Mann, I sympathetically traced von Aschenbach's journey into homosexual love? And, heretic in MBA financial circles, but faithful to the intent of Thomas Wolfe, I rejected that stony corporate giant, the Federal Weight, Scales and Computing Company?

Where was I going wrong? I had to admit that instead of playing devil's advocate—and meaning it—I promoted the author's point of view, *making it difficult for students to formulate any other arguable opinion.* Instead of crackling with dissent, the classroom smiled in easy agreement with Flaubert, with Ellison, with Mann, with Wolfe, and—most enthusiastically of all—with me. Danger: undue influence at work.

Impressionable students (impressionable people!) are always at risk, but my seniors in Advanced Placement Literature struck me as particularly susceptible. Although encouraged to disagree, they preferred to remain agreeable. Why, I wondered, when early adulthood is traditionally the stage of dissent? Pursuing answers to my own nagging questions, I located a few strong tendencies common to their age and habits . . . and began to suspect that, blandly unacknowledged, certain strains of undue influence are probably more pervasive than we realize.

Raised on television, young people are passive receivers of information. The images and ideas that follow each other in stunning succession on the video screen leave little pause for critical reflection. So experience has bred today's learners to listen and accept, not to question. They are comfortable just settling down and soaking up. Lively discussion, especially when it is subtle or indirect, demands intellectual caution, an active mind-set they are not used to mobilizing and do not want to assume right now. Advanced placement courses are a way station between the comforts and conflicts of home and the headier air of independent college life. Even though they haven't quite formulated the questions, my students are looking for answers. Impatient for maturity, they have little tolerance for ambiguity or irresolution; it's a spiky time of life, unnerving.

Opportunity to read and talk about the temptations of love and money, manipulation and betrayal, sex and constancy, all those commonplaces of behavior into which we reflex at the approach of others: this is the magnet that draws them to my class. Relationship fascinates them more than the cosmos. They are relieved to discover that classmates—and teachers, too—sometimes wear a public face that hides private pain. We are analyzing motive and behavior of make-believe characters, tracing and proving through a fictitious text. But talk branches out into real life and genuine worries. To remain on a purely literary level would be as educationally thin as defining scientific theory without observing concrete applications.

As our novels limn the shaky establishments we have erected and pledged allegiance to, my students lament the breakdown of marriage and family that many have already experienced through the divorce of parents. A volatile mix of youthful idealism and disillusion urges them to discard familiar conventions and adopt "better" standards, a search not always rational or generous. To claim themselves, adolescents often need to disclaim parents ("Don't teach them to think. We'll teach them to think."). Seeking substitutes, they are drawn to ideas that sound admirable and teachers who take life seriously. Craving certainty and coveting final answers, they are avid to rubber-stamp mine. Raising idols and accepting wisdom from them is a lot easier than thinking independently.

In the wake of these guilty pedagogic musings, I looked for techniques that would strengthen students without deadening my own responses. But a set of problems kept vexing my attempt to become a less dominating discussion leader. First: the interdependence, the simultaneity, of thought and language.

We draw attention to ourselves and lead others to perceive and value us through verbal activity. "In the beginning was the Word." Language, by far the most persuasive element of discussion, puts meaning into the universe. Since we cannot "think" without words, teachers who redesign or influence student expression may be altering some very basic relation to experience. Melodramatic? Actually the reasoning is solid and the angst justified: control language and you control thought and behavior, the horrible truth of Orwell's *1984*. Purveyors of language have the power to both form and inform the people they serve. The way we speak about our concerns, the distinctive vocabulary we choose, begins to substantiate selfhood. During our years together, many students adopt my ironic humor, the metaphors I sketch in an effort to clarify ideas too elusive for rigid definition. They move very gradually toward a manner of verbal impersonation. I am not describing mimicry or mockery or the misguided belief that repetition and note-taking are a synonym for understanding (the student as duplicating machine of jargon, clichés, and buzzwords: an allied educational grievance). What happens is different and much less deliberate. My students must often translate into words the whisper of a sentiment or the breath of an insight they are still struggling to grasp. When they begin to define the "human condition," a concept at first foreign to them but always the fountainhead of art, they falter. They try to press their feelings into new combinations of words and phrases. But they have not often thought out loud about such matters and tend to fall back on their English teacher's vocabulary, since it is only when examining literature that they need to formulate these inklings. As they assimilate my diction and patterns of speech, so gradual a digestion that it is scarcely discernible, students are somehow internalizing the way I process experience. And this insidious borrowing is probably going on to a degree in many other broadly humanistic classes where language is shared.

Prevention, however, has become easy. Early on now, my students must—sometimes awkwardly—devise their own verbal versions of experience. I simply no longer allow them to copy the way I talk. Explanations must be couched in fresh terms and virgin similes, the stamp of a personal vision. This struggle for new language and original expression takes valuable class time, but I have finally grown comfortable with the sounds of silence that must punctuate discussion when active critical thinking is taking place. (Rather naively, I had assumed that *constant* oral exchange meant better classroom debate.) Slowing down, giving students relaxed time to think things out and discover original and appropriate language to express themselves: not a bad idea.

But Pandora's box opened even wider. Leaders determine not only the rhythm and dynamics of language, but also more subtle strategies that inadvertently command thought. Although we teach through open-ended and open-minded examination, our role is shadowed. Granted authority as resident expert, we still pretend to be seeking answers (one voice among many, kin to our students). That's an ingenuous claim. The discussion leader is *thought* to be impartial, but perhaps *cannot* be. Turning again to George Orwell and parodying his formula for tyranny: "All members of a class are equal, but the teacher is more equal than anyone else."[2] Aware of this tug-of-war, we should compensate for its twists and turns. Even when the room resounds with inquiry initiated by students, the discussion leader directs the flow. Why else the term "leader," already implicit in its self-fulfilling prophecy? Discourse is flexible as long as each point has merit and relevance. But discussion leaders usually give the edge to responses and questions that illustrate and impinge on their own interests. And as long as the issue under fire falls into reasonable context, the class must, quite properly, "follow the leader."

Certain other characteristics of discussion attract students to the strong opinions of a leader. Given: teachers know the intricate ins and outs of their material, whether these sentiments are morally loaded or less emotional. A funny paradox arises from this mastery. Why, after all, are we so sure of our preferences? Because, committed thinkers, we once fought through the same critical process now entangling our students. Even when I acknowledge arguments that seem to offset my own, the deck is firmly stacked. In reaching conclusions I now favor, I once systematically judged the merits of these very alternatives being discussed— and rejected them. In the unguarded heat of discussion, I can repeat the logic that persuaded me at that time; logic that the passing years have since made bedrock. I can hear opposing views and dismantle them because I have passed this way before.

Good leaders would never deny a viable objection. Indeed, they welcome alternatives from students and invite serious dissection. But having once convinced themselves, how can they fail to influence a class? They are informed, discerning, candid, reasonable . . . and sure they are right.

During this period of self-assessment, I learned to curb my selfish desire to shed instant light. Exercising the restraint that wiser and more patient leaders have always practiced, I tried to create an atmosphere that encouraged alert but *unhurried* reflection. And I found, just as before, that when I allowed my students sufficient unpressured time for mulling and stewing in their own critical juices, they uncovered the same logical arguments I once helped them (too much, too quickly!) to assemble.

They discovered other insights too. Oh, I haven't retreated from discussion: radical withdrawal would wither the heart of my teaching and honesty compels me on occasion to a spirited defense of some position I hold dear. But we all argue a lot more now, thank goodness . . . nice, noisy counterpoints to those productive silences that fight undue influence.

A few other shifts in style have given greater critical responsibility to my students without dimming their pleasure or mine. Starting a major work, for instance, I used to read the first chapter or two out loud, pausing often for class comment. Students enjoyed hearing me read. Like most of my colleagues, I am a cultivated ham. Familiar with the fiction, loving it (hadn't I chosen the novel myself? more on this pivotal point later), I performed well, altering tone and stress so that nuances emerged, highlighting noteworthy details, obeying the author's creative will. But even though I interrupted with questions, this technique was more lip service than meaningful discussion because my dramatic delivery had already implied the important answers. (There you are: variations on the same old theme. Embarrassingly like television, I was nurturing passive receivers under the guise of active discussion. By making character and motivation so immediately accessible, I was denying my students the right to wrestle—no holds barred—with suggestive material.) In the private setting of their *own* imaginations, students might contemplate a range of motives, whereas my public reading urged uniform interpretation. Members of a younger culture that maintained its own social attitudes, they might measure with different yardsticks of acceptance and disapproval.

Still, reading out loud is such fun that I now routinely ask a few savvy students to rehearse the night before and come to class primed. So it is *their* dramatic fireworks that ignite discussion and bring life to the literary text. Capitalizing on some point I have previously overlooked, I acknowledge that it adds dimension to the story. Hey, teachers are only human, and a small sprinkle of fallibility seasons the day.

Moment of truth time: even though I act in good faith, elements of undue influence will continue to infiltrate my course through the choice of texts. Students are entering a make-believe world whose syllabus is so malleable that it takes the shape of teacher priority. What are we really looking at? "Surely one of the novel's habitual aims," wrote John Updike, "is to articulate morality, to sharpen the reader's sense of vice and virtue." (There are novelists of equal distinction who disagree, but I ignore them and send my students running after Rabbit.) Like a genie in a bottle, formidable value judgments push for release whenever a particular teacher opens a particular book with a particular class. Once given voice, great writers are hard to resist.

The wisdom of many authors lies waiting on bookshelves, ready to be tapped, but they can publicize their truths only through teacher invitation. I am the single arbiter, the whole program committee. So it is not just Tolstoy who initially forces students to face mortality and scorn those who won't ("The Death of Ivan Ilych"); or Henry James who leads them to a wry admission that money—or the lack of it—can corrupt ("The Pupil"); it is I. When Kafka's scuttling bug of a cloth salesman arouses pity and disgust, it is their English teacher who has unleashed the antagonism that embitters father and son.

We do not plow through a prescribed text heavy with scholarship and footnotes. Instead, I decide just which unsettling themes my students will read and think and talk and write about for a hundred and eighty days; literary conflicts that reflect my own badgering concerns about how we should live. The fictional landscape teems with genius, and I can always find an excellent work that presents social problems meaningful to me. The corollary is plain: these same problems will become apparent (and probably meaningful) to my students. The only dietician in the kitchen, I dictate the menu and cater to the moral health of my clientele.

Choices are not parochial. To the contrary, the books we read *seem* to survey a changing cast and scenery. And, in a way, they do. But they are all viewed through the same middle-aged range finder. In the end, they all convey a similar vision, imaged through different artistry. As we visit Flannery O'Connor's rigorously Catholic farm world and then Bellow's urban Jewish streets, mingle with Henry James's drawing room crowd and Tolstoy's peasants, and tour Forster's India, Joyce's Ireland, and Gordimer's South Africa, the same pungent morality flavors the trip. Mine. In effect, we take sides against an unnamed foe that I have custom-selected. Certainly nothing so blatant as branding heroes and villains or ranking one life-style over another. Still, there is a recognizable quality of character that begins to claim my students' affection.

No matter how uncomfortable I am in theory, I cannot quite avoid this kind of influence. It's hard to "teach" an author whose philosophy is not congenial. The Hemingway hero's macho stance and refusal to court sympathy turn me off. Saul Bellow's suffering Rain King, on the other hand, complains, spills over, waters the page with grievance and hurt feelings. Not for Henderson (and not for me!) Hemingway's stiff upper lip. So when I do business with Saul instead of Ernest, I am actually promoting a specific model for coping with distress. If the years have taught me that open communication and relationship offer solace, why should I teach fictions of impotence? Of loneliness without reprieve?

During that uneasy season of change I *did* teach Hemingway, and my discussion leadership was marked by a finicky pretense I tried to, but could not fully, conceal. I was too quick to give the nod to student criticisms or else, trying to be fair, countered their protests by condemning with faint praise. Although I truly admire Hemingway's art, I was an unworthy counsel for his defense.

Because my seniors are scrutinizing themselves and others so intently, the novels and plays we study (one after the other after the other!) can leave a deep effect. Too many former students have verified Samuel Beckett's abiding influence on them. I know that one of my nicknames is "Mrs. Godot"; that students end up sharing my affection for Beckett's courageous and hilarious—and depressed—clowns. They sense that I, too, yearn for answers but fear there are none except those I can create for myself with a little help from friends. Was it fair to lead suburban seventeen-year-olds away from secure pastures into the thickets of existential doubt and disorder? Unkind influence?

As they integrate real and imaginary events that move them, young people are deriving a philosophy that determines the kind of adults they will become. One learns about the world by roving in it or studying about it; one is not born with a personal ethic, only with the capacity to develop values, discard, and perhaps recover them. In the flux of experience we keep inventing ourselves. Make no mistake, art spurs powerful revelations. It is a genuine happening that invades and occupies. Under the aegis of close textual analysis, my students pity Prufrock and all those emotionally bereft who measure out their lives with coffee spoons. In rejecting gray, conforming Ivan Ilych, they are identifying and diminishing their own fathers.

I have come full circle. Fulfilling the high aims of literature enables my students to pass judgment on the people closest to them. And because they are young and relatively untried, they condemn . . . sometimes by rote, almost with relish.

One has to undergo the rough-and-tumble of adult life in order to learn sympathy for the frailties that riddle all of us. When I suggest that the road ahead is pitted with temptations and they should, perhaps, judge less harshly, my students fret and fume and finally demand, "Well, what do *you* think?" After all the conscientious theorizing and precaution-taking, the heart of this teacher's dilemma still beats most strongly at that moment when I am pinned against the blackboard and asked to tell the truth. I am no proselytizer, but the role I have chosen and the way I play it force my hand: I tell them what I think. Despite qualms about swaying students, I am not willing to sidestep. Refusing their need to hear a straightforward answer would affront the dignity of my profession.

Teachers are drawn to the classroom by a special kind of feeling. They like to talk about their subject and introduce others to its peculiar pleasures. They like to participate in its intricacies. Then why not simply become full-time sociologists or businesswomen or government employees? Why *teach*? I suspect that at the soul of our profession lies a wistful but unremitting desire to influence people. (There, I've said it!) It's an urge, not uncommon, to define ourselves by producing a significant impression on others. This is not a quest for power, subtly camouflaged. Our earliest memories of teachers, reaching way back to kindergarten and elementary school, recall nurturing men and women; caretakers, really, they have little to do with the technicalities of reading, writing, and arithmetic. They are, instead, the warm conductors of social and emotional attitudes evolved during childhood. Teachers play a formative role, teaching is a helping art.

Many discussion leaders practice an artless humanism, influencing without guile. Students seek them out as mentors. Despite a sincere distaste for imposition, these teachers want to move beyond the basic educative function of transferring knowledge and skills. In their heart of hearts, they want to help students become "better people." Aye, there's the rub, the fly in the ointment, the black spot of conscience: more than most, they distrust the slippery relativity of that pat phrase "better people." And yet, simply and profoundly, they also believe in these words. They are pledged to ambiguity.

What a bind! Far from being doctrinaire, these teachers want their students to think critically, question convention, and discover for themselves how hard it is to live by what Anthony Burgess called a "higher morality." These teachers are the talkers and listeners who put their faith in language—clearly, fairly, but also passionately used—to help redeem our failures.

The best I can do is try to "teach my students to think" by directing the flashlight of discussion into crevices that usually remain dark. Sometimes I want students to see through my eyes and measure with my yardstick. That's part of the whole literary scene that should be put on display. But I must also stimulate them to hold me off; to recognize that they are separate people who may be gratified by another version of maturity. Visions differ. I must give them strength to resist me and other ardent persuaders. Intellectual resilience, educated minds that remain open to influence but never imprisoned by it: Hasn't this always been our first defense against tyranny in the classroom or anywhere else?

NOTES

1. Joseph Epstein, ed., *Masters—Portraits of Great Teachers* (New York: Basic Books, 1981).
2. The original quotation is: "All animals are equal, but some animals are more equal than others." See George Orwell, *Animal Farm* (New York: Harcourt Brace, 1946), p. 123.

17

A Delicate Balance: Ethical Dilemmas and the Discussion Process

DAVID A. GARVIN

THE WORD "ETHICS" OFTEN evokes an image of pipe-smoking philosophers engaged in endless, abstract debate. All of their attention seems to be focused on first principles and fundamental questions, like the definition of good behavior. The importance of these issues is undeniable—how, after all, can we judge the rightness of our actions without well-defined ethical standards?—but strangely removed from the hurly-burly of everyday life. Ethical choices seldom appear in the abstract or otherwise undisguised; more often, they are embedded in the mundane and parochial, linked inescapably to our daily affairs. Most of us steer an ethical course through seemingly small decisions. Or as one of John Updike's characters puts it in A *Month of Sundays:* "Doing right is, to too great an extent, a matter of details."[1]

This is especially true of teaching, where ethical choices crop up at every turn. Selecting and assigning readings, presenting ideas, grading or evaluating students—the basic stuff of classroom life—involve decisions of unexpected ethical import. Instructors normally emphasize some readings at the expense of others and highlight those interpretations that support their own views; at what point does this process lose objectivity and become a form of indoctrination? Grading is equally sticky: Does one respect individual differences and apply different standards to various members of the class, or does fairness require the same treatment for all?

Since ethics, according to one definition, is "that set of mutual rights and obligations that ought to govern human relationships," the linkage between educational and ethical issues is hardly surprising.[2] In any classroom, disparities in knowledge and power between instructors and students are likely to create ethical dilemmas. These concerns are not new; they have been a staple of philosophical discourse since the time of

287

Socrates. Discussion teaching, however, presents a special set of ethical problems that has received far less attention.

These problems revolve around questions of *process:* how instructors decide whom to call on, how they balance out individual and group needs, how they deal with misplaced or incorrect comments, and how they keep their own views from stifling wide-ranging classroom debates. Such issues seldom arise in lectures. There, the instructor's primary goal is to impart information; process is secondary, and ethics is largely a matter of accuracy and evenhandedness—a willingness to give opposing views a fair shake by counteracting one's own prejudices—rather than a balancing act played out in classroom interactions.

Because discussion teaching pursues broader educational objectives, including the development of social and communication skills and the honing of critical thinking, it raises far more complex ethical issues. Discussions force students to articulate and defend positions, to display their reasoning to others, and to accept and respond to criticism. Values clash, and the instructor finds him- or herself juggling competing goals. An individual's desire to participate may conflict with the educational needs of the group: Should he or she be frozen out of the discussion temporarily, or is personal development more important? Sometimes a weak student offers a comment that would crumble under analysis: Should probing questioning be pursued because of what other students will learn, or is the risk of damaged self-esteem too great?

These examples point up two critical aspects of discussion teaching. First, ethical issues are unavoidable in discussion settings. Precisely because the classroom mirrors the fragile personal interactions of everyday life, human relationships and the associated ethical issues are continually at stake. Second, in such settings absolute fairness is impossible, and trade-offs and compromises are inevitable. Someone is likely to be disadvantaged or displeased by almost every action; the instructor's only hope is to establish a rough hierarchy of values, to monitor the personal and educational impact of the resulting decisions, and, when in doubt, to follow that priceless maxim "Strive to do no harm."[3]

We sometimes forget the power of the instructor. By leading the discussion process, he or she makes most of the ethical choices. Subtle decisions can have major impacts. Recognizing one student's hand at the expense of another's, heaping praise on some occasions while withholding it on others, assigning roles to individuals and expecting their comments to fit preestablished patterns—these choices illustrate the instructor's power to create "stars," to undermine self-esteem, to help and to hurt.

Instructors differ, of course, in their interpretations of what constitutes helpful and supportive behavior, and in the importance they attach to various ethical standards. Each is likely to have his or her own personal code. Moreover, circumstances differ as well, and the ethically appropriate action in one situation may be precisely wrong in another. This essay can do no more than chart the terrain. It is best viewed as a point of departure: one teacher's attempt to wrestle with the ethical dimensions of discussion teaching, and to work his way through several commonly experienced ethical dilemmas. The proposed courses of action are unlikely to meet with universal acceptance; other instructors will undoubtedly rely on different values when sorting through the same issues. The approach, however, should prove useful, if only because it identifies the ethical dilemmas embodied in such simple instructional choices as whom to call on.

Educational and Ethical Values

Any analysis of the ethics of discussion leadership must eventually wrestle with the question of fairness. Impartiality and equitable treatment are essential to effective discussions; without them, efforts to encourage participation, to juggle diverse viewpoints, and to balance educational and personal needs would meet with massive resistance. That much seems clear. Complications arise from the multidimensional character of fairness. In discussion settings, one must consider not only fairness to the individual, but also fairness to the class, the discussion process, the material, and the instructor's own individual morality. Because efforts to respect one type of fairness often lead to conflicts with another, instructors must frequently engage in a delicate balancing act.

Fairness to the group, for example, normally requires the evenhanded treatment of equals. Opportunities to participate, to open and summarize discussions, to criticize and be criticized are to be shared without favoritism. All students should be in the same boat, each as likely as any other to be called on unexpectedly, taken to task for faulty reasoning, or subjected to piercing cross-examination. Otherwise, some individuals will benefit at the expense of others. They will learn more quickly, or adjust more rapidly to classroom norms.

How, then, does one accommodate individual differences? All students are *not* equal. Some have advantages in prior training or knowledge, while others suffer from psychological or personal blocks that impede active participation. Should discussion leaders ignore such problems as shyness or excessive sensitivity to criticism? Do the norms of fairness require instructors to treat all their students the same?

Not if education is to be more than the simple transfer of information. Instructors with an allegiance to broader goals—a respect for individual self-worth, an interest in personal development, or the cultivation of humanitarian values—will bend over backward to provide special opportunities to the disadvantaged. Other class members may find this burdensome; their own opportunities are likely to be constrained as a result. Yet such behavior has a clear ethical basis. As John Gardner notes: "The good society is not one that ignores individual differences but one that deals with them wisely and humanely."[4] Put another way, fairness to the individual deserves the same standing as fairness to the group.

In practice, this principle often translates into a distinction between standards and standardized treatment. A group will seldom cohere unless efforts are made to apply some standards across the board. Among the most important of these are standards of analysis—what constitutes a solid argument and what does not—and standards of civilized discourse. Ad hominem attacks, for example, have no place in the classroom. Because these standards are essential to creating an environment that is conducive to shared learning, they cannot be compromised to accommodate individual students. To do so would imperil the very foundations of discussion teaching.

Standardized treatment, on the other hand, is seldom warranted. Students have different needs and temperaments, which call for varying educational approaches. Where students face special problems with class participation—for example, stuttering, shyness, or an inability to accept criticism from others—instructors are certainly justified in tailoring their approaches to assist in overcoming these problems. A shy student may be given a bit of advance notice about when he or she will be called on to open a discussion; someone likely to be supportive may be called on to follow up comments made by a student vulnerable to criticism. In these situations, students are not being evaluated any differently or being judged by different sets of standards; they are simply being offered equal opportunities to excel. Here, fairness means that individuals are being treated in ways that acknowledge their differences as individuals.

Fidelity to the discussion process is a third aspect of fairness, essential to real learning. Students must have faith in the *integrity* of discussion: unless they accept the process as legitimate, they will withhold participation and personal commitment. This is especially true where the ends of the educational process are ambiguous and ill-defined, or provide little in the way of motivation. How many first-year law students, for example, fully understand what it means to "learn to think like a lawyer"? How many are willing to engage actively in discussions because of their commitment to such a dimly understood goal? Especially in the earliest class sessions, students must accept a great deal on faith: the legitimacy of the process is often their only sure anchor. Instructors must therefore take great care to keep the discussion process untainted. Deviousness in any form—distortions of fact, the willful manipulation of opposing views, the exploitation of honest ignorance—should be avoided, even if the goal is simply to encourage active debate. While a class may be temporarily energized by such tactics, their long-run impact is more insidious. Trust erodes, students begin to lose faith in the justness of discussion procedures, and eventually personal commitment wanes. Without a process that students can believe in, little will be accomplished.

For similar reasons, instructors need to ensure fidelity to the material. This does not mean that discussions should be channeled in the direction of accepted solutions, or that students should be steered away from creative, personal interpretations. On matters of opinion—for example, the appropriate ruling in a legal case that is without clear precedent, or the best strategy for marketing a new product—instructors are without ethical obligation to rein in students' ideas, however unsound they appear. But where facts are at issue or analytical methods are involved, the imperative is quite different. Such material has its own truth and logic, which must be respected if learning is to occur. Especially early in the semester, when they are facing unfamiliar material, students need some assurance that they are moving in the right direction and working from a common base; otherwise they will see little point in cooperating. The instructor becomes their compass, pointing the way when all seems lost. As a practical matter, this means that discussion leaders must occasionally intervene actively and emphatically on matters of fact and method, to ensure that the material has been justly treated and the appropriate groundwork laid for subsequent classes.

The fifth element of fairness, fidelity to one's own individual morality, is particularly dear to most instructors. We teach, in part, because of deeply held views that we wish to communicate. None of us is a tabula rasa; our values, prejudices, and opinions infuse every encounter. These views, we believe, deserve the highest respect precisely because we have thought them through so carefully. It is for this reason that personal values and interpretations present such delicate problems of self-management for most discussion leaders and raise such difficult ethical issues.

For example, should instructors encourage a balanced and evenhanded discussion of material with which they violently disagree? Perhaps a business student has argued in favor of industrial espionage: Should the instructor who disagrees pointedly state his objections? Should discussion leaders ever proselytize for a favored point of view? More fundamentally, at what point does the instructor's obligation to classroom process end and loyalty to personal values begin?

These questions all center on a basic tension: the competing pulls of advocacy and evenhandedness. Their resolution requires a shift to a higher level of abstraction, and an examination of the larger themes of objectivity, neutrality, and indoctrination.

Indoctrination is the easiest to tackle: it has few defenders and many enemies. Most teachers agree that the goal of education is to develop independent thinking, not to encourage the uncritical acceptance of other people's views. The more difficult question is operational. Where instructors are powerful—possessing greater knowledge, skills, and authority—and students vulnerable, as is so often the case, how is indoctrination to be avoided? Is there any way for instructors to introduce their personal views—even, perhaps, arguing for them passionately—while protecting freedom of inquiry?

One critical element is the presence or absence of coercion. Students are quick to infer how much room the instructor is allowing for independent thought. Dogmatism flourishes only when opposing views are suppressed. As Derek Bok, the president of Harvard University, has observed:

> An instructor does not indoctrinate his students merely by disclosing his own ethical values. The critical line is crossed only when a teacher attempts to force his values on his students by refusing to entertain contrary arguments or by using his power as a grader and discussion leader to coerce students into accepting his views.[5]

Because questioning attitudes require constant cultivation, an open process—one that encourages students to make up their own minds, whatever the issue—is the best insurance against indoctrination.

Of course, instructors could go a step further, striving for neutrality on all major points. Discussions would then proceed without their personal views coming into play. The discussion leader faced with the issue of industrial espionage, for example, would simply keep his views to himself. This is the very opposite of advocacy. Unfortunately, it is seldom a practical alternative. Almost every action in the classroom—the hands that are recognized, the questions that are asked, the readings that are assigned—betrays a point of view. Moreover, concealing strong opinions borders on dishonesty. Instructors are entitled to have opinions of their own and to communicate them openly. To suggest otherwise would remove a critical human element from teaching.

The classroom ideal, then, is neither pure partisanship nor unblemished neutrality. It is closer to objectivity—what Larry Churchill has called "a scrupulousness about presenting accepted knowledge as knowledge, and opinion as opinion."[6] For critical thinking to flourish, discussion leaders must work hard to maintain the distinction. Their personal views should not be suppressed, but neither should they be disguised as facts or conventional wisdom. Personal views should be explained, not merely stated; if students are to make up their own minds about a subject, they need to be exposed to the reasoning that lies behind those views. Dissent should then be encouraged as part and parcel of the discussion process.

This is easier said than done. Years of experience have taught students to parrot the views of those in authority. Instructors should therefore be especially careful to tread softly in the earliest sessions of a course. They should, for example, save personal views until the end of most discussions in order to encourage debate; make sure reading lists include articles opposing their favored viewpoints; cultivate objectivity by pointedly distinguishing fact from opinion; publicly dissociate grading from the support of particular points of view; and initially limit their interventions on matters of opinion until an ethic of independence has been firmly established.

These five aspects of fairness—fairness to the individual, to the group, to the discussion process, to the material, and to the instructor's own morality—form the ethical core of discussion teaching. Each has its own imperatives, and instructors are certain to differ on the amount of attention that each deserves. Moreover, the imperatives often conflict; when they do, the dilemmas are especially difficult, because there are few clear ethical guidelines.

Ethical Dilemmas in the Discussion Classroom

The essence of discussion classes is active participation. But participation must be regulated, for an uncontrolled class produces little besides chaos. The instructor serves as the critical link: as leader, he or she allocates air time, decides whom to call on, and tries to ensure that all members of the group receive ample opportunities to speak. A relatively simple task, it would seem—until one recognizes the multiple goals that the process is designed to serve. Then a number of ethical dilemmas become apparent.

Consider, for example, the problem of the independent and unpredictable student whose comments are totally unrelated to those of preceding speakers. Calling on such a person is likely to divert, and perhaps derail, the discussion. Any sustained line of argument is lost. Is it fair to the class to allow a lone individual to disrupt the discussion? Is it any fairer for the instructor to freeze the individual completely out of a debate?

What about the student with expertise in a field who invariably has the correct solution to a problem? Should that student be treated any differently from other members of the class, called on more or less frequently or at different points in the discussion? Is it ever appropriate to keep such people from a debate precisely because they are likely to offer a knowledgeable response?

Even more difficult is the dilemma posed by the passive student who, with a few leading questions, will follow the instructor down almost any line of reasoning, however mistaken. The class may learn a great deal from an exposure to these dead ends, which contrast sharply with the correct approach. But is it fair to expose so glaringly the weaknesses of an individual student? Is it legitimate to call on someone precisely because one is hoping for a flawed response?

What of the instructor who involves an impressionable student, without warning, in a role-playing exercise of great emotional power? The class that results may have extraordinary force and immediacy, with the class reacting viscerally as well as intellectually. Suppose, however, that the success of the role play requires a temporary violation of discussion norms. Perhaps the instructor has to apply a bit of verbal jujitsu, deliberately misinterpret a comment, or create an artificially threatening environment. Is such behavior ethical? Do the deep lessons learned justify putting an individual at risk or compromising the integrity of the discussion process? More fundamentally, at what point does teaching end and manipulation begin?

These four dilemmas all involve the choice of whom to call on, in what circumstances, and for what purposes. Each requires the careful balancing of educational and ethical values. And each is without an obvious solution.

On matters this ticklish, even the most thoughtful instructors are prone to disagree. The precise solution that a discussion leader selects will depend on his or her ranking of the desired ends. Others may well set their priorities differently; my own preference is to err on the side of protecting the individual, and then in favor of preserving the integrity of discussion. Substantive learning can usually be repeated or replaced; a student, once turned off or tuned out, is almost impossible to retrieve. Such a ranking of values provides help in sorting out the dilemmas cited above. For example, it suggests that the risks of leading an unthinking follower through a faulty chain of reasoning are almost always too great: the side effects include damaged self-esteem, a loss of confidence in the discussion process (potentially by all members of the group), and the likely withdrawal of future participation (or, at the very least, reduced participation accompanied by high anxiety).

A persuasive case can, however, be made for the other side. Errors and flawed reasoning are integral parts of education. We almost always get things wrong before we get them right, and learn better as a result. Students need to understand this principle, the argument goes, living it out in the classroom by accepting a high level of personal risk. By the same reasoning, instructors may occasionally have to employ leading and directed questions.

There, of course, is the dilemma. The ends are indeed deserving: a richer understanding of what distinguishes valid from flawed reasoning, the recognition that mistakes have educational value, and a deeper appreciation of the logic of well-formed arguments. The means, unfortunately, are more problematic. A professor who relies heavily on leading questions is frequently guilty of *using* students, denying their individuality while focusing on the roles they can play in the instructor's grand plan. Even with a sensitive instructor, the usual result is feelings of hurt, loss, and betrayal. Worse, the students involved in such a question-and-answer process are frequently among the most vulnerable in class, and thus the most easily damaged.

Even when it is not prompted by instructors, flawed student reasoning presents something of an ethical dilemma. Exposing weakness may educate the group, but the individual suffers. Should the instructor then call attention to a misguided approach, if the student is likely to wilt under probing? Are there times when wrong answers should be overlooked because focusing on them would chill further discussion? Or is a single, unvarying strategy the best alternative?

Here again, there are few clear answers. My own view is that students normally benefit from discussions of their own, self-generated mistakes, providing both class and instructor are sensitive and supportive. Few of us enjoy making errors; still fewer enjoy being told that we are stupid or lacking in common sense. Epithets have little educational value, and no place in the classroom. Careful attention to students' views, however, *even when their reasoning is flawed*, affirms their value and shows that they are being taken seriously. This builds confidence in the discussion process, at the same time creating a more open and questioning environment.

Some students, however, are so lacking in self-esteem that a public airing of mistakes might cripple their confidence. In an effort to protect such sensitive souls, concerned instructors often exempt their comments from the more rigorous scrutiny applied to others. Unfortunately, this approach, while benign on the surface, threatens the evenhandedness of discussion procedures.

For one thing, such efforts frequently undermine students' commitment to shared inquiry. Applying different critical standards to different individuals leaves the entire class on shaky ground. Personality rather than substance becomes the focus of attention. Soon students are asking, "Why did Richard get off so easily?" rather than "Did the argument make any sense?" Nor is it clear that such protection actually benefits the students in question. Exemption from criticism often subtly undermines an already shaky self-confidence. The message is subliminal but unmistakable: not for you the parry and thrust of critical questioning, for you are too weak.

Many of these students would be better off if they were treated less delicately. The ability to survive public criticism, after all, is an important professional skill, and one that must be learned. Often, a supportive classroom is the best environment for such lessons. Providing ad hominem attacks are avoided and fellow students aim to be helpful, even weak students should be capable of rising above their mistakes. For many of them, the fear of error is likely to be worse than the reality; in a curious way, being wrong once makes it easier to risk being wrong a second time.

So much for the handling of flawed reasoning. A different set of problems is raised by thoughtful and expert answers, delivered time and time again by students with superior experience or background, and by sensible comments that fail to relate to the preceding discussion. Handling such behavior patterns is not simply a matter of classroom tactics; a broader ethical issue is involved as well. At what point does an individual student's need to participate outweigh the needs of the group? On what basis should such decisions be made?

The complicating factor here is the power of the instructor and the connection between participation and grading. In many discussion classes, students are graded on what they say; to a surprising extent, instructors determine the outcome of the process by their choice of whom to call on. A well-prepared student recognized early in a discussion is likely to present a long and detailed analysis; the same student can contribute far less after equally well-prepared classmates have had their say. A peripheral comment in one context may weaken or divert a discussion; the same comment drawn out at another time will move the class toward fertile, unexplored ground. The discussion leader is thus a kingmaker of sorts. Each student's performance, as well as his or her opportunities for learning, is shaped by the instructor's call pattern. A student who is recognized early and who is allowed to speak frequently stands a much better chance of success than one who is recognized less often and whose comments come only after the discussion has run its course. Students who assert their claims to excellence early in the term are normally rewarded as the year goes on. Students who begin with a poor showing may never catch up: they are likely to be called on less and less frequently, often only when the chances of making a major contribution are limited. There is something of a self-fulfilling prophecy in these behavior patterns. The instructor first decides, on relatively slim evidence, who is likely to offer substantial comments and who is not; the expectations are then confirmed because the instructor's own actions shape students' opportunities for making effective contributions.

How, then, should instructors respond to expert students who have all the answers, or students whose remarks are largely unrelated to the discussion at hand? The preferred strategy is to speak with them personally outside of class, explain the problems they are causing, and work slowly toward improvement. But what if such remedial efforts fail? Freezing these students out completely is not an option, for they do not deserve to be ostracized so harshly. Calling on them discriminatingly, however—when they are least likely to disrupt the flow of discussion or when their expert answers are likely to do the least damage—is also perilous. Offending students will find themselves with fewer and less desirable opportunities to speak; the quality of their contributions, and thus their grades on class participation, will decline accordingly. This is a heavy burden to bear, and one that has been imposed unilaterally by the instructor.

I believe that these students deserve better. Not in any given class perhaps, but over the course of the semester they should be offered the same opportunities to speak as their classmates. Occasional disruptions are a small price to pay for keeping opportunities open. Moreover, real improvement is likely if the disruptive comments are always followed up by pointed questions—asking the unpredictable student to relate his comment to what was said earlier, or requiring the seasoned expert to develop the implications of her analysis. Discussion leaders must provide such students with room to grow and change. Typecasting them as problems and narrowing their opportunities to participate fails to respect their potential as individuals.

Problems of typecasting arise in other discussion settings as well. For example, in an effort to encourage debate instructors may unwittingly cast students in predefined roles. One will be the radical, always contesting the status quo; another the libertarian, arguing for less government interference; a third the hard-line conservative, defending big business. Students soon recognize the roles that they have been assigned; since these typically reflect their true feelings—how else would instructors have cast them in the first place?—little prompting is required. The result is a well-tuned orchestra. The instructor has only to decide what notes he or she wants played, and then to seek out the appropriate soloist.

All discussion leaders follow this strategy to some extent. Knowledge of students can—and should—be used to give shape and texture to classroom debate. A student with an engineering background is more likely to introduce an unexplored technical issue, while a foreign student is often the one who highlights the importance of global competition. Knowing the class's resources and tapping them at the right time is part of effective discussion leadership.

The problem is that assigned roles can easily become ideological straitjackets. Students begin to take their parts *too* seriously: they start to see themselves in terms of the views that they have been assigned, and limit their participation to comments in which they parrot the party line. Instructors may suffer from a similar narrowing of perspective. They begin to see students as cogs in a giant machine, their individuality and potential for growth less important than the positions they represent. The result is frequently an environment that discourages personal exploration and the learning that comes with it.

How is this dilemma to be resolved? Instructors cannot simply ignore students' backgrounds or long-standing views, for tapping into them brings passion and commitment to class participation. They can, however, work occasionally against the grain, asking students who support a particular position to present arguments for the opposite side. The conservative may be assigned the Justice Department's view in discussing a leading antitrust suit, the libertarian asked to spell out the merits of government regulation. Such efforts to break the mold ensure that students will at least consider competing perspectives.

Other strategies can also be used to hold typecasting in check. An effective early warning system is a must: instructors need a way of determining quickly if students have begun to confine their comments to limited roles. Class participation must therefore be closely monitored, and patterns of response tallied. Equally important are efforts by the instructor to modify his or her call pattern, and to avoid forcing students into roles by recognizing them at the same juncture in every class. A student with liberal leanings who is called on only after more conservative classmates have already spoken will soon stake out an assertive and doctrinaire position; given other opportunities to speak, he or she is likely to range more widely.

From an ethical standpoint, the key issue is establishing limits. Some reliance on preassigned roles and students' backgrounds is useful for discussion; too much will compromise opportunities for individual growth. Each instructor must make an individual decision about where to draw the line, and on what basis. As always, well-intentioned and principled teachers are likely to disagree. My own preference is to rely frequently on student expertise—accepting the roles that accompany competence or interest in a field—while steering clear of typecasting that involves values or opinions. Tapping students' expertise gives them a base on which to build further participation, allowing them to gain confidence while teaching their fellow classmates. Injurious effects are few, as long as it is clear that no single student offers the last word on a topic. An emphasis on ideology or political position, however, is more confining. It requires students to view the world through a one-dimensional filter, narrowing their perceptions as well as their range of response. Positions quickly harden, and real dialogue soon disappears.

Typecasting is closely related to a fourth ethical dilemma: the emotional role play that, to be successful, requires surprise and a violation of classroom norms. For example, a business instructor who wants students to experience the hurt and anger that accompany being fired may decide to simulate the event in class. But since the impact of such a role play is often diminished by advance briefing, the instructor may conclude that the only way to induce the desired reactions is through an interchange that singles out an unsuspecting student and mimics an unexpected firing. Surprise is required for success, and also careful casting. The instructor must select a student who will react instinctively to dismissive remarks launched without warning. Classes are often galvanized by such tactics, but the fallout is frequently severe. The student who is "fired" may take the dismissal personally, suffering a severe loss of self-esteem. The discussion process, too, will never be quite the same. Trust will erode, and the instructor, who has masterfully stage-managed strong personal feelings, will be viewed with a touch of suspicion. Students will wonder whether they are slated to star in the next grand performance.

The dilemma here is obvious: fidelity to the material versus fairness to the discussion process. Certain topics can never be fully understood at a purely intellectual level, but must be appreciated emotionally as well. From this standpoint, the instructor who wants students to experience what it means to be fired, and not simply discuss it, is pursuing a laudable goal. But evoking the desired reaction requires changing the rules of the game, causing students to question their assumptions about how discussions are conducted. Once again, we have values in conflict. How should they be reconciled?

For me, protection of the discussion process comes first, because it is the bedrock of effective teaching. Without faith that the rules are secure and their personal safety nets will not be withdrawn, students are unlikely to continue to invest themselves in class either actively or enthusiastically. Most will participate to some degree after the emotional fireworks have passed, but only grudgingly. The instructor will have crossed an invisible line that determines whether he is "with us" or "against us." Unfortunately, once an instructor's motives have been questioned, it is often impossible to recover the desired openness and personal involvement from students.

As these dilemmas illustrate, respecting multiple forms of fairness inevitably requires trade-offs, and instructors must frequently settle on the lesser of two evils. Even at its best, ethical discussion leadership demands a delicate balancing act. But there are a number of simple steps that instructors can take to maintain their ethical vigilance.

Patrolling the Process

To become ethically sensitive, discussion leaders must first begin to see the classroom with their students' eyes. Many have lost touch with the student perspective: they are preoccupied with teaching rather than with learning. The two activities are separated by a vast psychological distance. Teaching is more stable and secure, with an unambiguous and dominant role accorded the instructor; learning, by contrast, is a delicate and fragile act, accompanied by great personal risk.

How can this shift in perspective be obtained? When preparing for class, instructors must continually ask themselves how students are likely to interpret events. Will their pattern of calling on students, for example, be perceived as fair, or will it seem to favor some members of the class at the expense of others? Are students likely to feel that volatile and value-laden subjects are being treated evenhandedly and that conflicting views, especially those opposing the instructor's, are receiving equal time? Will the class take well to planned criticism, or are the leader's remarks likely to be construed as disparaging and personally destructive?

Such private dialogue is essential for developing greater ethical sensitivity. Each instructor will have his or her own list of key questions; the particular issues that are chosen are less important than the existence of a list in the first place. Without such self-scrutiny, ethical concerns are easily overlooked.

The same is true of in-class behavior. Instructors must learn to sensitize themselves to a variety of warning signals—the tremulous voice, the stereotyped role, the sudden collapse of self-esteem, the withdrawal of participation, the angry, belittling response—that show all is not well. Students seldom hide their disaffections or vulnerabilities completely; the trick for instructors is to identify problems early, while change is still possible.

For this reason, careful attention should be paid to students' personal characteristics in the first few class sessions, because they are the key to ethical behavior. Who, for example, appears to wilt under criticism? Who has a sharp tongue? Who has trouble speaking up? Who are the ideologues, limiting their participation to a single point of view. Which students are friends with one another? Which are enemies?

With this information in hand, instructors will find it far easier to chart an ethical course. Problems of typecasting can be recognized and avoided more readily; individuals requiring special attention can be singled out for early assistance; and potentially damaging classroom dynamics can be held in check. The last issue is especially important if trust is to be established, and students are to develop faith in the integrity of the discussion process. A perceptive instructor can avoid calling on a scathing critic to follow up the comments of a weak and uncertain participant. Calling on friends to support one another can bolster confidence. And when emotional and value-laden subjects are under discussion, leaders can alternatively seek out partisans from opposing camps, ensuring that competing views are aired and that no single perspective gains unshakable momentum.

Finally, instructors should take pains to keep their own views from dominating discussions. One important step in this direction has already been mentioned: publicly dissociating grading from the acceptance or rejection of the leader's point of view. Another is to pause conspicuously to praise well-constructed arguments that stake out positions antithetical to the leader's. Here, timing is critical, for in most cases, the later the instructor's opinion is revealed, the more freewheeling the debate. Once the instructor has spoken, the topic of discussion normally shifts, subtly and imperceptibly, from the merits of the issue to the merits of the instructor's point of view.

Ethical choices are unavoidable in discussion settings. Because they are normally embedded in routine decisions about classroom management and the flow and direction of discussion, with few obvious ethical overtones, heightened awareness is the critical first step toward ethical discussion leadership. Most of us need to develop greater sensitivity to the ethical implications of our in-class behavior, and must learn to think harder about the trade-offs we face among various forms of fairness. One way or the other, these decisions will be made. A conscious weighing of values will undoubtedly accomplish more than decisions made by default.

NOTES

1. John Updike, *A Month of Sundays* (New York: Fawcett Crest, 1974), p. 228.
2. Daniel Callahan, "Should There Be an Academic Code of Ethics?" *Journal of Higher Education*, vol. 53, no. 3 (1982), p. 338.
3. This maxim, taken from the Hippocratic Oath, has been applied to teaching by David Riesman. See David Riesman, "Great Vocations: The Educator." Speech to the Cambridge Forum, May 23, 1984.
4. John W. Gardner, *Excellence: Can We Be Equal and Excellent Too?* (New York: Perennial Library, Harper & Row, 1961), p. 88.
5. Derek Bok, *Beyond the Ivory Tower* (Cambridge, MA: Harvard University Press, 1982), p. 127.
6. Larry R. Churchill, "The Teaching of Ethics and Moral Values in Teaching," *Journal of Higher Education*, vol. 53, no. 3 (1982), p. 304.

About the Contributors

James Austin, Richard P. Chapman Professor of Business Administration at the Harvard Business School, has been teaching by the case method for twenty years and has recently completed his thirteenth book on management in developing countries.

Colleen Burke, Harvard MBA 1970, spent a decade founding companies, and then a decade teaching undergraduates at Skidmore College.

C. Roland Christensen is the Robert Walmsley University Professor Emeritus, Harvard University and currently teaches a seminar at the Harvard Graduate School of Education. He taught Business Policy to MBA students at Harvard and developed and led faculty seminars on teaching by the case method from 1973 to 1990. He is co-author of *Business Policy,* and *Teaching and the Case Method.*

Heather Dubrow, Professor of English at the University of Wisconsin at Madison, formerly taught at Carleton College and the University of Maryland. Her most recent book is A *Happier Eden: The Politics of Marriage in the Stuart Epithalamium.*

Richard F. Elmore, Professor of Education at the Graduate School of Education, Harvard University, and Senior Research Fellow with the Center for Policy Research in Education, is senior author and editor of *Restructured Schools: The Next Generation of Educational Reform.*

David A. Garvin is the Robert and Jane Cizik Professor of Business Administration at the Harvard Business School, where he teaches in the MBA and Advanced Management programs and has also led seminars on teaching by the case method. His most recent book is *Operations Strategy: Text and Cases.*

Joyce Garvin directs the education of the gifted and talented in grades 7

Joyce Garvin directs the education of the gifted and talented in grades 7 to 12 at the River Dell Regional High School in New Jersey and teaches Advanced Placement English there. She is also a consultant on interdisciplinary education.

Daniel A. Goodenough in 1989 was named the first Takeda Professor of Anatomy and Cellular Biology at the Harvard Medical School, where he has made a number of discoveries in the chemistry, function, and molecular structure of gap junction proteins. He has won numerous prizes for teaching and participated in the New Pathways Program at the school.

Bruce Greenwald, currently at Bellcore, has taught at the Harvard Business School and Wesleyan University. He has done research for Bell Laboratories and for the Presidential Task Force on Market Mechanisms.

Abby J. Hansen is a writer and educational consultant. Formerly a Senior Research Associate at the Harvard Business School, she is co-author of *Teaching and the Case Method.*

Julie H. Hertenstein, Assistant Professor of Business Administration at the Harvard Business School, has written extensively on the use of inflation accounting within firms. She is currently writing and teaching about how firms manage resource allocation for capital and R&D projects.

John Hildebidle is a writer of short stories and Professor of Literature at MIT. His most recent book is *Five Irish Writers: The Errand of Keeping Alive.*

Herman B. Leonard is the George F. Baker, Jr., Professor of Public Sector Financial Management at the John F. Kennedy School of Government, Harvard University. He has served on numerous public policy task forces on fiscal problems at all levels of government.

Melissa Mead taught at the University of Texas at Austin and then, for four years, Managing Information Systems at the Harvard Business School. She then decided to become a physician and is in her third year at Boston University's School of Medicine.

Laura L. Nash, Adjunct Associate Professor, Boston University School of Management, has taught in the classics departments of Harvard, Brown, and Brandeis before joining the faculty of the Harvard Business School, where she taught Business Policy and conducted research in business ethics. She is author of *Good Intentions Aside: A Manager's Guide to Resolving Ethical Problems.*

Catherine Overholt, a health economist and former Lecturer at Harvard's School of Public Health, has taught workshops on discussion teaching in the United States and abroad. She has directed case development projects and is the lead editor of *Gender Roles in Project Development: A Casebook.*

Ann Sweet, Director of Alumni Relations at the Harvard Business School, formerly taught ancient and medieval history in the ninth grade in Wellesley, Massachusetts. She also served for nine years on the School Committee in nearby Weston.

James Wilkinson—AB, AM, and Ph.D. from Harvard—is Director of the Danforth Center for Teaching and Learning. Author of the Wilson Prize-winning book *The Intellectual Resistance in Europe,* he has been a visiting Associate Professor of History at Boston University, and Associate Professor of History and of History and Literature at Harvard.

Index